A WANDERER
IN THE PROMISED LAND

A WANDERER
IN THE PROMISED LAND

BY

NORMAN BENTWICH

NEW YORK

CHARLES SCRIBNER'S SONS

1933

Printed in England at The Chiswick Press

To
ARTHUR ELLIS FRANKLIN
A FELLOW-WANDERER

CONTENTS

vii

PREFACE

For fifteen years I have lived almost continuously in Palestine; and I have traversed many times the length and breadth of the country, and with my wife I have wandered in the surrounding countries which are within the borders of the land promised to Abraham, " from the River of Egypt unto the Great River, the River Euphrates." That is a much larger area than what we commonly call Palestine or the Holy Land: for it includes the countries on both sides of the Jordan, a large part of Syria, and Sinai. The whole of it formed part of the Jewish kingdom only for short periods; but it has been through the ages the principal scene of Jewish history. It is that Promised land of which I have tried to portray the historical pageant in this book. It is impossible not to meditate on the history of the scenes as one roams; for nowhere else are landscape and history so completely fused. Palestine is not only the most historical of countries: but it is also the cradle of the world's civilization, and the countries around it were the nurseries of that civilization. Our knowledge of the relations between the different peoples, races, and cultures of antiquity increases every year, as the spade of the excavators reveals, and the imagination of the scholars illuminates, the treasures of the past. For that reason, amid the many books on Palestine, there may be place for another which takes account of the studies of the archaeologists and historians, and tries to fit them into the framework of Jewish history.

What Anatole France says of truth may be applied to Palestine literature, that it has always something unexpected which renders it tolerable. And the observation that it is the special interest of the Jewish nation that it

alone is met with at every turn of history, applies with
particular force to its place in the history of Palestine.

From time to time I have written impressions of my
travels in and about the land; and several of the papers
in this collection are founded on those earlier sketches.
Nearly all are of the nature of historical geography, by
which I mean that they deal with the country in its historical aspects. And they all touch upon the evolution of
the Jewish people at various periods of their history. I
have made no attempt to cover the whole ground, or to
produce a treatise on the lines of Sir George Adam Smith's
famous work. I have sought rather to portray the less
known parts of the country, and the less trite aspects of
Jewish history. While I have not dealt specifically with
modern developments, I have here and there described the
Jewish settlements and enterprises of to-day as a contrast
or a complement to the older civilization.

The papers fall into three divisions. Two deal with
Jerusalem, five describe parts of Palestine, and the last five
are concerned with the surrounding lands in their relation
with Palestine and the Bible. By way of prelude I have
reproduced a chapter from a little book which I wrote
fifteen years ago, to summarize the place of Palestine in
Jewish history.

My sketches make no pretence to scholarly accuracy in
matters of archaeology. I am only an amateur in those
matters, and I expect that many errors and obsolete statements will be found. My aim has been to give a picture of
the passage of civilization through the Promised Land,
using freely the scholarly work of many hands. I should
like to think that my impressions may make the scenes of
Palestine and the neighbouring lands more vivid to those
who have not seen them, or recall an image to those who
have had the good fortune to visit them.

I have had the privilege of going over some of their
excavations with Sir Flinders Petrie, Professor Garstang,
Mr. Guy, Mr. Rowe and Mr. Crowfoot, who have made

these buried cities live again. My debt to the Publications
and the Quarterly Statements of the Palestine Exploration
Fund and to the Journal of the Palestine Oriental Society,
in regard to the account of recent archaeological study, is
obvious, as is also my debt to the records of Jewish medieval travellers, edited by that doyen of modern Jewish
travellers, Dr. Elkan Adler. I am also under obligation
to the Hebrew book of my friend, Mr. Ben-Zevi, *Shear
Yashub*, which contains an illuminating series of studies on
the theme of Jewish survival on the soil as well as in the
towns of Palestine through the ages since the destruction
of the national independence. And lastly, I have to thank
the proprietors of the *English Review*, the *Bnai Brith
Magazine*, and *The Near East and India*, for permission to
use material originally contributed to their reviews.

Abbreviations used:

P.E.F.Qy. = Palestine Exploration Fund Quarterly Statement.
J.P.O.S. = Journal of the Palestine Oriental Society.

I have referred to dates as B.C.E. and C.E., as these abbreviations
are common to Jews and non-Jews.

Inset — Ancient Jerusalem:

Temple
Tyropoeon Valley or Mill
Palace of Herod
ZION
OPHEL
Water Gts
Gihon
En Rogel
Pool of Siloam Old Pool
Valley of Hinnom
ANCIENT JERUSALEM
Brook of Kidron

Main map labels:

ASIA MINOR

HITTITES

Aleppo
Antioch
Daphne
R. Orontes

Latakia

Hamath

CYPRUS

Aryad
Tartus
Homs
Kadesh
Tadmor
(Palmyra)

Tripoli
Gebal

MEDITERRANEAN

Beirut
Zidon
Baalbek

Zarephath

LEBANON
ANTI LEBANON
SYRIA

SEA

Tyre
Mt. Hermon
Damascus

Ras en Nakurah
Safed
Water of Merom
Acre
Capernaum
Bethsaida
Haifa
Tiberias
Sea of Galilee
Mt. Carmel
Hippos
Gadara
Atlit
Mt. Tabor
R. Yarmuk
Megiddo
Bethshean
Caesarea
Taanach
Gilboa
Ajlun
Gerasa
Dothan
Samaria

Jeb el Hauran

PALESTINE

Joppa
Shechem
Mt. Ebal
Shiloh
Rabbath Ammon

Mt. Ephraim
Bethel
Ashkalon
Ashdod
Jerusalem
Bethany
Heshbon
Beth Shemesh
Herodium
Callirhoe
Hebron
Machaerus
Engedi
Arnon

River of Egypt

Mons Casius

Zoan

Ar of Moab
Masada
Kir of Moab

Daphnæ
Pelusium
L. Sirbonis
The way of the land of the Philistians
Gaza
Beersheba

Succoth

Suez Canal

Auja Hafir
Zoar

NEGEB

Wilderness of Shur

Kossaima
Kadesh Barnea
Petra

EGYPT

Bir el Themed

Mt Hor

LAND OF EDOM

ARABIA

ARABIA PETRÆA
Tor

Ezion Geber
Elath

Mt. Horeb

MIDIAN

Mt. Sinai

Gulf of Akaba

INTRODUCTION: PALESTINE
IN JEWISH HISTORY

As the Jews are the most historical of peoples, so Palestine
is the most historical of countries. To the whole land
there may be applied the words which Cicero used of
Athens: " Wherever we plant our foot we are treading on
history." There is hardly a hill-top in Judaea which is
not covered with the vestiges of a fortress or city of former
ages, hardly a village which does not hide the site of some
ancient centre of civilization. Here we find the stone implements of the palaeolithic age illustrating the first
attempt of man to conquer Nature; sunken catacombs
and Dolmen circles constituting prehistoric cemeteries;
the foundations of colossal walls that encircled the fortified
cities of the early Semites; towns and temples piled in
layers on each other, that illustrate the pageant of
Egyptian history as faithfully as the cities of the Nile;
ruined streets of Ionian and Corinthian columns, and the
remains of amphitheatres and basilicas which tell of the
settlement of Greeks and Romans; Byzantine churches
and mosaic pavements of extraordinary variety; stern
monasteries and castles of Crusaders perched on almost
inaccessible rocks; bastioned walls of the Middle Ages
to-day enclosing a collection of mud huts; spacious
mosques and graceful minarets soaring out of the plain;
and, of our own day, vast stony palaces, convents and
hospitals of the European peoples, vieing with each other
in bigness and solidity to cover the hills. Cave-dwellers
and Hittites, Hyksos and Egyptians, Amorites and Phoenicians, Hebrews and Philistines, Babylonians and Assyrians, Hellenes and Romans, Persians and Arabs,
Franks and Saracens, Egyptians and Turks, have in turn

fought for the country, and conquered it and left their traces.

To humanity, therefore, Palestine is a country of peculiar interest. But for the Jews it has a surpassing importance. For nearly two thousand years it was the centre of their nation; for nearly two thousand years more, since their capital was destroyed, it has been the centre of their hopes and aspirations. From the very beginning of their history they have regarded it with affection greater and more lasting than that which any other people have for their native land. To the Hebrews, sprung from tribes of Arab nomads and delivered from the slavery of Egypt, Canaan was the land of promise, flowing with milk and honey, the chosen place for the chosen people, " a land on which God's eyes rest from the beginning of the year to the end of the year." (Deut., xi. 12.)

Israel was a nation " dwelling by itself, not counted among the peoples " (Num., xxiii. 9); and the territory of Israel likewise was set apart and aloof from the other lands, possessing unique features and " not counted among the countries." The desert isolated it on the east and south, a rocky inhospitable shore on the west cut it off from communication with the Mediterranean kingdoms, and only on the North was it at all accessible; and there the mountain ranges of Lebanon offered but narrow and difficult passes. Small as it was in extent, even when measured from Dan to Beersheba and from Carmel to beyond Jordan, it contained an extraordinary variety of climes and soils, from the sub-tropical country of the Jordan valley sunk hundreds of feet below the sea-level to the temperate zone of the uplands of Judaea, and from the scrubby wilderness of the Negéb to the rich pastures of Gilead. The Jewish sages, noting that the word Ha-aretz (The Land) was used twelve times in the description of the country in Deuteronomy, taught that the land of Israel consisted of twelve different provinces, each of which constituted a country with its separate characteristics unlike those of the others. Egypt, Mesopotamia, and Syria are lands of a single nature, and therefore they have each produced a people of one type. But the diversity of the different parts of Palestine fostered a striking diversity of ethnic types. Ephraim and Judah were two separate nationalities, which were held but for a short time under one sovereignty. Yet, though the influence of each part was different, the impression made by the land as a whole was extraordinarily deep.

When the division of the people of Israel had brought about the fall of either part before the military powers of Assyria and Babylon, and the conquerors, pursuing the policy by which they had destroyed other nationalities, tore up the people from their roots in the soil, and deported them to the banks of the Tigris and the Euphrates, the Jews' love of their land did not die out. The other conquered peoples accepted their new home and let their individuality decay; the captives of Israel and Judah wept by the rivers of Babylon for the country from which they were exiled, exclaiming: " If I forget thee, O Jerusalem, may my right hand forget its cunning! "

There were some to whom the fertile plains and teeming cities of Mesopotamia seemed more attractive than the ravaged highlands and the ruined homesteads from which they had been dragged. But a sturdy remnant—and in all ages it has been the remnant which has saved Israel—cheered by the prophets and taught by the scribes, nourished the hope of return till the day came when Cyrus, " the anointed of the Lord," gave the order that they should go back. Then to the number of 60,000 they started on their way home, " filling their mouths with laughter, and their tongues with rejoicing " (Ps. cxxvi. 2). Led by a scion of the house of David they settled round the old centre of the nation; and proceeded to rebuild there the Temple which was the outward sign of their religious unity. The new sanctuary was less magnificent than that of Solomon, and when it was dedicated some of those who had seen the splendour of the first wept; but it was invested with a fresh glory. It was henceforth in their eyes the religious centre not only of Israel but of the world, covering God's holy mountain to which many people and mighty nations should come to seek the Lord and pray before Him. Their national ideal had deepened in exile, and they now regarded Zion not as the seat of political grandeur but as the " City of Truth."

Judaea for the next three hundred years had a political history which was not distinguished. It was a tributary state, first of Persia, and then of one or other of the Hellenistic Kingdoms which were carved out of the Persian Empire. The Jews did not aspire to State independence; they had no great military leaders, no ambitious kings. They erected no striking buildings, they created no enduring art. But Judaea had an excellence of its own. It continued to nourish a spiritual development which found expression, partly in books of religious literature, partly in a religious ordering of the life of the people. The books have been an inspiration for mankind; the religious ordering of life has given the Jews a distinctive national character. The children of Israel were scattered far and wide in all the countries of Hellenistic civilization, in Persia and Babylon, Egypt and Cyprus, the isles of Greece and the coasts of Asia Minor. " Earth and sea are full of them," said the Sibylline oracle. And at Alexandria, the intellectual capital of the world, they were gathered in hundreds of thousands and occupied two of the five quarters of the city. By their numbers and their commercial prominence they held a position there, at the centre of the Orient, analogous to that which the Jews hold in the metropolis of the New World to-day. The Alexandrians and the other communities outside Palestine preserved their close connection with the Temple by the deputations which came up to Jerusalem at the three great festivals of the year bearing the free-will offerings of every family to the central shrine. As Philo puts it, " the delegates of the Diaspora traversed desert and sea, finding the way easy because of their joy in the goal which awaited them." The pilgrimages marked outwardly the unity of the whole congregation of Israel; inwardly they secured the catholicity of the religious life.

The Maccabaean struggle against a debased Hellenism in the second century B.C.E. vindicated the political, as well as the religious, liberty of Judaea, and stimulated the spiritual consciousness of the nation. The teaching of the prophet that they should be " a light to the Gentiles " was now a real inspiration. Their enthusiasm took indeed different forms in Palestine and the Diaspora; here they became zealous for the Law, there zealous for proselytes, but everywhere proud of their special mission and their special wisdom. A new period of trial began when Palestine passed under the heel of Rome, who with her policy of " warring down the proud " had broken the national spirit of every other people. The Jews still maintained their unyielding separateness, still obstinately preserved their ideals, and still acted as one whole when their religion was attacked. The mad emperor Gaius (Caligula) in the first half of the first century of the Christian era sought to set up his statue in the Temple; and straightway the communities rose in the East and West so menacingly that the Roman proconsul refused to march on Palestine. Caligula was murdered before the order was carried out. But the inevitable conflict came to a head in the great rebellion of C.E. 66-70, which led, after five years of bitter warfare, to the ravaging of Jerusalem and the destruction of the Temple by Titus.

Palestine had been laid waste, the Jewish metropolis was no more, and a Roman legion was encamped on its blackened ruins. The central sanctuary had been blotted out of existence, and its most sacred vessels and the scrolls of the Law had been carried in triumph through the Forum of Rome. Tens of thousands of the land's inhabitants had been slaughtered, hundreds of thousands more

B

were sold as slaves. The towns were depopulated, the villages were desolate, the fields were ravaged. It might have been expected that the communities of the Diaspora would accept the fall of the national centre and lose their national cohesion, remaining a separate religious body but abandoning their struggle for separate national existence. That indeed happened with a section of the people. The Christian heresy taught that the followers of the true faith had passed beyond the narrowness of nationalism, and the new Jerusalem on which its hopes were set was a City laid up in Heaven. But the main body held firm to the old ideals, and cherished with passionate ardour their hopes of re-establishing the Sanctuary on its old foundation. Twice they broke out in desperate revolt—in the reigns of Trajan and Hadrian—and for years they withstood the power of Rome. Roman legions had to be recalled from farthest Britain to put them down; but in the end the rising was crushed, and an attempt was made to exterminate a people who would not be subjugated. Whole Jewish communities were wiped out in Cyprus, Egypt, and Cyrene; in Palestine itself the country ran with blood; and on the site of Zion arose a pagan Roman city, Aelia Capitolina, from which Jews were excluded.

But though the national aspiration was defeated, the national hope was undimmed. In place of the outward visible bond of the Temple, the inner bond of the Torah (The Law) was strengthened. And despite massacres and pillage, Jewish life went on uninterrupted in Palestine, maintaining its hearth of learning and of thought. Driven from Jerusalem the sages set up their schools in the smaller towns of Judaea; and when, after the rising of Bar Cochba, these too were destroyed, they found refuge in Galilee. The Sanhedrin moved its seat ten times, it was said, till at last it was located in Tiberias, the lowest city of the country, to fulfil the words of the prophet: "Thou shalt be brought very low."

Most of the Jewish teachers of the first centuries of the

civil era came from the Holy Land; and the heads of the
Palestinian schools, the Patriarchs, held almost a sovereign
sway over the whole of Israel. The scattered congregations
sent contributions to them which took the place of the
former offerings to the Temple services, typifying the cord
of learning which united the people. Rabbi Judah Hanassi
(the Patriarch or Prince as the Jews called him) at the
beginning of the third century ordered the tradition in the
code known as the Mishna, which sealed the development
of post-Biblical Judaism. A little more than a century
later Hillel the Second of Tiberias fixed the calendar by
which the calculations of the Jewish holy-days and feasts
are still reckoned. There were other seats of learning in
Babylon and Nehardea, in Rome and Carthage; but for
long they were not deemed to compare with those in the
Jewish land.

The people's love for the country appears over and over
again in quaint Rabbinical hyperboles; as, for example,
when it is said: " Only he who has eaten the bread of the
land of Israel knows how bread tastes ": or again, " He
who has walked four miles in the land of Israel is assured
of a place in the next world." More prosaically the feeling
finds expression in the reiterated appeals in the liturgy for
the rebuilding of Jerusalem and the restoration of the
Temple. There is not a service nor a religious occasion in
which that appeal is not voiced: morning and evening,
working-day, Sabbath and holiday, at marriage and death,
at home and in the synagogue, the Jew from generation to
generation has offered these prayers, which were originally
composed by the teachers of Palestine. And time and
again during the early centuries of the civil era they
sought to give effect to their intense hope by rising against
the oppressors whenever they could ally themselves with
their enemies.

The triumph of Christianity in the Roman Empire at
the beginning of the fourth century inaugurated a new era
of repression for the Jews. By the bitter irony of history

the branch of the Jewish people which carried part of its teaching to the heathen became the oppressors of the parent trunk, and the new missionaries of Hebrew morality sought to crush out their religious rivals. The victorious sect were anxious to exclude the Jews from the place where their founder had been put to death, and to purge the land of the unfaithful who had denied him. A short-lived ray of hope was vouchsafed to the Jews during the reign of Julian the Apostate, who, hating the Christians with the hatred of a backslider, looked for allies in those whom the Church itself hated. He invited the Jews to return to Jerusalem and rebuild their Temple, and they responded with alacrity. But before the building had proceeded far Julian died; and since his day Christian Emperors have ruled the Western world.

Persecution caused a decline of the Palestinian schools, and little by little the pre-eminence passed to Babylon, where a new " Land of Israel " had been settled by refugees from the West. Yet Babylon never commanded the affection of the Jewish people. Its schools might claim their respect for a period by reason of the authority of learning; but the heart and the soul of the people were fixed as immovably as ever on Palestine. From time to time a false Messiah would arise claiming that he would lead back the people to their land—such as Moses of Crete, who was followed by thousands into the sea. And when the Persian monarch Chosroes sent an army to invade Palestine against the Byzantine forces (C.E. 614), thousands of Jews joined it and took part in the capture of Jerusalem. Again their victory was short-lived; for in 627 the Byzantine Emperor Heraclius marched on the city, re-took it, and avenged the previous defeat by killing all the Jews who lived in Palestine.

Five years previously (C.E. 622) Mohammed had fled to Medina from Mecca (the event from which dates the first year of the Hejira, the Mohammedan era). In the first years of his preaching Mohammed regarded Jerusalem

as the appointed centre of the religion, and he instructed
his followers to turn to the Holy Mount of Moriah in
prayer. But later, when he was anxious to dissociate his
followers from Jewish practices, he decided that the religious centre must be changed, and he altered the " Kibla "
from Jerusalem to Mecca. Jerusalem, however, was one
of the first goals of the Mohammedan armies. The prophet
himself died on the way to capture it; and in 638 the
battle of the Yarmuk, one of the great engagements of the
world's history, left the holy city at the mercy of the
Khalif Omar. The conqueror guaranteed freedom of religious worship to all denominations, but he erected a new
shrine of the new creed on the site of the Temple.

The sting of persecution was relaxed in Palestine for a
spell. Then came a long epoch when the Cross and
Crescent were struggling for the possession of the Holy
Land, and the Jewish people resigned themselves to passive
longing. Though no longer the centre of learning, Palestine had still a considerable Jewish population; and when
the Karaites who rejected the Oral Law were driven from
Babylon by the Rabbinist schools, many of them emigrated to Jerusalem and the other towns of Jewish association, and revived there the tradition of scholarship. The
intensity of the hope which the congregations of the
Diaspora still felt towards the land of their fathers, whether
in good times or in bad, is manifest in the writings of the
most brilliant of the Hebrew poets who flourished in the
golden era of Jewish thought in Spain. Jehudah Halevi
(1085-1140) poured forth there his songs to Zion, and
finally set out on the perilous journey to the land he loved.
" I am in the West, but my heart is in the East " was his
theme in Spain; and when he came to Jerusalem, and
saw the lowly condition of its few Jews, his heart broke.
According to one story, he vanished in the ruins of the
Temple; according to another, celebrated among the
lyrics of Heine, he was pierced by a Crusader's lance as he
uttered his dirges. His fate is symbolical of the hopeless

love which the Jews of the Middle Ages felt for the national
home.

In the twelfth century a new power obtained sway in
Palestine. The Crusaders in 1100 captured it for Christendom and divided it into a number of feudal fiefs. Jehudah
Halevi must have found Jerusalem ruled by a Latin King,
and the Temple site and the Moslem shrine, the Dome of
the Rock, occupied by the Knights Templar. The
Christians were less tolerant than the Mohammedans, and
they signalized the capture of Jerusalem by a butchery of
the Jews. But the Jewish merchants and craftsmen had a
place in the lively civilization to which the meeting of
East and West gave birth. At Damascus, the chief centre
of the caravans, there was a community of over 3,000
Jews. They carried their mercantile adventures to
Eastern Asia and Africa, and brought the wealth of
China and India, Nubia and Abyssinia, to enrich the
castles of the lords of Palestine.

Benjamin of Tudela, another Spanish Jew, who wandered over the Holy Land about 1170, describes the
communities which he found not only in the large towns
but in smaller places such as Ascalon and Tanturah,
where there were skilled dyers and glass-makers. But
while the struggle between Frank and Saracen was
raging, the condition of the Jewish settlers grew more
wretched. As in feudal Europe, so in feudal Palestine,
the Jew was outside the State and outside the law, and in
such an atmosphere high thinking could not flourish.
Maimonides, fleeing there from the fanatical Moslems of
North Africa, found no congenial resting-place, and he
passed on to Egypt, where a broad-minded and liberal
Moslem held sway. The Emir Saladin, to whom he became physician, was a few years later to wrest Jerusalem
from the Christian knights, and to bring the greater part
of the country again under the sway of the Khalifs.
The intervention of Maimonides with the victor was instrumental in opening the door to Palestine again for

Jewish settlers. Scholars and rabbis from France and England turned to what seemed again a land of promise and of freedom, and Jewish learning revived in Jerusalem and Tiberias. Intermittently, incursions by Tartar hordes spread destruction; but the settlement continued to grow. The final expulsion of the Crusaders from the coast towns occurred in 1291, synchronizing with the expulsion of the Jews from England.

The land, even under the rule of the rude Turks, became increasingly the refuge for the persecuted Jewish scholars of Europe. The philosopher Crescas declared that the excellence of the Jews was due to the excellence of the land of Israel. Most distinguished of these settlers was Nachmanides, who emigrated from Spain at the age of seventy, and brought to his new home the ardour for mystical speculation which marked his era. The dream of the restoration, though darkened by the smoke of oppression, was still alive, and the hope of the Kingdom of God was translated into an inner vision. Ten centuries of exile had transformed the love of Zion from an active to a contemplative feeling; and the sages in Palestine sought to hasten the advent of the Messiah by pondering on the mysteries of the world and penetrating the hidden meaning and secret wisdom of God's law.

The expulsion of the Jews from Spain at the end of the fifteenth century brought to Palestine a revival of Jewish culture. The bulk of the fugitives turned eastwards and settled in the Turkish Empire, now the dominant power of the Moslem world, and they introduced into the Holy Land not only the Castilian dialect (the Ladino) of the Peninsula, but a revived Hebrew ardour. The land had lost its old fertility and prosperity through the repeated devastations of Tartar hordes. Its countryside was deserted; its houses were ruined; its ports were empty; but the light of learning still shone. In the new flowering of Jewish scholarship Safed, the hill-city of Galilee which had been a Crusader stronghold, leapt into fame. It was filled with Rabbinical schools which exercised an authority over the whole of Jewry like that which the schools of its neighbour Tiberias had enjoyed a thousand years before. The Holy Spirit seemed again to be vouchsafed to the sages of the Holy Land. And one notable attempt was made to give practical direction to the ideal of Israel's restoration. Don Joseph Nasi, the descendant of a Portuguese exile, who had become the trusted diplomatist of the Ottoman Empire and had been created Duke of Naxos, after entertaining and then abandoning the idea of a Jewish colony in an island of the Greek archipelago, obtained from Sultan Selim II the grant of a large tract in Galilee with permission to rebuild the town of Tiberias and populate it exclusively with Jews. It was the anticipation of the modern movement for the return of the Jews to their ancestral soil, the first practical expression of the reviving national consciousness.

Lady Mary Wortley Montagu, writing from Constantinople at the end of the seventeenth century, says of the Jews: "These people are an incredible power in this country. They have many privileges above all the national Turks themselves, and have formed a very considerable commonwealth here, being judged by their own laws, and have drawn the whole trade of the Empire into their hands." Yet the Jewish people as a whole was not ready for a large movement of repatriation. The influences of the Ghetto crippled the wings of its imagination, and at the same time impaired its power of action. Under the leadership of the pseudo-Messiah, Sabbatai Zevi, the Eastern Jews indeed rose in their thousands to inaugurate a new Kingdom of God in the Holy Land. Two of his chief supporters are described as " Nathan of Gaza " and " Joseph of Ascalon," proving that Jewish congregations still flourished in the ancient cities of Palestine. But with the downfall of its leader the movement collapsed even more quickly than it had sprung up. And the effect of their hopeless enterprise was to sap for generations the

vigour of Oriental Jewry, and to bring about the secession
of a sect who continued to believe in the pseudo-Messiah.

In Palestine itself the decay of the Jewish communities
set in as the government of the Turks weakened and left
the country a prey to the roving tribes of Bedouin. Yet
Israel is never altogether deserted; the undying love of
the people for their land received a new outlet when the
famous Rabbi Elijah, known as the Gaon of Wilna, at the
end of the eighteenth century, revived in the form of the
Chalukah the old contribution to the Jewish schools of the
holy cities. His aim was to preserve a centre of Jewish
learning in the place of Israel's hopes, and his project was
received with enthusiasm throughout Russia and Poland,
Galicia and Germany, Hungary and Holland. Hundreds
of scholars settled in the Holy Cities. The Chalukah
system has been abused in recent times, but for years it
had the merit of maintaining a remnant in the land, and
of giving a concrete form to the spiritual yearning of the
people.

The hope of the return had for seventeen centuries
never been dried up or become outworn. It had given to
the harried, hunted, and persecuted Jewish people,
driven from land to land, denied in places human rights,
nowhere at home, nowhere accepted into civil society, the
vision without which it must have perished. It had lived
in their imagination, endowed with an ideal life in their
prayers and their religious observances, called to mind on
every occasion of joy or sorrow. It had been the magnetic
lodestar by which the ship of the Jewish nation, often
rudderless and often without any captain, had held on its
course. And if the hope of the physical return had, in the
blurring process of time, become dimmer, this ideal of the
Yishub (the " return " of the nation) remained to illumine
the obscurity of the Ghetto, and to give a meaning to
Jewish suffering.

The French Revolution, which heralded a new era for
humanity, ushered in also a new era for the Jew. In

France, in Germany, and in England, under the influence of liberal ideas and the belief in the rights of man, the gates of the Ghetto were broken down; in the United States of America, where, from the time of the Declaration of Independence, the idea of human equality was accepted as an integral part of the polity, the gates were never erected: and in these countries, though the clouds of prejudice might still hover, it was possible for the Jew to become a freeman and a citizen of the world. The genius which had been cribbed, cabined, and confined for generations, wasted if it could not find scope in the preservation of Judaism, burst forth to display itself in a more spacious field. While the Gentile peoples were proclaiming Liberty, Equality, and Fraternity, from among the Jews a cry was raised, " Out of the tribal into the human." That idea was implicit in the Mendelssohnian " enlightenment," and it guided the Paris Sanhedrin of 1796 which sealed the Concordat between the Jews of France and the French Republic.

It is noteworthy, however, that Napoleon, who, as First Consul, pressed for the Concordat, realized on invading Egypt and Syria in 1799, the undying appeal of Palestine, and issued an invitation to the Jews of Asia and Africa to settle under his aegis in Jerusalem. He published a political manifesto to this end in the *Moniteur Universelle*. His attempt to be the modern Cyrus had even less fruition than the attempt of the Emperor Julian 1,500 years previously. His Eastern campaign collapsed before Acre, and Palestine remained under the misgovernment of the Turks.

Within a short time, indeed, Palestine was conquered by Ibrahim the son of Mehemet Ali, the Pasha of Egypt, who had made himself independent. Under his strong rule there was a promise of better things. When Sir Moses Montefiore paid his first visit to the Holy Land in 1837 he met Ibrahim, and negotiated with him as to the Jewish colonization of the deserted plains and villages of the country. The Jewish philanthropist entertained, in common with the best of the emancipated Jews of the time, a profound feeling for the country of Israel's past, which found expression in the effort to re-establish there a Jewish peasantry. But before his plan of colonization could be started Mehemet Ali had been compelled by the European Powers to renounce his sway over Syria and to restore the country to Turkey. There was at the time no chance of negotiation with the Turks; and Sir Moses Montefiore had to restrict his efforts to the betterment of the conditions of the few thousand Jews who were already living in the country.

The Crimean War, which arose immediately out of the trouble between rival churches as to the custody of the Holy Places in Jerusalem, directed the attention of the Great Powers, and the outbreak some years before of the Blood Accusation at Damascus directed anew the attention of the emancipated Jewish communities, towards Palestine. The Christian Churches began to vie with each other in building religious institutions on the sites secured by them in Jerusalem; and the Jewish communities of the West founded schools, hospitals, and other philanthropic institutions for their brethren in various parts of the country. In the latter half of the century a more radical change in the outlook of the Jews towards Palestine, the transformation of the idea of the Restoration to Zion from the region of dreams to the region of reality, was brought about by an intensification of the national feeling of Europe, and a revival of their own national consciousness.

As the permanent influences of the French Revolution worked themselves out, the idea of the rights of man was amplified by the idea of the rights of nationalities. It was claimed that every aggregation of men conscious of forming a separate nationality, whether united by language or tradition or history, or all these, should be an autonomous nation; and in the light of this principle Greece, Belgium, and Italy, and later the Balkan and Scandinavian peoples,

asserted and established their political independence. At
the same time, in the gradual decline of the respect for
the rights of man by themselves, the old feelings of dislike
and contempt for the Jew, fanned by inherited prejudice
or bureaucratic machinations, began to get the upper
hand in the less enlightened parts of Europe. The pro-
gressive spirit of the age combined with the reaction of the
time to revive the Jewish feeling of nationality, and to
shatter the philosophy of the early leaders of the " enlightenment," who sought by denial of any national
individuality to smooth the way for the absorption of the
Jews into the European polity.

The idealist movement " Back to the Land " began
before persecution came to spur it: but the relapse of
Russia into medieval barbarism, which threatened the
destruction or demoralization of six million Jews, brought
it home anew to the whole of Jewry that in the words of
their daily prayer: " God hath not made us like the
nations of other lands and hath not placed us like other
families of the earth." A new exodus began which carried
every year something like 150,000 souls to new homes.
True that the main tide of emigration has flowed to the
New World; yet Palestine has become year by year the
common goal of the Jewish people and its most living ideal.

Thirty years of pioneer work made the Yishub already
a pride and inspiration to the whole of Jewry. And
during the Great War the sentiment hardened into a
conviction that the opportunity for the Jewish restoration
has come. It found its consecration in the Declaration of
the British Government on 2nd November 1917, proclaiming that England views with favour the establishment in Palestine of a national home for the Jewish people;
and will use her best endeavours to facilitate the achieve-
ment of that object.

At the Congress of Vienna in 1815, with which the war
era of the French Revolution came to an end, the Jewish
representatives who hovered on the outskirts of the gather-

ing were concerned to secure for the Jewish communities of Central Europe, what the communities of France had already secured—civil and political rights. They wanted Jews to be counted of the nation, but not as a nation. At the Conference which followed the war of our own era representatives of the Jews, admitted as the spokesmen of a nationality, asked of the assembled Powers that their claim to return to their historic home as a people might be granted in order that they should make Palestine again a fruitful land, fruitful with the products of nature and fruitful also with the products of the human mind.

I

ATHLIT: AN EPITOME OF PALESTINE CIVILIZATION

(*With a Note on Caesarea and Megiddo*)

It is one of the striking features of Palestine that it is full
of the meeting-places of ages and civilizations. Amidst its
hills and caves primitive man developed from the brute
beast, as is witnessed by the skull found a few years ago
in the caves of Tabgha by the Sea of Galilee, and by the
thousands of flint implements of the Musterian, the
Palaeolithic and Neolithic periods which have been
gathered in various parts of the land. Here the conquering races of antiquity—Hittites, Egyptians, Assyrians,
Philistines and the rest—piled their fortresses and their
temples one on the other, as witness the layers of the Tells
of Beisan, Megiddo, Tel el Farah and others which the
scientific excavator is now laying bare. Here later the
Seleucids and the Romans encircled the Jewish Kingdom
with their columned towns, Sebastiya, Jerash, Ascalon, of
which the ruined theatres and temples still strew the
ground: and, after the Jewish Kingdom was brought to
an end, the Byzantines multiplied their monasteries and
the Crusaders their castles. And so we come to the epoch
of the Arabs and the Turks whose walled cities, mosques
and domed huts rise in rhythmic lines from the hills.
And lastly to the red-roofed villages and the orange
orchards and the pylons carrying electric power through
the length and breadth of the country, which mark the
return of the renascent Jewish people to its ancient home.

All this development through the ages may be seen in an epitome within the area of the single village of Athlit which lies on the coastal plain of Sharon some fifteen miles south of Haifa. There is a station of the Palestine Railways which, on the board announcing the name of the place, states " For the famous Crusaders' Castle." The castle rising on a bold promontory from the sea in a rugged mass of towers and walls is, indeed, the most striking thing on the landscape. Yet near by, in a break of the foothills of the Carmel at the eastern edge of the coastal plain, lie certain deep dark caves which are likely to be as famous in the annals of pre-history as is the castle of Athlit in the chronicles of the Middle Ages. The caves are now under exploration by Miss Garrod of the British School of Archaeology, who started on the work some years ago with three other women. Her party have penetrated far into the labyrinth. They were led there through the discovery, in one of the caves, of the first prehistoric work of art unearthed in the Near East. It was a carving of bone representing a bull-calf beautifully executed. The government inspector who made this discovery in his turn was led to the place, because it was originally proposed to quarry from these very caves the stone required for the Haifa Harbour now under construction. But before the destruction of the ancient was begun for the sake of the industrial enterprise of to-day, the Department of Antiquities carried out a survey. So much light was thrown on the prehistoric age by this preliminary examination that it was decided that quarrying must not be allowed to ruin what had been preserved for tens of thousands of years, and that the tons of stone to be thrown into the sea should be obtained from a less precious cliff.

The excavations of the group of women revealed a number of human burials which are among the earliest known to archaeologists, and a vast treasure of palaeolithic industries, ranging from the Musterian to the Bronze Age. The weapons and implements of bone and flint are heaped feet deep on the floor of this earliest habitation of man. In 1932 further remarkable discoveries were made. Eight human skeletons of adults were found close together. They were of the type of the so-called Neanderthal Man, but with differences so definite that the anthropologists have had to christen a fresh species, Palaeanthropus Palestinus. The cranial vault of these skulls rises higher than in the Neanderthal Man, and the head is somewhat rounder. The face and jaws jut out more markedly, so as to approximate still more closely to the ape; and the scientists are already building up a case for putting further back the evolution of man.

The latest diggings in the caves of Athlit, and in another series of caves, some ten miles to the south beneath the Jewish village of Zicron Jacob, have revealed also traces of an earlier " mesolithic " civilization than was known in pre-history. A new local name has been given to it, the Natoufian, from the name of the Zicron cave. It is dated at about 6000 B.C.E.; and besides other objects of primitive art, bracelets of bone-beads and carved animal heads, the caves have yielded a store of large perfectly-formed tools of flint, including sickles and other agricultural implements. These demonstrate that cultivation of the soil was known in Palestine in that remote age. In no other part of the hearth of civilization, which is placed by anthropologists and archaeologists in the " fertile Crescent " between the Nile and the Euphrates,[1] has there been such a definite indication of this early progress of man to the practical arts. It is remarkable that Palestine should have furnished both the first specimens of wild wheat, which was found by the late Aaron Aaronson of Zicron Jacob, and the first examples of agriculture, and that the neighbourhood of Athlit is associated with both discoveries. Civilization, it seems, moved in the earliest epoch from Palestine to Egypt; though Egypt was to make repayment in a later age. In the days when the caves of Athlit

[1] See Breasted, *The Conquest of Civilization*. Harpers, 1926.

were inhabited, the climate and nature of Palestine were
different. For the Fauna whose bones were discovered
include deer which require a damp and wooded country,
and the rhinoceros which must have trampled through a
primitive swamp. Though nature has changed, the march
of civilization through the valley has been uninterrupted
for 7000 years.

At the other end of the ages and the march of civilization
we have the quarry for the harbour, now placed at the
long barrier of rocky hill which separates the foreshore and
the castle of Athlit from the cultivated plain. And here
daily some 800 workers assemble; 600 Arabs and 200
Jews, who with the most modern machinery remove the
vast slabs of rock. The waiting railway trucks then carry
the stone some fifteen miles; and there men hurl it into
the sea by the point of Carmel beneath the Monastery of
Elijah, whence a mole runs out more than a mile to make
what will be the third largest harbour of the Mediterranean.

The whole coast indeed is dotted with worked-out
quarries, and strewn, in the words of Sir George Adam
Smith, with " the fiercer wreckage of harbours." Every
little promontory, every islet that was formed off the
sandy coast, became in Biblical times a port for the hardy
Phoenician mariners from northern Syria. And it was on
one of these promontories that in the twelfth century the
Crusaders placed their strongest and most famous harbour.
Before and after their time the place was known as Athlit;
but it was renamed by them " the Fortress of the Pilgrims." Athlit has its ancient as well as its medieval record under that name, though it is not mentioned in
scripture. Some years ago Jewish archaeologists found,
amid its ruins, a slab bearing the two letters Ayin and
Teth: and scholars have conjectured the origin of its
name in a Semitic root meaning a cranny of the rocks.
They have identified it indeed with the fortress of Magdiel
or Magdalel, " the castle of God " which is referred to
in the book of Genesis (xxxvi. 43) amongst the list of

places governed by Ishmaelite chiefs. In the fourth century Eusebius writes of " Magdiel in the land of the tribe of Naphtali, on the way to Acre, five miles from Dor." Now Dor was one of the great fortresses which guarded the land of Israel from the Northern invaders. It was transformed later into a Hellenistic town and port, and has been identified with the village of Tantura, which lies five miles south of Athlit. There on another rocky promontory you may still see the rounded columns and the strewn capitals of the Greek and Roman temple, gleaming in the sun, and the rocky shelves fashioned for the beaching of the galleys. And if that identification is correct, then Magdiel five miles to the north would be the predecessor or successor of Athlit.

The road that runs along the coastal plain from Acre southwards to Jaffa, and on again to Gaza and the River of Egypt, is one of the main highways of the world's history, the Via Maris—the way of the sea. These ruined harbours of Athlit, Dor, Caesarea, and Apollonia lay along its course. The road was protected too by a number of fortresses, of which one lay near Athlit and may still be distinguished in a rounded Tell which keeps a historic name. In Roman times it was known as Districtum; to the Crusaders it was Detroit, and its ruins to-day are called by the Arabs Khirbet—that is, the ruins of— Dustri. Recent excavation has revealed below the Tell a cemetery of the seventh or eighth century B.C.E. with bodies and ornaments of Egyptians and Phoenicians, and scarabs that help to fix its date. Here there must have been then, nearly 2,000 years before the Templars built this fortress of the Pilgrims, a place of commerce and seafaring men. The fortress commanded the pass which led through the reef of rocks, and was known to the Byzantine chroniclers as Petra Incisa.

But it was the Crusaders invading the country, and for less than two hundred years its rulers, who raised at Athlit the vast fortress of which the ruins still arouse

amazement. After the disastrous defeat of the Frankish
knights on the Horns of Hattin, when Saladin broke the
power of the Latin kingdom of Jerusalem, the Crusaders
were pinned down to a line of castles along or near the sea
coast. New fortresses were built which should be free from
the corruption and sinfulness of Acre. Athlit was the
strongest of these new castles and the home of the Knights
Templar; and stood the unceasing attacks of the Saracens
longer than the rest. But in 1291 it fell before the Emir
Saladin Khalil, who finally broke the power of the Franks
in Palestine. St. Jean d'Acre had already fallen a year
earlier; and with the capture of Athlit the Crusaders lost
their remaining foothold on what is still sometimes called
the Crusader Coast.

To-day the Department of Antiquities of the Government of Palestine is restoring the form of the old fortress
which, with its outworks and faubourgs where the bur-
gesses and merchants lived, covered an area of over fifty
acres and was surrounded by a moat. The line of the moat
is still intact—marked by evil-looking and evil-smelling
pools. But it is proposed to let in the water so that the sea
once again may engirdle the castle. And while the ancient
and medieval stronghold is being restored, modern industry, working side by side with archaeology, is changing
the face of the land. The moat of the castle of Athlit
borders the salt pans laid out by the Palestine Salt Company on what were hitherto malarial marshes. The company supplies nearly all the salt which is required for the
people of Palestine, over 7,000 tons a year, producing it
from the evaporation of the sea water in these pans. At
the border of the pans facing the massive ruins of the castle
stands a factory where the salt is cleaned and crushed.
And at the northern end of the pans the cranes lift the vast
chunks of stone hewn from the quarry for the Haifa
harbour.

They are the same quarries from which in the Middle
Ages the Templars obtained the stone for making their

castle and their harbour. The stone has proved its sea-
worthiness in withstanding the waves these 700 years.
The noise of the blasting is the daily music of Athlit. But
the pastoral pipe of Arab shepherds is still heard along the
foreshore; though those shepherds who have squatted
within the castle's precincts are now to be moved to a
place where they cannot ruin the ruins.

The little Jewish agricultural village, planted on the
plain by the Jewish Colonization Association some thirty
years ago, has now become the home of a thriving population. In addition to the farmers' cottages, it includes the
huts of the Jewish workers in the salt-pans and the quarries.
One other ruin, however, and that a modern ruin, lies
within the village lands of Athlit. It is the wreck of the
Experimental Agricultural Station, founded by Aaron
Aaronson some years before the War. It still displays its
former functions by a shady avenue of Washington palms,
and is approached by a metalled road that before the War
was the best piece of highway on the plain of Sharon.
Its plantations are sadly deserted and withered, as they
have been since the Turks laid them waste during the
War, believing that the Station was being used for the
purposes of the British Intelligence Service. The only
signs of activity are the pylons of the Palestine Electric
Corporation, striding through the fields and waiting to
receive the power from the Jordan which will bring a new
prosperity to the plain of Sharon.

Save in this one corner, the lands and the foreshore of
Athlit are humming with activity as they have not hum-
med for six hundred years. In this God's acre the ages
have met; prehistoric, ancient, medieval and present;
and the Jews who are now restoring the fertility of the soil
where their ancestors ploughed, and helping to build the
harbour where another Semitic people had its haven
three thousand years ago, form the link of continuity in
this epitome of civilization.

If Athlit was the medieval stronghold on the coast, the

older fortified town which guarded the Via Maris was Dor. It has been identified, as we have seen, with the Arab village of Tantura at the side of which a rocky promontory is protected from the waves by two rounded reefs. Dor was one of the four forts—Baisan, Taanach and Megiddo are the other three—which in the epoch of the Egyptian campaigns commanded the highway from the sea to the Jordan Valley and Syria beyond, and guarded the passes against an invader coming from the north. Like the other coast-towns it was occupied by the Philistines when the Egyptian power declined; but Solomon ruled it and placed it under his son-in-law, Abinadab (1 Ki., iv. 11). When the kingdom of Israel and Judah was divided, it must have become a principal port of Israel. But after the captivity it fell to the Phoenicians who occupied the whole coast and together with the other neighbours of the Jews were Hellenized. Dor then became a centre of Hellenic culture. The Maccabee conqueror Alexander Jannaeus made himself master of it; and his name is perpetuated in the Iskanderun (*i.e.* Alexander) rivulet which runs near here through the plain of Sharon; but it returned to its Hellenistic autonomy when Pompey overthrew the Jewish authority outside Judaea.

Palestine, it has been said, eats up harbours. The artificial ports along its straight sweep of coast disappear, one after the other. Dor had its day when Herod built a new and greater haven some twenty miles to the south, Caesarea ad Mare, to be a stronghold of the Roman naval power on the Mediterranean Coast. Josephus describes how the harbour formed the centre of surrounding sections of the city.[1] All the streets led in radial directions to it, and were intersected by parallel avenues. The haven was always free from the waves of the sea. It was as large as the Piraeus (the port of Athens), and had towards the city a double station for the ships. Subways have survived to this day which lead to the beach, and must have once

---

[1] Jos., *B.J.*, I. xxi.

connected different parts of the city. Herod constructed also two great aqueducts, of which the ruins, partly covered by the encroaching dunes, still stretch over some twenty kilometres. The higher channel carried the water for the town, and the lower served to drain and irrigate the plain of Sharon. Of the vast harbour all that remains is an amorphous block of stone, some 100 metres out in the sea. The temple to the honour of Caesar, his royal master, which the Jewish king built at the mouth of the haven, has disappeared without a trace. The temple in the town itself, which in the Middle Ages was transformed into a cathedral, is now a cattle-yard, though Greek sculpture may still be seen on its walls. The theatre in which a successor of Herod, King Agrippa, acted and died, can be traced only by a slope of circular tiers on a hillside. Before Herod magnified and glorified the city, it was known as Strato's Tower, probably after some Sidonian king of the fourth century, but it has borne now for 2,000 years the name of Herod's patron.

After the destruction of Jerusalem, Caesarea was to remain the capital city of Palestine and the seat of government for six centuries, throughout the periods of the Roman, Byzantine, and early Christian Empires. The fatal rebellion which ended in the destruction of the Temple (c.e. 70) had its inception in a riot between its Jewish and Gentile citizens. According to tradition, Rabbi Akiba was executed here by the Roman conqueror after the desperate Jewish rising of Barcokbah was crushed in the second century. Here in the third century Jewish and Christian learning flourished side by side: the Jewish under Rabbi Abahau, to whom is ascribed the so-called Talmud of Caesarea, and the Christian school of Patristic philosophy, of which Origen was the chief master. Centuries later Benjamin of Tudela in his travels through Palestine found there 200 Jews and 200 Cutheans or Samaritans. He wrongly identified it with Gath of the Philistines. St. Louis, the pious and warrior French King,

who in the thirteenth century led a forlorn Crusade to the
Holy Land, built a castle which still stands with its
medieval walls, and houses to-day a poor village. The
town about the castle was entirely destroyed by the arch-
destructor, the Sultan Baibars, about 1290; and the place
was derelict for hundreds of years. An age of anarchy
followed the destruction of the Christian kingdom in the
Holy Land. The country was overrun by semi-barbarian
tribes of Turcomans and Mongols, till the conquest of the
Ottomans in the sixteenth century. It is to this period that
we must attribute the long desolation of a land which was
once smiling and prosperous as well as holy.

Caesarea offers to-day one of the few examples of
Turkish colonization in Palestine. After the loss of Bosnia
and Herzegovina in 1878, the Ottoman Sultan placed in
the ruins of the medieval fortress a colony of Moslem
Bosnians who still live there. They have made a wreck
of the classical ruins which, before their coming, were
spread over the ground for miles. The columns and pillars
and capitals, which must have been brought by Herod
from afar, were sold for building stone, and were taken, it
is said, to build palaces for the merchant-princes of
Alexandria. The places marked on the map as the King's
Palace, the Forum and the Hippodrome are now rough
cornfields; and all that remains of the breakwater is a
small ridge visible at ebb-tide. Where once 200,000 lived,
to-day barely 100 have their home.

Besides the Bosnians planted by the Turks, another
group of colonists have been planted more recently by
the Jewish Colonization Association in the lands between
Caesarea and Athlit, and are reclaiming them to their old
fertility. Jewish pioneers are draining the marshes, and
planting the sand dunes which, unchecked for centuries,
have invaded and overwhelmed the cultivable lands, and
they are making Sharon bloom again like the rose. At
Tantura too in our day Baron Edmond de Rothschild,
the father of Jewish colonization, sought to revive the old

Jewish industry of glass-making. But malaria drove away the workers; and the factory stands gaunt and derelict amid its deserted wood of eucalpytus. The Baron has made a more auspicious attempt to revive another Palestinian industry in this region, by the perfume factory of Benyamina: and the country is fragrant with jasmine and narcissus which are grown for the purposes of the factory.

From Dor an ancient track, going almost due east, leads through the Carmel ridge to the pass of Megiddo, most famous of the historical routes of the warriors of antiquity. It is mentioned on the pylon of Thotmes III, the conquering Pharaoh of the fourteenth century; in the Tel-el-Amarna tablets of the following century; on the stele of Shishak the conqueror of Rehoboam who set up a triumphal monument in Karnak; and frequently in the Bible. Scarabs of Thotmes and a cartouche of Shishak were found in the Tell itself. Near it Shalmaneser broke the bow of Israel, and King Josiah fell in his battle with the Egyptian Neco. The Romans named it Legio, because it was the station of a legion; and to this day the Arab village at the mouth of the pass is Lejjun. But in the Book of Revelation it is marked as the place of the great battle before the Last Judgment, with its old name slightly disguised as Armageddon, *i.e.*, the Hill of Megiddo. And the latest conqueror of the Holy Land, who sent his cavalry galloping through the pass in September 1918, has appropriately taken his title as Lord Allenby of Megiddo.

History is piled up here like storeys in an American skyscraper. Before the War a German expedition made soundings and had one remarkable haul, a seal marked " Shema, officer of Jeroboam." It was of the time of Jeroboam II, the King of Israel in the eighth century. And the pre-war excavation was only a prelude.

The secrets of the vast Tell—known as Mutesellim—overlooking the pass are being systematically given up to-day as the mound is removed, layer by layer, by the excavator. The expedition of the University of Chicago has set itself to carry through the exploration, in a period of twenty years, more thoroughly perhaps than any other expedition has explored a Biblical site. The Tell will be removed: every stone and object will be preserved: or, if not preserved, surveyed, docketed, and photographed. The expedition, working backwards through the ages, has already disposed of the Arab, the Byzantine, the Roman and the Hebrew layers. The last displayed a wall four metres thick and a vast system of stables, where King Solomon must have stabled his war-chariots and their horses. The foundations are complete, with the stalls for 300 horses, the mangers, the tethering pillars. They are of hewn stone and of long rectangular shape. The workman-ship is Phoenician, and the masonry is like that of the relics of the Temple of Solomon; and the Seal of Solomon was found graven on the wall. Similarly the Tell el Hesi in Southern Palestine, on the site of the Lachish mentioned in the Bible and the Egyptian monuments, which was early excavated by Flinders Petrie for the Palestine Exploration Fund, revealed a vast stable that is ascribed to the same period. The two discoveries confirm the re-cord in Kings and Chronicles of store-cities which the King built for the chariots and horsemen (1 Ki., ix. 19 and 2 Chr., viii. 6).

It is the essential romance of Palestine that the scenes of the day-to-day struggle with nature, of modern enter-prise and agriculture, are steeped in human history, so that the associations of the Prophets of Israel, the Sages of Judaea, the warring Kings of the nations, the knights of the Crusades, and the paladins of the East are continually about the worker, and inspire him to a greater purpose. That thought is finely expressed in the lines which the English poet, Thomas Hardy, wrote of Allenby's victory in 1918 in this pass of Megiddo.

Did they catch as it were in a vision at shut of the day—
When their cavalry smote through the ancient Esdraelon
    Plain,

And they crossed where the Tishbite stood forth in the
    enemy's way—
His gaunt mournful Shade as he bade the King haste off
    amain?

On war-men at this end of time—even on Englishmen's
    eyes—
Who slay with their arms of new might in that long ago
    place,
Flashed who drove furiously? Ah, did the phantom arise
Of that queen, of that proud Tyrian woman who
    painted her face?

    .   .   .   .   .

Could such be the hauntings of men of to-day, at the
    cease
Of pursuit, at the dusk-hour, ere slumber their senses
    could seal?
Enghosted seers, kings—one on horseback who asked
    " Is it Peace? " . . .
Yea, strange things and spectral may men have beheld
    in Jezreel!

II

THE OLDEST CITY OF JERUSALEM

They that Trust in the Lord shall be as Mount Zion,
which cannot be removed but abideth for ever.

(Ps. cxxv)

Bernard Shaw, who visited Jerusalem in the spring of
1931, suggested that a board should be placed by each of
the holy sites in the Holy City bearing the legend, " N.B.—
This site is not genuine." That legend indeed could be
justified of many of the reputed places of pilgrimage; and
in general it is the scene and not the particular site, the
out-of-doors, and not the building, in Jerusalem—and in
Palestine—which is impressive.

One Biblical monument in Jerusalem, however, which
is the work of man's hand, is not only indisputably genuine,
but is absolutely unchanged from the Bible days. It is the
tunnel built by King Hezekiah during the invasion of the
Assyrian hordes to carry the waters from the spring which
lay outside the walls of his fortress-capital to the enclosure
of the city, so that those within might have to drink, and
the invaders might not cut off the very life of the defenders.
The many invasions and sieges of Jerusalem have not
destroyed or impaired this ancient piece of engineering.
And though in the winter months it is not possible to pass
along the tunnel, during the long summer spell of rainless-
ness when the waters subside, it may be penetrated—in
waders. The knowledge of its course, indeed, was hidden
for centuries. Some fifty years ago, however, one of the
pioneers of Palestine archaeology, M. Clermont-Ganneau,
the French Consul in Jerusalem, after a Jewish schoolboy
had passed through the channel then thought to be impassable, recovered a tablet which records its making in one

31

of the oldest Hebrew inscriptions extant. The inscription, which was in the Assyrian script, runs thus simply:

" Behold, the boring through [is completed]; and this is the story of the boring through. While yet the excavators were lifting up the pick, each towards his fellow, and while yet there were three cubits to be bored through, there was heard the voice of one calling to another, for there was a crevice in the rock on the right hand. They rose up, they struck on the west of the boring, the stonecutters struck each to meet his fellow, pick to pick, and the waters flowed from the source to the Pool for a thousand and two hundred cubits; and three quarters of a cubit was the height of the rock above the heads of the stonecutters."

The carving was cut by a Greek ruffian out of the rock where it was found, and broken and damaged. But it reposes now in the Museum of Constantinople.

The inscription is striking, not only for the human appeal of the record of the two working parties, whose joy at the success of their work we may experience again, but also as an example of Hebrew script in the days of the Kingdom of Judah, and as a sure measuring-rod of the cubit. The passage is 1,700 feet in length, so that we may fix the cubit at $1\frac{7}{12}$ of a foot.

One evening in September a party of us set out to walk through the tunnel. We started by walking round the Old City and across the hill under which the channel was conducted, so that we might gain afresh our historical bearings, and recall the crowded chapter of history which had this hill as its subject. The Jebusite city, which was the capital of the Kingdom of Judaea till the first Captivity, lies outside the present walled city of Jerusalem. It was built on and around the hill named Ophel, which has a circumference of some 1,300 metres. This mound has been excavated with remarkable thoroughness in recent years by Capitaine Weill on behalf of Baron Edmond de Roth-schild, by the British School of Archaeology in Palestine, and by the Palestine Exploration Fund.

Ophel, it may be mentioned, means simply a hump or swelling, and so is used generally for a mound or knoll (see 2 Ki., v. 24). It is used in connection with the Jebusite fortress rather as an epithet than as a name; and the height itself is more commonly called Zion (1 Ki., viii. 1). That name is said to mean a watch-tower; and it would correspond in connotation with the other hill to the east which is now known as " Scopus " and is the site of the Hebrew University.

The excavations have cleared up the doubts and settled a long-drawn controversy, with regard to the site of Mount Zion and the City of David. Josephus, who is more often than not inaccurate, and medieval tradition, which is generally misleading, had identified the hill of Zion and the City of David and Solomon not with Ophel but with the south-western part of the height, in spite of strong indications in the Bible to the contrary. That hill rises some 200 feet above the Ophel, and is dominated to-day by a battlemented citadel, commonly known as the Tower of David. The Gate in the existing walls that opens on the hill is known as the Zion Gate. Till the beginning of this century the learned generally regarded this upper and higher hill as the site of the original Jerusalem, and scoffed at the idea that the lower spur of Ophel, with its mere fifteen acres, could have accommodated the fortress-city of David. As is usual in Jerusalem the holy sites were dup-licated: there were two Zions and two Ophels, just as there were two Calvarys and two Gethsemanes.

Confusion as to the original Zion arose in the period when the two hills that were divided by the Tyropeon valley were included in the walled city of the Maccabees and the Herodian Kings, and the limits of the early city were forgotten. Herod placed his palace on the highest hill, and secured this part of the city by four towers.

Here too he kept his mercenaries. Hence the south-western hill came to be recognized as the seat of power and authority. The palace of Herod became the residence of the Roman procurators—or High Commissioners—and the camp of the Roman legions abutted on the present citadel. The name of Zion, which was applied by the prophet and Psalmist to the whole city, and had been used more particularly for the seat of the governing power in the City of David, was now transferred to the new stronghold. It remained there through the ages, " and perverted the whole tradition of Old Testament topography."

It was on the new Zion that Byzantine tradition placed the tombs of the earliest Jewish Kings, and the early Christian Community built its first churches in Jerusalem. The sanctuary of Nebi Daoud built over the supposed tomb of David was identified by them with the place of the Last Supper. And for centuries it was known as the Coenaculum. The Moslems venerated it as the burial-place of David and Solomon; but they for a time in their tolerance allowed the Franciscan Order to hold it as their headquarters.

The new Mount Zion was covered during the nineteenth century with aggressive religious buildings of the Christians, the German Church of the Dormitium, and a vast unsightly church of the White Fathers which rose over the ruins of the traditional house of the High Priest Caiaphas. The original Zion or Ophel, on the other hand, was largely bare of building and given over to market gardens.

The false identification had the fortunate result that the site of the Jebusite city was left relatively free for the spade of the archaeologist; and that spade has in recent years done its work faithfully. It has revealed a part of the Jebusite ramp sheer above the Kidron valley and the spring. The ramp which David's men scaled when they took the city about 1000 B.C.E. is the most impressive monument of Canaanite fortification which has survived; and as one stands upon it, one may yet feel the sense of impregnability which those within the fortress boasted. The spade has exposed also the gutter or the watercourse[1] through which Joab led his mountaineers into the heart of the enemy fortress and captured the city. The Bible tells the dramatic story of the capture:

> "And the king and his men went to Jerusalem unto the Jebusites . . . which spake unto David, saying: 'Except thou take away the blind and the lame thou shalt not come in hither': thinking, David cannot come in hither. Nevertheless, David took the stronghold of Zion; the same is the city of David. And David said on that day, Whosoever getteth up to the gutter and smiteth the Jebusites, and the lame and the blind, that are hated of David's soul, he shall be chief and captain. . . . 'So Joab went first up, and was chief.'"[2]

The archaeologist without a spade, as we saw at the beginning, has explored the greater tunnel which, some 300 years later, King Hezekiah made to preserve the waters of the spring for the inhabitants when they were threatened with invasion and famine by the Assyrian host. Excavation has exposed also the foundations of two fortresses which guarded the Mount. On the eastern side is a bastion which, it is surmised, was built by Solomon at the flank of the Jebusite rampart, and is identified with "Millo" that stopped the breach in the wall of David's town.[3] The other fortress stood on the western side of Ophel, where the hill is bounded by the valley of the Tyropeon. The valley of old separated the hills of the plateau, but is now almost entirely choked up. The indications of "a great and strong wall with mighty towers" have suggested the identification of this fortress with the

---

[1] Some scholars deny the interpretation of the Hebrew word "Zinnor" as a water-course; and interpret it as a trident, referring to a strange weapon of David's men. See *David's Capture of Jerusalem*, by Sukenik. *J.P.O.S.*, xiii. p. 12.

[2] 2 Sam., v. 6 and 8; 1 Chr., ii. 6 and 7.   [3] 1 Ki., ii. 9.

citadel or Akra which was built by Antiochus Epiphanes
in the second century B.C.E., to hold down the city, and
was captured some thirty years later by Simon the Maccabee King. The lower part of the wall, indeed, is ascribed
to the period of Nehemiah who, as we are told in his book,
rebuilt the walls of the City of David after the return from
the first Captivity, and placed the gates " around Ophel
where dwelt the Nethinim." The wall ran over the pool of
Siloah by the King's garden, and was built " over against a
great tower which lieth out even unto the wall of Ophel."

The Bible records dramatically the desolation of the
city when Nehemiah came to rebuild the walls.

> " And I rose about night, I and some few men with
> me: Neither told I any man what God put in my heart
> to do in Jerusalem; neither was there any beast with
> me save the beast that I rode upon. And I went out by
> night by the gate of the valley, even before the dragon
> well, and to the Dung-gate, and viewed the walls of
> Jerusalem which were broken down, and the gates
> thereof were consumed with fire. Then I went on to
> the gate of the fountain and to the King's pool—[which
> must be the pool of Siloam]—but there was no footing
> for the beast that was under me "—because of the mass
> of ruins. (Neh., ii. 12-14.)

And Sanballat, the leader of the Samaritans, mocked at
the Jews when they began to rebuild, saying: " What do
these feeble Jews? Will they fortify themselves? Will
they revive the stones out of the heaps of the rubbish
which are burned? " (Ib., iv. 2).

Of the Seleucid fortress which was built 250 years later
the writer of Maccabees tells us in detail:

> " And they fortified the city of David with a great
> and strong wall, with strong towers, so that it was made
> the citadel for them. And they placed there a sinful

nation, lawless men; and they strengthened themselves therein. And they stored up arms and provisions; and collecting together the spoils of Jerusalem, they laid them up there. And it became a sore menace; for it was a place to lie in wait against the sanctuary, and an evil adversary to Israel continually." (1 Macc., i. 33 *ff.*)

It was beneath this Citadel that Antiochus and the Hellenizers built the Gymnasium which was an abomination to the pious Jews. Judah did not succeed in taking this citadel, when he recovered the Temple mount and restored the Temple worship. It is recorded that he appointed a number of men to fight against those who were in the citadel until he should have cleansed the Holy Place. (*Ib.*, iv. 41.) It was left to his warrior brother Simon to capture by siege the last stronghold of Hellenism and the Hellenizers in the Holy City. As it is said:

" But they of the citadel were hindered from going forth and from going into the country . . . and they hungered exceedingly. And they cried out to Simon to take right hands; which thing he granted them. But he cast them out from thence, and he cleansed the citadel from pollution. And he entered it with praise . . . and palm-branches . . . and with hymns and songs, because a great enemy had been destroyed out of Israel." (*Ib.*, xiii. 50.)

It was one of his titles to fame that he ruled over this citadel.

" In his day things prospered so that the Gentiles were taken away out of their country, and they also that were in the city of David, that were in Jerusalem, who had made themselves a citadel. . . . And he made the Jews to dwell therein, and fortified it for the safety of the country, and he made high the walls of Jerusalem." (*Ib.*, xiv. 36 and 37.)

D

With regard to the later fortification of Ophel, Josephus recounts that the Maccabean prince caused the level of the hill, which was higher than the Temple mount, to be lowered, and the work of the people was required for three years. But there is no evidence of any such huge operation; and the balance of scholarly opinion is that he misunderstood the record of some destructive measures ordered by the Maccabean victor, or exaggerated it, as was his manner, to a fantastic exploit. The book of Maccabees records only that Simon made stronger the hill of the Temple that was by the citadel (1 Macc., xiii. 32).

The Mount of Ophel, under the name of Zion, is the symbol in the Psalms of that which cannot be removed but abideth for ever (Ps. cxxv); and, unlike Moriah, the hill of the Temple,[1] it has not been smoothed away by man's hand. It is now fairly certain, therefore, that it was not only the primitive Jebusite stronghold, but also the city of David and Solomon, the Ophel of King Hezekiah and King Manasseh " who built an outer wall on the slope to the west of Gihon and raised Ophel to a great height: "[2] the restored city of Zerubbabel and Nehemiah which Cyrus permitted the Jews to rebuild: the Zion of the Prophets and the Psalmist; the citadel of the Maccabean struggles against a debased Hellenism; the Acra and Lower City of the struggle with Rome.

Some archaeologists indeed would ascribe to the hill a still greater antiquity as a centre of government from the prehistoric age.

Whether it was the site of a place " Awsamm," which occurs in hieroglyphs upon a collection of early potsherds of the age of the eleventh dynasty (2000 B.C.E.) that contain the names of towns and princes hostile to Egypt, and were consigned to perdition by the Egyptian priestly magicians;[3] or whether it is to be identified with the city of Salem from

---

[1] See p. 55.   [2] 2 Chr., xxxiii. 14.

[3] *Jerusalem et les Documents Egyptiens*, by Mallon: *J.P.O.S.*, viii. p. 1.

which Melchizedek came to bless the Patriarch Abraham—
that is not yet proved for certain. But there can hardly be
doubt that it was the " Urusalim " which is mentioned as
a seat of Egyptian rule threatened by the dread Habiri in
the Tel-el-Amarna letters of the fifteenth century B.C.E.
The governor of the place Abd-Khiba writes frantically
to his overlord in Egypt:

" Behold this land of the city of Urusalim, no man
aids me, no tribe supports me. Lo, it is done to me as was
done to M. and the sons of L. who have given the King's
land to the Habiri. . . . Lo the King has established his
law in Urusalim for ever, and will not rashly speak of
the desertion of the lands of Urusalim. To the scribe of
the King thus says thy servant. I bow at thy feet: I am
thy servant. Render the news well to the King." [1]

Definite traces of Egyptian occupation have been found in
the excavations of Ophel, principally in the form of
pottery marks on jar-handles. And an Egyptian head of
black granite, with a form of headdress that marks it as of
the eighteenth dynasty, has been dug up on the neighbouring hill. The statue might, indeed, have been brought
to Jerusalem by some Roman lover of the arts of a later
age; but the evidence of the Ophel pottery is said to be
unmistakable.

Urusalim must have been a place of importance, if we
may judge from the concern of the Egyptian governor;
and there is no part of the hilly plateau of Judea which is so
suited for a large habitation as this Hill of Ophel. Professor
Sayce has given the weight of his opinion to the theory
that Urusalim was a Babylonian name, and that a pre-
Jebusite city here goes back to the days when Babylon
bore sway in Canaan. Another authority, the late Dr.
Hall, put forward the hypothesis that the delay in the
capture of the Jebusite fortress by the children of Israel

[1] Berlin Collection of El Amarna: No. 103.

after their occupation of the land of Canaan (as is recorded
in Jud., i. 18), was due to the presence of an Egyptian
garrison. Other scholars have suggested that the Hebrew
name Yerushalaim, which is a dual form, refers to the two
parts of the town which lay one above the Kidron and the
other above the Hinnom ravine. One part was occupied
by the men of Benjamin, and the other by the conquered
Jebusites until David captured the fortress. As it is said
in Judges:

"And the children of Benjamin did not drive out the
Jebusites that inhabited Jerusalem, but the Jebusites
dwelt with the children of Benjamin unto this day."
(i. 21.)

Be this as it may, the fortress Jebus, which is Jerusalem,
and which became the City of David, was built up around
the perennial spring of pure water that bursts forth by the
Kidron under the precipitous scarp of the hill. The spring
determined the site of the one city on that arid plateau.
And it is not surprising that the spot where it breaks out
was chosen by David as the place for the crowning of
Solomon and his successors. (1 Ki., i. 33.) In the Bible
the spring is called Gihon, and, as many think, is identical
also with En Rogel (Josh., xviii. 16) which was the boundary between Judah and Benjamin. To-day it is called
by the Christians the Virgin's Fountain, and by the Arabs
the Spring of " Sitt Miryam " (their name for the Virgin):
but it has a second Arab name, Ain Um el Daraj, the
Spring of the Steps. For the cave where it rises lies now so
deep in the valley that it must be approached by a descent
of thirty steps. The level here, as everywhere in the Old
City of Jerusalem, has been fundamentally changed by the
heaping of the rubbish of ages. The course of the stream,
too, has been changed. In days of old it flowed free and
unrestrained from its cavern to join the Kidron. The
Bible speaks of " a river the streams whereof make glad

the City of God," and in the eighteenth century the religious English poet Heber writes in his lyrics:

> By cool Siloah's shady rill
> How fair the lily grows.

and a still greater English poet wrote before him of:

Siloah's brook that flows fast by the Oracle of God.

In days of old the description may have been justified. In our day, however, the stream is intermittent; it flows four or five times a day in the rainy season, once or twice in the dry season. And it is diverted for the domestic needs of the inhabitants of the village of Siloam. They fetch water for their households and they wash their clothes at the spring itself; and the Kidron valley is a dry-bed during most of the year, save when a sudden rain fills its stony waste.

We passed from the spring to the slopes of Ophel, and saw the excavations in the rock made a year before the Great War by Capitaine Weill. He was searching for the tombs of the Jewish kings which have been a magnet for archaeologists. He found tombs, but empty; and whether they are of kings or of commoners none may say for sure. We saw, too, the shaft sunk some fifty years ago by an English explorer of " underground Jerusalem " who was the pioneer of modern methods of excavation. Colonel Warren it was who found a tunnel leading from the spring of Siloam to the Tyropeon that is identified with the water-course of Joab's exploit. And it may be the channel of which the prophet spoke when he describes " the waters of Shiloah that flow gently " (in the Authorized Version, " go softly ") and were despised by the people. (Is., viii. 6.) For the word Shiloah means " sent " or " conducted "; and may refer to the system of aqueducts.[1]

Next we saw the remains of a Roman aqueduct which

[1] Sir George A. Smith, *Jerusalem*, vol. ii. p. 128.

led the waters of the Pool of Siloam to the town that in Roman and Byzantine times covered the hill. We saw, too, other channels which led off the water of the once bountiful spring to irrigate the fields of the Kidron valley. The Spring of the Virgin indeed is the source of a network of surface and subterranean channels, which may be compared with the network of underground and overground railways and sewers that form the communications and the drainage system of a modern capital. Père Vincent, the great authority on Jerusalem topography, has shown that the exterior opening of the spring was covered and concealed, while the water was diverted into subterranean channels communicating with the city by shafts.

So we came at last to the Upper Pool of Siloam itself, by which there is the ruin of a Byzantine church built by Justinian in the sixth century, and the minaret of a mosque built over that ruin and in daily use. Here our subterranean expedition was to begin.

The Pool, which was hollowed by Hezekiah to be the reservoir of his fortress city, must have been one of the beauty spots of old Jerusalem. We may imagine it filled with the pure waters of the spring and set amid the grateful shade of the trees. A channel was led off from it to the lower pool a few hundred yards down the valley to irrigate the King's gardens that were planted in the level ground by the junction of the Kidron, the Tyropeon, and the Hinnom ravines. To-day, in place of the King's pleasures, you have vegetable gardens in this hollow, productive enough but not lovely; and the waters do not run in a pure stream, but are fouled with the sewage of the city above that is fertilizing but not sweet. The beauty has gone from the scene, as it has gone from another scene, almost equally famous, in the other great hearth of our civilization. The stream of the Ilissus outside Athens, by which Socrates sat with his disciples and debated the question of justice, as is recorded in the *Phaedrus* of Plato, is likewise noisome with the sewage of the city of Athens; and it is as hard to picture by its banks the pleasant greensward as it is at Siloah's rill.

The Rabbis believed, because of the ebb and flow of the water, that the spring communicated with the Great Sea. It was from this pool that the water was brought for the Water Festival in the Temple which was celebrated on the nights of the Feast of Tabernacles. The priests, setting out in solemn procession from the Temple area at the break of dawn, fetched the water in a golden vessel and poured it with a libation of wine over the altar. Then the palm-bearers proceeded with their circuits. Of this feast the Rabbis declared that he who has not seen the celebration of the drawing of the water has not seen the true joy. The libation was designed as an appeal for rain; and it is replaced to-day by the special prayers for rain which are sung in the synagogue at the Feast of Tabernacles.

The tunnel runs between the Upper pool of Siloam and the Virgin's spring; and the reason of the making of it is thus recorded in the book of Chronicles:

"King Hezekiah took counsel with his princes and his mighty men to stop the waters of the fountains which were outside the city, and they helped him. So there was gathered much people together, and they stopped all the waters of the fountain and the brook that flowed through the midst of the land, saying, why should the kings of Assyria come and find much water?"

And again, it is recorded of the king:

"This same Hezekiah stopped the upper spring of the waters of Gihon and brought them straight down on the West side of the city of David." (2 Chr., xxxii. 3, 4, and 30.)

The occasion of the work was the invasion of Sennacherib, King of Assyria, about 700 B.C.E. The Northern Kingdom of Israel had already fallen, and Judah was in

sore straits. Jerusalem herself, the fountain and centre of
the nation's life, seemed impregnable with her sheer
ravines topped by her walls; but her weakness was the
danger of cutting off the water of her inhabitants. So
Hezekiah covered the opening of the cave in which the
water issued, and led the water under the City of David
into a reservoir in his city. An Assyrian inscription of
Sennacherib describes the King of Judah as shutting himself up like a bird in a snare in Jerusalem. But the bird
could not be taken.

The subterranean channel winds more like a labyrinth
than a tunnel. Some authorities opine that the deflections
were deliberate, to avoid the tombs of David and Solomon
and their successors which lay above the tunnel. Others
maintain that the Hebrew engineers of that day could not
direct the tunnel in a straight line, but worked by the
method of trial and error. Certainly the path seems every
now and then to go astray and is corrected. While the
straight line between the entrance and the exit would be
some 1,000 feet, the actual length is over 1,700 feet. The
passage admits only one person between its rough walls,
and over a large part he must needs stoop to avoid the
rock. The water in the dry days of autumn rises half-way,
and reaches to the hips and sometimes to the waist. Its
rushing is like the noise of a train in an underground railway.
There is no shaft to admit light anywhere in the course.

At the end of the passage we plunged into the Pool of
the Virgin itself, where the water has a depth, even in the
dry season, of over five feet. We emerged into the starlit
night, and saw the cliff of Mount Moriah and the compact
city of Jerusalem towering above us. When once they
were assured of water and food, the defenders of the city
must have felt themselves invincible in their fastness
against the invader below, protected by the ravines of
Kidron and Hinnom. But on the west side the hill of
Ophel was vulnerable, and in a later age was protected by
the strong works of man. There it sloped to the valley of

the Tyropeon (or " of the Cheesemongers "), as it was called in the later kingdom. Josephus states that the valley, which divides the hill of the Upper City from the hill of the Lower, extends as far as Siloam.

" That is the name " [he adds] " of the fountain which hath sweet water in it in plenty. But on the other sides the hills are surrounded by deep valleys, and by reason of the precipices to them belonging on both sides, they are everywhere impassable." (*B.J.*, v. 4.)

So it was on this side towards the valley that the Seleucids built their fort of the Akra which has been disclosed in these last years.

After that fort was razed by the Maccabees, the defence of the Jewish sanctuary was planned by a line of walls round the Temple itself. The first of the three Walls of Jerusalem indeed still surrounded the Hill of Ophel, Siloam, and the Lower City; but the stronger defence was the Second Wall around the Temple Mount. In the struggle with Titus the Lower City was abandoned; and after the destruction of the Temple itself by Titus all the buildings must have been hurled down into the hollow of the valley by the ruthless conquerors, of whom their historian (Tacitus) says: " They make a solitude and call it peace." The destruction has altered the level for all time, so that the valley can hardly be distinguished any- where in its course. Recently an old Roman sewer in the Old City of Jerusalem fell in, and the Municipality of Jerusalem was forced to repair it; and to do for the sake of practical drainage the work which is usually left to archaeo- logists. During the reconstruction operations the workmen came across remains of the old First Wall of which the foundations were at a much lower level than the present street. The sewer itself, which is now laid far below the ground, had been an open Roman drain, passing under a viaduct which ran from the Temple enclosure across the Tyropeon valley to the hill on the opposite side.

A section of that viaduct which was identified nearly 100 years ago by an American divine, the pioneer of scientific topography into Palestine, and named after him " Robinson's Arch," is still visible. It is the one fragment of the engineering in Herod's city that is left above ground.

The excavations revealed also two streets from the Roman times, the first $3\frac{1}{2}$ metres below the existing street level; and the second at a further depth of $1\frac{1}{2}$ metres. The water-conduit which brought the water to the Temple Area from the Pools of Solomon—fashioned not by King Solomon but in the Roman epoch, and still one of the reservoirs of Jerusalem—passed through the spandril of the viaduct which bridged the valley. The viaduct itself must have been a beautiful structure composed of a number of trimmer arches descending the eastern slope of " Zion "—as it was now called—and ending in an arch of some forty-five feet span which sprang over the deepest portion of the valley and gave directly on to the Temple wall. The viaduct was destroyed with the valley when the Romans razed the Jewish stronghold; and it is interesting that a Jewish coin of the period of the last struggle was found during the excavations. But the modern David Street, which leads from the Jaffa Gate to the Holy area, passes along an ancient causeway which bridged the Tyropeon valley further to the North.

Jerusalem, renamed Aelia Capitolina after the Roman Emperor Aelius Hadrian, who crushed another desperate Jewish revolt and sought to root out Judaism from its home, was an inferior military station of the Romans and in no sense a metropolis. It was altogether closed to Jewish habitation for five centuries, so long as the Roman Empire, Pagan or Christian, held sway in Palestine. Christians may have been allowed to live in it, because they were no longer counted as Jews. But its inhabitants were mainly pagans. It is recorded indeed in early Christian chronicles that Jewish synagogues were found by Hadrian on Mount

Zion; but if they were there, they must have been destroyed by that enemy of the Jews.

The excavation of Mount Ophel, which was conducted immediately before the outbreak of the Great War, disclosed on the hill the existence of an older synagogue of the Herodian period, the only synagogue before the destruction of the Temple of which we have trace in Jerusalem. The diggers lighted on a large block of limestone with a Greek inscription, in characters similar to those on the stele in the Temple of Herod warning the Gentiles against entering the inner court. The inscription runs:

"Theodotus, son of Vettienus, priest and chief of a synagogue ... built this synagogue for the reading of the Law and the teaching of the Commandments; and also the hostel with its chambers and water-installation for the needs of those who, coming from outside [the Diaspora], would lodge there, an establishment founded by his father of old and the elders and Simonides." [1]

The stone was found immediately above Hezekiah's aqueduct; and it would seem from the words at the end that the synagogue was rebuilt on the site of an older place of worship. The name of the dedicator is given in Greek, but may correspond with the Hebrew Nathaniel or Mattathias. The name of his father is definitely Roman, and suggests that the father was a freedman, *i.e.*, a freed slave, and possibly among the captives transported to Rome after the capture of Jerusalem by Pompey (63 B.C.E.). M. Clermont-Ganneau, the French savant who has illuminated the history and topography of Jerusalem, hazarded the suggestion that it was a synagogue of the Freedmen, such as is referred to in the Acts of the Apostles. Still more ingeniously, he suggested that the father was a famous moneychanger of Rome, who is referred to in the letters of Cicero. Be this as it may, the inscription throws

[1] *P.E.F. Quarterly* of Jan. 1921.

light upon the organization of the synagogue in Jerusalem at the time when the Temple was still standing. The head of the synagogue was not a spiritual leader, but a lay dignitary, like the present Parnass, and often held an hereditary office. The synagogue was already the place of study as well as of worship; the Beth Hamidrash as well as the Beth Hakeneseth. Attached to it was a hostel, and seemingly a bath-house, corresponding, perhaps, to the Mikveh of to-day.

The other scant records of Jewish life on the hill in the period before the last national struggle are principally of jar handles stamped with Hebrew letters, and potsherds with Hebrew inscriptions. Most of them bear the name of God and not of persons, which is taken to indicate the theocratic character of the Jewish State in the period between the return from the Captivity and the Maccabean Kingdom. Hebrew epigraphy of any kind is a rare fruit to be plucked by the explorer; and it is not until we come to a later civilization that the life of Ophel can be again vividly portrayed.

The hill has given recently to the digger a new level of occupation, of which the date is placed in the fourth and fifth centuries of the Common Era. That was a period when holy sites were multiplied and holy relics were principal articles of commerce, when the wilderness of Judaea was populated with monks, and the barren Negeb blossomed with religious houses. The Christian Queen Helena, mother of Constantine, yearned to identify the holy sites, and priests and monks were ready enough to help her in the search. For when the Emperor Constantine in the fourth century was converted to Christianity, and what had been an illicit cult became the dominant and militant religion of a world-empire, then Jerusalem, resuming her proud name and functions, was once more a metropolis. She became a religious centre of the Christian world, and was thronged with pilgrims, covered with monasteries and churches, spread over her diadem of hills;

and indeed she grew to be a greater city than at any time till our own day.

The chronicles of the pilgrims start with the famous record of the Pilgrim of Bordeaux, C.E. 333. The Empress Eudocia, wife of Valentinian, who lived in the city for sixteen years during the fifth century and died there, restored and extended the lines of the walls; and Ophel and the Tyropeon valley with the Pool of Siloam were included again in the walled area. The Jews were still excluded, save on the one occasion in the year when they were permitted to enter the gates and lament by the site of the fallen glory of the Temple. At the south-east corner of the site there now arose a Christian Basilica, the predecessor of the Mosque El Aksa. The place of the sanctuary itself was abandoned and became a dust-heap.

From this period of Byzantine reconstruction of Ophel, a paved street and a row of houses, with an excellent system of drainage and a water-supply and mosaic floors almost unimpaired, have survived below the market-gardens and been brought to light in recent years. The eye of the excavator—who, it has been said, is not exactly a forger but good at reconstruction—sees these houses inhabited by Christians who made their living by catering to the wants of pilgrims, selling them cheap relics and providing them with refreshment as they toiled up to the city from the Pool of Siloam.[1] Ophel was no longer the favoured residential part of Jerusalem or the governing quarter. It corresponded rather with the David Street and Christian Street of our own day—or at least of the Jerusalem before the Great War—and was the hucksters' bazaar. But the Pool of Siloam was one of the holy sites. By its side Justinian in the sixth century erected a great pilgrim church; and the Pool itself, surrounded by a colonnade, became a baptistery.

Ophel, Christian Ophel, must have been destroyed again after a short period of prosperity, either by the Persians

[1] Crowfoot in *P.E.F. Annual*, 1928, p. 55.

who, with Jewish allies, sacked Jerusalem in the early years
of the seventh century, or by the Moslem Arab conquerors
who entered it in C.E. 638, or by the Tartar or Turkish
invaders of the thirteenth century. There was only scattered habitation on the debris of that complete destruction
until our own day. The walls of the Saracens left it outside
their ambit and their defence. Of the old gates only one
remains, the Dung Gate, which is at the northern end of
Ophel and the southern corner of the present wall, giving
entrance to the Moorish quarter around the Kotel
Maaravi, the Western Wall of the Temple.[1]

Jewish medieval travellers who visited the Holy Land
regularly refer to the waters of Siloam. Rabbi Jacob of
Paris, writing in the thirteenth century, speaks of waters
which come out of the Temple Mount under earth till the
pool, and thence descend to the gardens of the city. They
were said to heal the sick, and therefore the Moslems
bathed in them. He noticed that the city was now to the
north of the Temple Mount, though according to the
Book of Ezekiel (xl. 2) it lay to the south of that Mount,
i.e., on Ophel.[2] A later scribe, Obadiah de Bertinoro, of
the fifteenth century, writes of the waters of Siloam that
flow underground in the valley of Jehoshaphat:

" Siloam is not exactly a stream, but a spring which
rises every morning till about noon, then falls and flows
under the mountain to a place where there is a large
ruin."

While the village of Siloam on the opposite side of the
Kidron remained a place of continuous dwelling, Ophel
was for centuries a deserted hill-top with a few stone walls
dividing its surface into gardens irrigated by the sewage
of Jerusalem.[3] The mistaken identification of the south-
eastern hill with Zion induced, as we have seen, its neglect

[1] See ch. ii. p. 62.   [2] *Jewish Travellers*, p. 120.
[3] *P.E.F. Quarterly*, 1929, p. 148.

by Cross and Crescent. The hill has been restored to its proper historical prerogative in our time. A part of it, containing the Jebusite ramp and the Eastern bastion, has been acquired by the Government of Palestine as a national monument; most of it has been excavated, and has disclosed a wealth of knowledge about the history and topography of Jerusalem A part remains to be explored, and may yet yield the tombs and the treasures of the Kings of Judah, which have been already the special object of quest. It is remarkable that in 1931 the archaeological lecturer of the Hebrew University discovered in a derelict museum of the Orthodox Russian Church on the Mount of Olives an Aramaic inscription which purports to be a funerary tablet of Uzziah King of Judah. The Book of Chronicles records that he died a leper, and was " buried with his fathers in the field of burial which belonged to the kings." (2 Chr., xxvi.) That would point to a separate place of burial, and makes it more possible that his tomb escaped the rifling which overtook the graves of the other kings. But whether the inscription is not too beautiful to be true has yet to be decided by the archaeologists.[1]

A party of adventurous Englishmen, a few years before the War, tried to make their way through the channels and tunnels under the hill of Ophel to the sub-structure of the Haram el Sherif, the sacred Moslem area on the site of the Temple. They had hope of finding the treasure of the Hebrew sanctuary, of which the site was revealed to them by a Finnish savant who found a cipher in Ezekiel. Failing in that, they contrived by bribing the guardians of the Haram area to carry on excavation there by night. But they were soon detected, and had to run for their lives from an infuriated Arab crowd. Nobody has sought to repeat that experiment.

It is the way of archaeological research in Palestine, as

[1] It is interesting in this connection that during the Middle Ages the waters of the Pool of Siloam were believed by Christian pilgrims to be a cure for leprosy.

is perhaps fitting for the most historical of countries and among the poorest materially, to give up the secrets of history and to expose the wall foundations, but not to reward the digger with intrinsic wealth, such as has been upturned from the mounds and tombs in the neighbouring countries of Egypt and Chaldea. Elsewhere you may excavate for loot; here for knowledge only.

Most of the Old City of Jerusalem cannot be upturned; for it is covered with sacred buildings and cemeteries which may not be moved. Yet bit by bit scholars are building up an exact knowledge and a clear picture of the Eternal City, the city of David and of Solomon, of the Kings of Judah, of Hezekiah and Isaiah, of Zerubbabel and Ezra, of the Maccabees and Herod, of the last struggle with the Romans, of the pagan and Christian Empires, of the Saracens and the Crusaders, of the monastic orders and the Turks, and lastly of Montefiore and Ibrahim Pasha in the last century. Throughout that long stretch of 3,000 years, Ophel and Siloam have not ceased to be inhabited; and, more than any other part of the City, they preserve their old physical character on the stark landscape.

III

THE WESTERN (WAILING) WALL
OF THE TEMPLE

Jerusalem is a Golden Bowl Full of Scorpions.
(Arab proverb)

Palestine is the land of the three faiths, Judaism, Christianity, and Islam; and the followers of those faiths in the land are readily roused to fierce passions over religious questions. For they regard themselves as the spearheads of contending forces, and are not prepared to give up a single inch of the religious ground to their rivals. The Arab people, Moslem and Christian, which is normally kindly and friendly, can be roused on a sudden to a wild, and indeed savage, fanaticism over the question of a holy place, just as in India the Hindu and Moslem communities may be turned, on some slight religious provocation, from peaceful citizens to fighting factions.

In Palestine indeed the religious strifes were mainly waged until this century between the different Christian sects, and particularly between the Orthodox or Eastern Church and the Latin or Western Church, over the Holy Places connected with the life of Christ. Originally in the custody of the Latins from the days of the Latin Kingdom of Jerusalem, the Church of the Holy Sepulchre at Jerusalem, the Church of the Nativity at Bethlehem, and other Holy sites passed in the eighteenth and nineteenth centuries, as Russia grew strong and more menacing, to the possession of the Eastern Orders. The struggle between the two Churches was one of the causes of the Crimean War. France and Great Britain protected Turkey against the pretensions of Russia, who was the champion of the

E

Easterns. The quarrels were still unsettled at the end of the war; and the Treaty of Paris, 1856, laid down that the *Status Quo ante Bellum*—ominous words in Palestine—should be maintained. That prescription was repeated in the Treaty of Berlin, which was concluded at the end of the Russo-Turkish conflict of 1877-8.

The Holy Places remained one of the unsettled problems of European diplomacy; and it was with a view to the settlement of this problem that the Palestine Mandate contained two articles specially dealing with them. Articles 13 and 14 of the Mandate provide:

Article 13. " All responsibility in connection with the Holy Places and religious buildings or sites, including that of preserving existing rights and of securing free access to the Holy Places, religious buildings and sites, and the free exercise of worship, while ensuring the requirements of public order and decorum, is assumed by the Mandatory, who shall be responsible solely to the League of Nations in all matters connected therewith; . . . provided that nothing in this mandate shall be construed as conferring upon the mandatory authority to interfere with the fabric or the management of purely Moslem sacred shrines, the immunities of which are guaranteed.

Article 14. A special commission shall be appointed by the mandatory to study, define, and determine the rights and claims in connection with the Holy Places and the rights and claims relating to the different religious communities in Palestine. The method of nomination, the composition and the functions of the commission shall be submitted to the Council of the League for its approval, and the commission shall not be appointed or enter on its functions without the approval of the Council."

Soon after the British Occupation, however, it became apparent that the mandatory would have to deal with

rival claims of two of the principal communities regarding
holy places, in addition to the claims of the contending
Christian sects. There was a vexed question between
Jews and Moslems over the most historical monument of
the most historical city of the world, and that question
imperilled the public peace. The monument is the Western
or Wailing Wall of the Jewish Temple.

One other site in Jerusalem beside Mount Ophel is in-
contestably genuine. It is Mount Moriah, the Temple
Mount, or as the Hebrew name describes it, the Mount of
the House. It rises above the other hill, and is still more
crowded with sacred memories and history. It was not a
part of the original Jebusite fortress-city, but at the time
of the conquest of Ophel by David was the threshing floor
of Araunah, or Ornam, the Jebusite. It was chosen by the
warrior-king to be the site of the Temple of God, when the
angel of the pestilence that followed the sin of the number-
ing of the people of Israel put up his sword, and commanded
David to set up there an altar to the Lord. (1 Chr., xxi.)
The threshing floor must have been already a level place;
but David and Solomon levelled the whole hilltop with
the labour of tens of thousands of men, and made it so that
it had no longer the appearance of a hill. On that huge
square platform Solomon built the sanctuary which was
the age-long pride of the Jewish people, and among the
Gentiles was counted as one of the wonders of the world.

The Temples of Solomon, of Zerubbabel, and of Herod,
which were successively erected on the same site, were all
modelled on the first shrine of Israel, the moving Tabernacle of the Wilderness. They had the form of a square
enclosure, with the altar of sacrifice and the Holy of Holies
in the midst of the square. Around this shrine the people
were massed in pillared courts at the great festivals which
brought together myriads of pilgrims from the Diaspora.

In the last Temple which was built by Herod over a
period of forty years, from 20 B.C.E. to C.E. 20, and is fully
described for us by Josephus, there were four rectangular

courts, contained one within the other. The first or outer-most court, of the Gentiles, was accessible to Gentiles as well as to Jews. Within it was the second enclosure, the Court of Women, which was restricted to Jews and their wives. An inscription in Greek, warning the penalty of death against the Gentile trespasser who should enter within the balustrade round the enclosure, has been pre-served, and reposes with the Siloam inscription in the Museum of Constantinople. Then came the Court of Israel, which was open to men only and was entered by seven gates. Last was the innermost court of the priests surrounding the " House " itself, and enclosed by a low wall, the " Soreg," which was accessible to the priests alone. The sanctuary of the House contained the " Stone of Foundation " (Even Shetia), which was reputed to be the centre of the whole world. A Rabbinical Midrash de-clares that Palestine was the centre of the earth, Jerusalem was the centre of Palestine, the Temple the centre of Jerusalem, and the Stone was the centre of the Temple. An ancient map of the world which has come down from the fifteenth century shows Jerusalem as the meeting-place of the three continents, Europe, Asia, and Africa; and the Temple Mount rises resplendent from the centre of Jerusalem. So was the sanctuary of Jerusalem the cynosure of all eyes.

Josephus reports that the Roman conqueror Titus held a Council of War to discuss whether he should destroy a shrine that was venerated by all the world as well as the Jews. He was anxious not to destroy it; but a soldier set fire to the place. Be this as it may, the glory of the Jews was burnt to the ground. One section only of the contain-ing wall of the outermost enclosures of Herod's Temple has survived the destruction and the ages. It is part of the western section, which must have looked down of old upon the deep ravine of the Tyropeon, but now lies actually below the level of the surrounding quarter of the City. One has always to remember in Jerusalem that the

level of the ground has almost everywhere been changed.
A modern scientific historian of the city, the late Col.
Conder, points out that

> " on the outside of the Temple, as we stand on the
> pavement at the Jews' Wailing-place, and gaze on the
> mighty rampart towering above, we only see less than
> half its present height, and it goes down beneath us
> nearly 40 feet, to the older pavement of Herod's age,
> which was itself 20 feet above the foundation rock."

Moreover, the ridge of Mount Moriah presented of old an
almost precipitous slope on the west side, sinking nearly
200 feet from the level of the rock on which the sanctuary
stood to the valley in which this Wall was built.[1]

In the days when the Temple stood the valley divided
the hills which were called, in this later period, Zion to the
west and Moriah to the east. It was then spanned by
bridges supported on great arches. The bridges evoked
the admiration of the stranger not less than the buildings
upon the hills, the palace of the king on Zion, and the
Temple on Moriah. To-day the bridges and the glory are
gone. The slopes of Zion where the royal palace stood are
covered partly with ignoble buildings and partly with
gardens of prickly pear. The bed of the valley itself, filled
with the accumulated rubbish of centuries, is occupied
with the houses and alleys of " the Moorish quarter,"
which huddle almost up to the relic of the Temple. Ever
since its destruction by Titus, the Jews have prayed and
wept at this relic of their sanctuary. It is for them the
" Kotel Ma'aravi," or Western Wall of the Temple: for
the Gentiles it is the " Jews' Wailing-place." There
through the generations they have uttered the lament:
" We sit in solitude and mourn for the palace that is
destroyed, for the walls that are overthrown, for our
majesty that is departed, for the great men who lie dead."

[1] *The City of Jerusalem*, by C. R. Conder.

The Talmud records that the heads of the Jewish schools in the first generation after the destruction of the Temple, Rabbi Gamaliel, the President of the college of Yavneh, Rabbi Joshua, Rabbi Eliezer Ben Azriah and Rabbi Akiba, went up to Jerusalem, and reaching the Temple mount saw a fox coming from the place of the sanctuary and began to weep. Another tradition tells that this Kotel Ma'aravi would never be destroyed, because the Shechina, that is, the holy spirit, dwells in the west. The same legend is repeated several times. In the Dark Ages indeed, the Jews located the Gate of Mercy at this fragment of the wall.

After the desperate revolt of the Jews against the might of Rome in the days of Hadrian (about C.E. 130), the Jews were forbidden for a time not only to live in Jerusalem, but to visit it. Their Holy City was now renamed Aelia Capitolina—after the Emperor Aelius Hadrian and Jupiter of the Capitol. Later the full severity of the sentence was relaxed a little, and the Jews were allowed once a year to visit the Holy site. From the period of the Pilgrim of Bordeaux (C.E. 330), the first Christian pilgrim who has left a description of Palestine, there is an unbroken record of their visits to the spot. He learnt that " all the Jews come once a year to the Holy place, weeping and lamenting near a stone which remained to the Holy Temple." The Roman Empire had now adopted as the State religion the Christian faith which had sprung from Judaism; but the Christians, who for centuries had been persecuted as enemies of the State, now that they had come to power, became persecutors more ruthless than the Pagans. The Jews were excluded from the city save on the one occasion which was the anniversary of the double destruction of the Temple, by the Babylonians and the Romans—the ninth day of Ab.

The Emperor Julian, who was an apostate from Christianity, and sought to revive a philosophical paganism, planned later in the fourth century to bring the Jews back to the city and rebuild their Temple. They responded eagerly, and the Golden Gate of the Temple Area is ascribed to their work at this epoch. An earthquake interrupted the construction, and Julian fell from power before it could be resumed. The harsh decree against the Jews was again enforced. The Christian historian, Jerome, writing at the end of this century, describes the scene when, for the privilege of staying a little longer and pouring out their tears, the Jews had to bribe the Byzantine soldiers on guard. It is not surprising that Jews joined the Persian army which stormed Jerusalem at the beginning of the seventh century, and for a short period established the creed of Zoroaster in the Holy Land. They were thrown out again from the city when, after a few years, the Byzantine Emperor Heraclius recaptured it and marked his triumph by a massacre of all the Jews in the Holy Land.

A more tolerant era was ushered in when Christian Jerusalem capitulated in the seventh century to the Arab conqueror Omar. It is said that the Christian ecclesiastical heads stipulated with the Moslem victor that no Jews should reside in the city. But Jewish chroniclers tell that Jews in the Arab army showed Omar the site of the Temple, which had been turned during the Byzantine domination into a heap of refuse, and obtained the right for their people to return and live in the city.[1] They bought the Mount of Olives to be a place for prayer for their community, and held services there to which the pilgrims came from the Diaspora. And the Mount of Olives, where to-day the Hebrew University is rising, remained the Jewish possession throughout the Arab epoch. The Moslem conqueror caused the place of the Temple to be purified, and he erected on it a simple, unadorned shrine

---

[1] Isaac Chelio, a Jewish traveller of the fourteenth century, records how Omar took a vow to build up the ruins of the Temple. When none knew where the ruins stood, an old Jew declared that he would show the place if the conqueror would swear to preserve the Western Wall as it was. (*Jewish Travellers*, p. 131.)

in front of the Stone of Foundation. That shrine is not the splendid building, widely but wrongly known to-day as the Mosque of Omar, which was erected a century later by the Caliph Abdul-Malek, and is properly called the Dome of the Rock. Omar did, however, erect a mosque on the site of the church which occupied the southern corner of the Holy area and had been built by Helena, the pious mother of Constantine and rebuilt by Justinian, the great law-making Emperor of the sixth century.

The Ommayad Caliph Abdul-Malek, who ruled in Damascus from 685-705, sought to make Jerusalem the Moselm religious centre of his Caliphate, to rival Mecca and Medina that were not within his dominion. It was El Kuds, the holy town, and has borne that name among the Arabs ever since. To this end he collected vast sums of money, " seven times the revenue of Egypt," and erected over the Rock itself one of the most beautiful shrines in the world. He encouraged a Moslem tradition which venerated the Temple Area, and particularly the Rock on the highest point of the Mount Moriah, as the place where Abraham offered up Isaac, and whence the Prophet himself was carried to Heaven in his miraculous ascent. A phrase in the Koran spoke of:

" Glory to God who carried his servant by night from the Haram place of prayer [in Mecca], to the place of prayer that is more remote."

The words at the end were interpreted to refer to the converted Mosque in the Sacred area, which received the name of " El Aksa," meaning " the more distant Mosque." The whole of the Temple area became a Moslem sacred place known as " Haram el Sherif " (the Noble Precinct), and in a gatehouse near the southern part of the Western Wall was shown the ring to which the wondrous cherub-horse was tethered to await the return of the Prophet from heaven, and to carry him back to Mecca. This steed,

known as El Burak (the glittering) had the wings and tail
of a peacock, and a shining face.

While the Moslems took the place of the Temple for
their own, the Jews were now allowed freely to live in
Jerusalem and to pray by the relic of the Wall. The
Karaite writer of the tenth century, Salman, writes in a
commentary to the 30th Psalm:

> " When, by the Grace of God, Rum [*i.e.*, the Byzan-
> tine Empire], was expelled and the kingdom of Ishmael
> followed, the Jews were given permission to reside in
> the City."

The Courts of the House of God were given over to them,
and they prayed there for many years.[1] Another Jewish
writer of a century later records that during the Arab rule
till the time of the Crusaders the Jews were permitted to
enter the Temple area, and pray therein at festivals.
And a famous Moslem chronicler of the tenth century
who was a native of Jerusalem, and hence called Mukad-
dasi—(meaning, from the holy city)—complains that
everywhere the Jews and the Christians have the upper
hand, and the Mosque is void of a congregation or learned
men.

From Benjamin of Tudela, who wrote in the twelfth
century when the Latin kingdom of the Crusaders still
held sway in Jerusalem, we learn that there were 200
Jewish residents living by the Tower of David, and at that
time they could still pray in an open court before the
Western Wall. In front of them rose the Dome of the
Rock, which had been converted into a Christian shrine,
and, under the belief that it was the Jewish Temple, received the name of *Templum Domini*. And Maimonides,
the sage of the Middle Ages who came from Acre to
Jerusalem in 1165 for a sojourn, records " how he entered
the court of the Holy House and prayed there." At the

---

[1] *The Jews under the Fatimids*, by Dr. Mann, 1920.

time of his visit the Holy town had come again under
Moslem rule. So long as the Arab Caliphate remained,
the Jews and Christians enjoyed a measure of tolerance;
but in the thirteenth century Palestine was invaded and
laid waste by rude hordes from Turkestan and Mongolia.
The Caliphate and hegemony of the Moslem world passed
from Arabs, who were pre-eminent in civilization, to the
ruder Turks. In that century a Moorish Emir established
a pious foundation, or Wakf, of the land to the south of the
Wall, and erected there houses for the reception of pilgrims. When the Moslem rulers became less tolerant, the
place where the Jews could assemble for prayer was restricted to a passage between these houses and the Wall;
and so it remains to our day.

We have a sad but vivid picture of Jerusalem in those
days after the Mongol incursions, from one of the Rabbinical sages, Nachmanides, who came from Spain to
settle in the Land of Israel in 1267, and founded anew
there a seat of Jewish learning. He writes to his son from
Jerusalem:

" What shall I say of this land? Great is its desolation. The more holy the place, the greater the desolation. Jerusalem is the most desolate of all, Judaea more
than Galilee. It contains about 2000 inhabitants, of
whom 300 are Christians who escaped the sword of the
Sultan. There are no Jews. For since the Tartar invasion [1244] some fled, others died by the sword. The
only Jewish residents are two brothers, dyers by trade.
[The Jews were the chief masters of dyeing in this age
throughout the East.] There the ten men meet [for
prayer] and on Sabbath hold service at their house. . . .
The city has no master, and he that wishes may take
possession of the ruins. We have procured from Shechem
Scrolls of the Law, which had been carried thither from
Jerusalem at the time of the Tartar invasion. Thus we
shall organize a synagogue, and shall be able to pray

here. Men flock from Damascus, Zobah [Aleppo], and
from all parts to Jerusalem, to behold the Place of the
Sanctuary, and to mourn over it. May you, my son and
your brothers, and the whole of our family, see the
salvation of Jerusalem, and be witness of the consolation
of Zion." [1]

A long period of darkness was ushered in from the
thirteenth to the eighteenth century, during which Jerusalem was derelict and moribund, no longer a centre of
enlightenment or of government, but a splendid name and
a hope. During that period the expression of Jewry's love
for Zion was in Lamentations. (Kinoth.)

The Western Wall of the Haram where they lamented—
and still lament—is more than 100 metres in length and
about 20 in height. Part, however, is screened by Moslem
buildings. The part where the Jews have gathered for
centuries is only about 30 metres long. In front of it is a
stone pavement with a width of 4 metres, which is used
as a passage also to the Moorish houses. The Wall itself
is composed of three distinct strata of stone. At the base
are large blocks of drafted masonry which are ascribed to
Herod's Temple. Above them are courses of undrafted
masonry which are Roman work; and the upper stratum,
which is of smaller blocks, is Arab work of the Middle
Ages. Beneath the Wall, and not visible, are courses of
Solomon's structure; for the present level is sixty-five feet
above the ancient foot of the Wall which ran from the
Rock.

The conquest of Palestine by the Ottoman Turks in the
sixteenth century made little difference to the Jewish
practice. The first record of dispute as to rights at the
place occurs at the time of the occupation of the land in
1840 by the Pasha of Egypt, Mohamed Ali, who was
seeking to make himself independent of the Ottoman
Sultan. In general, he was favourable to Jewish progress;

[1] See Schechter, *Studies in Judaism*, i. 131.

and it was with his son that Sir Moses Montefiore negotiated for a resettlement of Jews in the Holy Land. Perhaps, the Jews were encouraged too much; anyhow, they
asked to be permitted to remake the pavement, and received a rebuff. They were told that they might visit the
place as of old, but they must not carry out repairs. Their
right of visit was, it is believed, expressly confirmed by a
Firman which Sir Moses Montefiore later obtained during
one of his visits to Turkey on behalf of his people. But
although referred to by several writers, the Firman is not
extant. The Jews had been in the position of having to
buy favours of the Guardians of the Wakf. Baksheesh in
those days was the key which unlocked all doors and locked
all consciences. It would appear from the *Memoirs* of
James Finn, who was British Consul at the time of the
Crimean War, that the community submitted to these
exactions in order not to be disturbed at their prayers.

A similar incident with regard to claims at the Wall took
place a few years before the outbreak of the Great War.
It was in 1910, after the Young Turks' revolution, when
more liberal ideas were beginning to make their way, that
the Jews sought to obtain permission to bring chairs and
benches to the pavement so that they might pray in more
decent fashion. The request, which was dealt with locally
by the governor and the Administrative Council and was
not referred to Constantinople, was refused.

There is something pathetic in the attachment of the
Jews to this relic of the past glory. A former American
Consul in Jerusalem wrote in 1905: [1]

" Here, in the shadow of the Temple wall, the meagre-
ness of their privileges is sufficient to suggest the bitter-
ness of their experiences."

Zangwill was justified when he declared that the Jewish
people would not be saved either by the Jew at the Wall

[1] Wallace, *Jerusalem the Holy*, 1905.

or by the Jew of Wall Street. And Ahad-Haam, in one of
his notable calls to his people to create a new heart,
pointed to the Jew praying at the Wall as an example of
the lack of true national consciousness. Nevertheless, the
Wall remained to thousands the symbol of the hope of the
national restoration of the Jerusalem to be rebuilt. And
I may be allowed to repeat here what I wrote years ago
about the scene as it struck me on my first visit to Jerusalem:

" It represents the exile of the spirit which is bitterer
than the exile of the land. Yet this bare fragment marks
in a wonderful way the unity of Judaism through time
and space, and its abiding spirit. The faces of the whole
community are turned towards it in prayer; and it is a
national monument, not the resting place of any individual, which for the Jews is the supremely holy spot.
Refusing to recognize it as the symbol of ruin, they
make it the corner-stone of regeneration."

Early after the Occupation of Southern Palestine by the
British Army, in 1917, an attempt was made, with the aid
of the British military governor, to secure more ease for
the Jewish worshippers. Before the war eminent Jews had
been anxious to come to an understanding with the
Moslem guardians of the Wakf for the removal of the
hovels around the pavement, with a view to affording a
less cramped and confined space for worship. While sale
of Wakf property was forbidden, exchange could be permitted by a religious court if it were satisfied that the
beneficiaries would thereby gain advantage. It was hoped
that in the new conditions the scheme could be accomplished. But Moslem political feeling was engaged over
the Wall, and Moslem apprehensions were aroused lest
the Jews should seek to encroach on their holy places.
They looked at the Wall through a prism of suspicions
and antagonisms; and the negotiations for the transfer of
the Wakf houses had to be abandoned. The Moslems were

in the same stage of credulity about the Jews as were the English in the seventeenth century. When the request was made in the time of Cromwell to allow the Jews to resettle in England, the objection was taken that they would try to seize the English shrines and turn St. Paul's Cathedral into a synagogue. So the Moslems of Palestine were told that the Jews would try to seize the Haram and turn it into a synagogue or Temple.

After the Palestine Mandate was confirmed by the League of Nations in 1922, the British government made efforts to secure the establishment of the Holy Places Commission which was envisaged as the authority to decide finally on disputes between the communities as to religious sites. At one time it put forward a proposal for a commission of five Christians, three Jews, and three Moslems; but the Latin Powers were suspicious of each other and of the whole project, and no understanding was reached. The Mandatory was left to deal with the problems unaided, and had to restrict its action to the preservation of the *status quo*. Various small incidents occurred from time to time; and in 1922 Jewish feeling was excited when the governor of Jerusalem caused benches to be removed on the day of Atonement. The Moslems continually complained of trespasses by the Jews, and the Jews complained of obstruction by the Moslems. The complaints were laid by both sides before the Permanent Mandates Commission when that body began in 1924 to be concerned with Palestine; but the Commission could not do more than recommend to the Mandatory to seek a way of peace and understanding.

The serious trouble started out of another incident on the day of Atonement of the Jewish year 5689, corresponding with the 28th September 1928. The Deputy-District-Commissioner of Jerusalem, visiting the Wall on the eve of the Holy day, was met by the guardian of the Wakf who complained of innovations by the Jews in the arrangements of prayer, which infringed the Moslem rights of property. A large matting had been placed on the pavement, and, most serious of all, a screen to separate men and women at prayer had been fixed to the ground by an iron bolt. The Commissioner, having viewed the transgressions, directed the Jewish beadle at the wall to have the screen removed before the morning service. The morning came, and the beadle did not remove the offence; but went with a deputation to ask for a stay of execution. The stay was not granted, and the Commissioner directed a British Police officer to take action. Waiting till there was a silent interval in the prayer, and in ignorance that this was a moment of solemn devotion, the officer seized the screen, and forcibly removed it, while some of the worshippers resisted frantically what seemed a wanton sacrilege. It was an act parallel in its momentousness with the attempt of Pontius Pilate, some 1,900 years before, to introduce the Roman Eagle into the Temple. The Jewish people were aroused to passionate indignation. Failing to get satisfaction from the local Government which could do nothing heroic, the Zionist organization laid a petition before the League of Nations. The Permanent Mandates Commission, then in session at Geneva, could likewise do nothing heroic; but again invited the Mandatory to bring about an agreement which would assure to the Jews decent facilities of worship. That attempt was foredoomed to failure; and the government could only define what it understood to be the *status quo*.

This it did in a White Paper issued in November 1928, the first of a series with which Palestine was to be blessed during this epoch. The essential points of the State-paper were these: the Western Wall was holy to the Jewish people, and their custom of praying there extended back to the Middle Ages, and possibly further. The Wall was also holy to the Moslems, and legally the absolute property of the Moslem community; and the strip of pavement facing it was Wakf property. The government was bound to maintain the *status quo*, which they regarded, in

general terms, as being that the Jews have a right of access
to the pavement for the purpose of their devotions, but
may bring to the Wall only those appurtenances of worship which were permitted under the Turkish regime.
The government was, however, unable to specify at once
the appurtenances for which the Jews could claim a pre-
scriptive right from the former regime. And that was a
moot point; for the Moslems alleged that the Jews were
bringing the ceremonial of public worship, and aimed at
founding a synagogue at the Wall, contrary to the pre-war
practice.

The Jewish spokesmen had converted a local incident
into a world-question, and appealed to an international
Caesar to render unto the Jews what was theirs by sentiment. The Moslem leaders made a counter-appeal to
their Caesar, the world of Islam. They contrived to rouse
that public opinion by representing that the Jews were
threatening the holiest places of Jerusalem. The cry went
forth that the Haram and the holy Aksa Mosque were in
danger, and that Jewish aggression aimed at the restoration
of the Temple on its site. Passion conjured up passion, and
innovation engendered innovation. The Moslems proceeded to emphasize their legal rights of ownership by
building an extension upon the northern part of the Wall.
And they introduced a call to the faithful to prayer by a
Muezzin on the roof of the houses that abut on the pavement. The Jews sent protests to the government which
decided to submit the questions for legal opinion to the
highest authority in England. In the fulness of time the
law-officers of the Crown advised that the building by the
Moslems on their Wakf property could not be stayed provided that it did not cause, or was not likely to cause,
actual disturbance to the Jewish worshippers. Thereupon
the Moslems converted the house at the end of the
pavement into a Zawia or religious meeting-place, and
opened a way to this Zawia from one of the approaches
to the Haram, which involved that, for the first time,

there would be a passage from the Haram to the praying-place.

The terrible events of August 1929 which followed on these little changes made it abundantly clear that two things must be done. There must be an immediate pronouncement as to the conditions of Jewish prayer at the Wall; and there must be an authoritative determination of the Moslem and Jewish rights. The High Commissioner issued at once temporary regulations which declared that the Jews should have access to the Wall for prayer at all times, and specified the objects and the size of the objects which they might bring down for ritual purposes. This action evoked Arab protests, but was effective.

The Commission of Inquiry into the Palestine riots made a preliminary recommendation that the mandatory should take steps for the early appointment of a commission to determine the rights and claims at the Wall, which was necessary to the peace and good government of Palestine. The British government accordingly applied at the first opportunity to the Permanent Mandates Commission; but that body was unable to get over formal difficulties. In January 1930, however, it obtained a more helpful response from the Council of the League. A resolution was passed for the appointment of a tribunal to be composed of three persons, none of whom should be subjects of the mandatory power, to determine the rights and practices at the Wall. The three commissioners who arrived in Jerusalem in the summer of that year to take evidence were a former minister of Foreign Affairs in Sweden, who was Chairman; the Vice-President of the Court of Appeal at Geneva; and a former governor in the Dutch Indies. The pleadings were conducted on the Jewish side by local representatives of the Rabbinate, the National Council and the Orthodox dissenting body, the Agudat Israel; on the Moslem side by leading Arab advocates of Palestine and by two ex-ministers of State from Egypt. But the historical Jewish case was prepared by Dr. Cyrus Adler of

F

America; and to give proof of Moslem solidarity, delega-
tions came from many parts of the Orient to testify to the
opposition to Jewish claims.

The Jewish representatives disclaimed any right of
ownership to the Wall or the pavement, but asked that the
Jews should have the right of access to the wall for devotions in accordance with their ritual and without interference; and that it should be permissible to continue the
Jewish services under conditions of decency and decorum
proper to a sacred rite that had been carried on for centuries, without infringement of the religious rights of
others. The Moslems demurred to the jurisdiction of the
tribunal on the ground that only a Moslem court was
qualified to pronounce on a Moslem sacred place; and,
subject to that objection, urged that the Jews had no
rights at the Wall at all, and their visits were merely
tolerated by the Moslems.

The commission attempted in vain to bring about an
agreement between the two communities, and postponed
their finding to give a further opportunity for a peaceful
settlement. But, despite the earnest efforts of the government of Palestine and of peacemakers on both sides, the
attempt failed. The commission then rendered its report
to the British government at the end of the year 1930.
That report was published in June 1931; and is vested
with the impressive authority of an international judicial
body. In large part it confirms the findings of the White
Paper of 1928 and the temporary regulations of 1930, and
it contains no dramatic revelations or recommendations.
The Wall, as being an integral part of the Haram-el-Sherif,
is Moslem property, and the pavement in front thereof
where the Jews perform their devotions is also Moslem
property. The Wall was a sacred place for the Moslems,
but the pavement was not so; while both were sacred
places for the Jews. The claim of sanctity for the Wall is
based by the two parties on wholly different motives;
and each party can perform its devotions in separate

places, the Temple area being open to the one, while the other only makes claim to the space in front of the Wall. That religious site is used as such exclusively by Jews.

" No sort of legal servitude could be claimed by them over the pavement; but there existed a right *sui generis*, the basis of which is an ancient custom that has arisen under the protection of one of those ancient tolerances that are wont to serve as origins for what come to be valid legal customs."

As to the manner of Jewish worship and the appurtenances which they might bring to the Wall, the commission held that usage, in order to serve as a basis for a right, must be of fairly long standing. They examined the evidence as to the bringing down of the Scrolls of the Law and other objects, and concluded, on these principles, that the Scrolls could be used only on New Year's Day and the day of Atonement, and at the time of holding special fasts or prayers proclaimed by the Chief Rabbis of Jerusalem on account of some extraordinary calamity. The other articles mentioned in the temporary regulations, such as the memorial lamps, and objects carried by hand or worn, such as prayer-books or the Talith, may continue to be used; but benches and chairs, curtains and screens may not be brought. With a view to avoiding disturbance of the devotions of either community the Jews are not to blow the Shofar (the Ram's horn used in the New Year and the day of Atonement ritual) near the Wall, and the Moslems, on the other hand, shall not carry out the ceremony of the Zikr—the loud invocation of God which, accompanied by drums, had been one of their later forms of disturbance—close to the pavement at times of Jewish prayer, or cause annoyance to the Jews in any other way. The privileges of the Jews are not to have the effect of establishing any sort of proprietary right to the Wall or the pavement; and, on the other hand, the Moslems shall not construct or repair any building adjacent to the Wall in such a manner as to encroach on the pavement, or impair the access of the Jews to the Wall, or involve any disturbance to or interference with their devotions.

The Commission concluded their Report by expressing an anxious hope that the two sides would accept and respect their judgment with an earnest desire to attain mutual understanding. That hope was echoed by the Permanent Mandates Commission when it considered the Report. The British Government accepted the finding, and passed legislation to give effect to the specific proposals.

The question is before the Jewish and Moslem communities whether they will allow this judgment to usher in an era of humanity and mutual respect of religious feeling, or whether they will seek to maintain the status with the same jealousy as the various Christian sects maintain the status at the Church of the Holy Sepulchre. The award assures to either party the thing on which it laid most stress; to the Moslems the right of property, to the Jews the right of prayer undisturbed. It may be hoped that faction will give way to goodwill, that the Wall will no longer be a wall of partition, but will become the symbol of tolerance instead of the symbol of strife. The Moslem Congress, indeed, which was held in Jerusalem in December 1931, passed a resolution rejecting the competence of the Commission. But the action they called for was the better education of Moslem opinion throughout the world. And with an increase of knowledge there may be an increase of wisdom and humanity.

IV

THE BAY OF ACRE, THE HILLS OF GALILEE, AND THE EMEK

It has been said that the strongest visible impression which Palestine makes to-day is not Hebraic or Greek or Roman, but of the Crusaders. That is felt in the narrow streets of Jerusalem and on its battlemented walls. It is felt equally in the narrow streets, the battlemented walls and the half-ruined jetty of Acre, the most picturesque coastal town of Palestine. There are few sights in the world more lovely than the Bay of Acre seen from the height of Carmel in the early or the late hours of the day. The crescent blue of the sea, the crescent whiteness of the sands, the dappled green and gold of the Kishon marshes with the silver stream of the River Kishon itself threading between them, the azure haziness of the hills of Galilee topped here and there with their village-cluster, some bright with the red tiles of modernity, others merging more quietly into the grey stone of the hill; and, closing the horizon, the stern majesty of Hermon with its venerable white pall above its furrowed flanks of amethyst. The busy town and road-stead of Haifa and the harbour that is being built from the point of the Carmel are in the front of the seascape, and the gleaming pearl-like point of Acre breaks into the line of sandy beach which stretches from the bold promontory of the mountain of Elijah to the commanding cliff of the Ladder of Tyre. In all the lovely picture the detail which is both most lovely and the most full of historical associa-tion is the town and port of Acre, the Akka of the Arabs, and the Accho of the Hebrew Bible.

The history of Acre goes back to the days before the Children of Israel were in Palestine. It is mentioned on

the Egyptian monuments among the towns that
Thothmes III conquered when he made his triumphant
campaign against the Hittites some 1500 years B.C.E., and
it occurs again in the Tel-el-Amarna letters.[1] When Israel
conquered the land of Canaan the coastal region in the
north was allotted to the tribe of Asher; but it is recorded
that the tribe could not drive out the inhabitants of Acre
(Jud., i. 31). The Phoenicians held the coast-towns and
Acre remained a Phoenician city. It is mentioned in the
writings of the Greek orator, Isaeus, of the fourth century,
as a trading colony of the Athenian merchants. And it was
here perhaps that Hellenism and Hebraism had their first
contact. It was not until the days of the Maccabees, when
at last the coast of Palestine was subjugated by the Jews,
that it became part of the Jewish kingdom. Medieval
tradition placed in it the grave of the Hasmonean Eliezer,
and believed that the great church was on the site of a
college founded by him.[2]

Its name during the Hellenistic period was changed to
Ptolemais, probably in honour of one of the Ptolemies of
Egypt who ruled Palestine from about 300-200 B.C. The
city did not remain long in the Maccabee kingdom; for
the more powerful neighbours and invaders have always
had their eye on it. When Pompey invaded Palestine, he
made it, with several other of the coast-towns, a free
Greek city-state. Paul refers to his stay there on his way
from Damascus to Jerusalem (Acts, xxi. 7). It was an important military station in the campaign of Vespasian and
Titus, just as with the Crusaders a thousand years later it
was the chief port which the invading army held as its
base. It was captured by the Caliph Omar in C.E. 668 and
thenceforth resumed in history its Semitic name. But
when the Christians captured it 400 years later and made
it their first maritime fortress, they added a Christian
description to the old name and called it after the principal

---

[1] See "Egypt in Palestine," *inf.*, p. 162.
[2] See *Jewish Travellers*, Adler, p. 97.

church, St. Jean d'Acre. It changed its masters and its religious character many a time, from the day when Omar conquered the Byzantines and converted its church into a mosque, to the days when the last Knightly defenders surrendered to the Mameluke Sultan, Malek-el-Ashraf, in 1291. In the interval it was the chief place of arms in the Latin kingdom, and after the fall of Jerusalem in 1187, the headquarters of the Templars. It was captured by Saladin and recaptured by our English Richard. During the epoch of the Crusaders, it was also a great place of commerce, where the Venetians, Genoese, and Pisans gathered and built their factories, " the meeting-place of crafts and caravans; a place where Moslem and Christian merchants mustered from all sides."

It is to be remembered that during these three centuries of Crusading adventure, from C.E. 1000 to 1300, Palestine was to Europe what America was to it in the eighteenth and nineteenth centuries, the magnet of the adventurous; and it held in the commerce of the world much the same place as the British Isles holds to-day as a nodal point between East and West. Few Jews lived there; for in the Latin and Christian kingdom they were scarcely tolerated. Benjamin of Tudela, who passed through the place in 1173, records that they did not number more than 200; but they were reputed for their skill as glassmakers. The white sand of the Bay of Acre had been famous for the making of glass from the day of the Phoenicians. It was by the river which runs into the Bay close to the town and carries down the sand, now called the Numan, and known of old as the Belus, that, according to tradition, man first accidentally discovered glass by lighting a fire and finding the strange matter in the embers. Some have associated with this sand the words in the blessing of Zebulun: " the treasures hidden in the sand " (Deut., xxxiii. 19); for Zebulun was the tribe which possessed the Bay of Acre.[1]

---

[1] It is remarkable that another invention is ascribed to the neighbourhood of Acre. During the last of its many sieges, in 1832, a

A few years before Benjamin's visit, Maimonides, driven from Fez by Moslem fanaticism, landed at Acre and was rescued from apostasy. He remained for some months, and from it visited Jerusalem. But the Christian kingdom offered little freedom of life and thought to a Jewish thinker, and he continued his way to Egypt. Nevertheless he may have regretted in later years that he had not made his home in the land of Israel; at least he wrote in his Mishne Torah that it was better for a Jew to live in that land in a town where the Jews were a minority than in another place where they were a majority. Several famous writers who taught and died at Acre after it had been recaptured by the Moslems, including the lover of the land of Israel, Nachmanides, were buried in Haifa, because it was doubtful if Acre was part of the Land of Israel and therefore was in the Holy Land. Benjamin of Tudela says that it is on the borders of Asher and the commencement of the Land of Israel. But he too records that the great number of Jewish graves were at the foot of Carmel that sheltered Haifa at the southern end of the Bay.[1] In the seventeenth and eighteenth centuries famous Rabbis like the Kabbalist Moshe Haim Luzzato and the heads of the community were buried in the northern village of Kefr Yassif,[2] because of the same doubt. That practice remained till the present century.

Acre was captured and pillaged in 1291 by the Mameluke Sultan Baibars from Egypt, and thereafter the proud fortress was reduced to a fishing village and a place of encampment for the Bedu. The conquest of the country by the Ottoman Turks in the sixteenth century brought no revival of prosperity or commerce. It was not till the eight-

cannon ball destroyed the hookahs which the Egyptian soldiers of Ibrahim Pasha who were besieging the town used to smoke. An ingenious soldier bethought himself that the " Dutch tubes " which contained the powder for the charges of the guns would serve as a wrapper for the tobacco—and so made the first cigarettes.

[1] *Travels*, ed. Adler, p. 31.   [2] See below, p. 81.

eenth century that it becomes again a place of importance. In the interval Palestine was a prey to the strife of local feudal chiefs, like Europe in the Dark Ages. Then a powerful chieftain from Safed seized it, and made himself master of the surrounding lands and villages. He favoured Jewish settlement in Acre and Galilee. He was followed by one Ahmed of Gaza, surnamed Jezzar (the Butcher), who built the Green Mosque that crowns the old city, and the aqueduct which still gives the city a better water supply than that of any other town in Palestine. Jezzar had a Jewish Treasurer, Farhi, who procured him the means for his enterprises but was blinded by his jealous master.

It was in the days of Jezzar's tyranny that Napoleon made his bid for world-empire, and laid siege to the fortress which he described as the Key to the East. The hill on which his forces were encamped still bears his name, and an Arab survives who claims to have been in the army that defended the place. He was defeated by the Arab defenders with their stiffening of English sailors under Sir Sydney Smith. The strategic importance of Acre was recognized again thirty years later when another aspirant for Empire, Ibrahim Pasha of Egypt, occupied Palestine in his march to supplant his Suzerain, the Sultan of Constantinople. He was checked by the Great Powers of Europe; and when he would not accept their terms, was besieged for six months in Acre by English and Austrian naval forces and, in the end, forced to surrender. We owe to his energy, however, a restoration of the walls and towers of the City. The Turks, regaining authority, realized the importance of the place and made it the chief town of the Sanjak or county, which included Haifa and all Galilee.

New economic circumstances, however, have made the town which is situate at the southern end of the Bay of Acre its successful rival. While Acre remained mainly a Moslem city, Haifa was settled during the nineteenth century by Christians who venerated Mount Carmel in whose shade it was built, by Jews who divined its coming importance, and by German " Templars " who, coming to the Holy Land in the latter part of the century to establish a more Christian way of life, placed their chief settlement on the promontory of Carmel and made the town the most civilized in the land. And while Acre was a natural harbour of the ancient and medieval eras, Haifa offered better conditions for a modern harbour for big ships, and has been chosen for the chief British port of the Eastern Mediterranean. Haifa, too, at the beginning of this century, became the outlet of the Hedjaz Railway; and the joining of that line with the Railway which the British built from Egypt through the Sinai desert to Palestine during the War has destined it as the entrepôt for the trade of the growing hinterland.

Nevertheless, Acre to-day is growing and expanding as an appendage and satellite of Haifa, and Jewish settlement has begun to penetrate its walls. Its fortress still stands superb, and its ramparts form the most picturesque city girdle in Palestine. During the riots of 1929 the Jewish populace was placed for safety within the fortress, which is the principal prison of the Government; and it was reported by the Arab District Officer that " the Jews were in safety in the British Museum." Beneath the prison is a Crusader church, which is now being excavated; and the garden of the fortress has been made lovely as the garden of an English cathedral close.

Another beautiful garden which makes Acre a place of pilgrimage, but is in the Persian and not in the English character, is known as El Bahshi. It is the burial-place of the Persian Reformer Baha-Ullah, whose name means the glory of God. He was the leader of the Universalist movement which was derived from the Shia branch of Islam in Persia one hundred years ago, and is known to-day as Bahaism—after the first part of his name. His coming was foretold by an ardent Shia Moslem, Mirza Ali

Mohammad who assumed the title of the Bab, that is, the Gate: because he claimed to be the gate to the new era, " the channel of grace for some great being still behind the veil of glory." Mirza was martyred in Persia; but his body was brought later by his followers to Palestine and is buried on the slopes of Carmel above Haifa in a Persian garden. Above and under his resting-place his followers are making a series of nineteen terraces, corresponding with the number of his disciples, that are designed to lead from the top of the Carmel to the town. No monument or tablet mars the simple beauty of the flowered and terraced garden.

Baha-Ullah was one of the nineteen disciples of the Bab, and was persecuted with his master. He was rigorously imprisoned for some years in his native Persia, and subsequently exiled to Bagdad (then under Turkish rule), where he claimed to be the Prophet and preached the universal teaching. The Sultan of Turkey took alarm at the spreading of the new religion, and caused Baha to be brought to Constantinople, and later exiled him to Acre and imprisoned him in its fortress for many years. Eventually he was released, and he made his home in Acre and Haifa. He wrote to the Kings and other rulers of Europe announcing his mission, and calling on them to bend their energies to the establishment of the true religion, just government and international peace; and after his death he was revered as a prophet by a vast number of followers in Persia and the Orient. His son Abbas Abdul-Baha (that is, the servant of the glory), was born in Persia and imprisoned at Acre with his father when a young man; but most of his life he lived a free man at Haifa and was revered as a sage by the people around. He carried the preaching of the new faith to Europe and America, but his home was in Haifa. He was there during the war, and remained after the British Occupation, respected by the British authorities. He died in 1924, and is buried with the Bab in the garden on the Carmel. In 1914 he had a vision of Haifa as the coming commercial capital of the Orient:

" In the future the distance between Acre and Haifa will be built up and the two cities will clasp hands, becoming the two ends of one mighty metropolis. The great semicircular bay will be transformed into a fine harbour wherein the ships of all nations will seek shelter and refuge. . . . The flowers of civilization and culture from all nations will be brought here to blend their fragrances together. . . . A person standing on the summit of Mt. Carmel and the passengers on the steamers coming to it will look upon the most sublime and majestic spectacle of the world."

That vision is being remarkably fulfilled in our day.

When Abbas died in 1924, the headship—or guardian-ship—passed to his grandson who, educated at Oxford, continued to live at Haifa. His house and the hostel of the Bahais which have sprung up beside it are an oasis of religious peace. Palestine may indeed be now regarded as the land of four faiths, because the creed of the Bahais, which has its centre of faith and pilgrimage in Acre and Haifa has attained the character of a world-religion. The main ideas of its universalism are the oneness of mankind and the harmony of religions. Baha-Ullah its principal teacher proclaimed: " Let not a man glory in this that he loves his country, but let him glory in this that he loves his kind "; and Abbas used to declare that the supreme gift of God to this age is knowledge of the oneness of man-kind and of the fundamental unity of religions.

When you pass from the Bay of Acre to Galilee, on every side you come across remarkable relics of the period between the first and the fifth century of the common era, when Galilee was the principal centre of Jewish life and thought. After the destruction of the Temple by Titus, the seat of the Sanhedrin was at first in Judaea. Yabne and Lydda had in turn that honour. But when the Jews had been goaded into another violent outbreak by the Emperor Hadrian, and their desperate resistance had been crushed still more ruthlessly, Judaea, as well as Jerusalem, was closed to them, and for a time indeed they could not openly maintain their schools in the Holy Land. Babylonia was thenceforth for nearly 1,000 years the principal centre of learning. The succession of the more tolerant Antoninus Pius (*c.* C.E. 160), who was a philosopher on the throne, enabled the Sanhedrin to be set up again in the land of Israel; and it was placed in towns of Galilee which are now humble villages. The disciples of Rabbi Akiba, the spiritual hero and one of the martyrs of the last outbreak, returned from Babylon, where they had taken refuge, and settled first in Usha, and later in Sepphoris and Tiberias. Learning was to be for many generations the Jewish Dreadnought; and deprived of their Temple and excluded from their old capital, the Jews were in the schools of Galilee to secure the integrity and the permanence of their spiritual heritage. " If the legions could raze the Temple, they could not destroy Judaism."

The Jews maintained, too, for long ages, in the hills of Galilee their agricultural life. They were freemen of the highlands. A few miles north-east of Acre, perched on a hill that rises steeply from the plain, is a village Kefr Yassif which has a long tradition of their settlement. A local legend ascribes its foundation to Josephus. While the story has no warranty in the works of that worthy— who was not used to hide his light under a bushel— historical records prove the continuity of the Jewish population until the end of the eighteenth century. To-day the ruins of a synagogue and a Jewish cemetery, which, as we have seen, served also the Jewish congregation of Acre, bear witness to the decay of the Yishub. Here as in other Talmudic places of this neighbourhood,

Kabul, Usha, Abelin, it is surmised that the link of the
people with the soil was not broken. If interrupted by
short periods of oppression, it was resumed as soon as
circumstances were more propitious.

Again, a few miles further east of Acre in the foothills of
Galilee, is Seffurieh, which is the successor of that town
Sepphoris that plays a big part in the histories of Josephus
and the records of the Rabbinical schools. In the reign of
Herod Antipas, who Hellenized like the greater Herod, it
was renamed Dio Caesarea. It was the royal capital; and,
like Caesarea on the coast built by the other Herod, was
adorned with the outward magnificence of a Greek city.
Jesus must have spent some of his youth in the town; for
the village of Nazareth was only a few miles away; and
Sepphoris was the centre of trade and of civilization in
Galilee. When Jesus was a child, Judas the Galilean
started here one of those desperate revolts against the
Romans that preceded the great rebellion.

The ruins of an ancient synagogue, which was later the
church of the Crusaders, are still shown; but to-day the
Arab village contains no Jews. When it was the chief town
of Galilee, Rabbi Judah, the prince, lived there in the
second century and compiled the Mishnah, the collection
of the Oral Law which is the core of the Talmud. So
populous was it in those days that another rabbi declared
with punctilious hyperbole that he saw the booths of
180,000 sellers of salt in its markets.[1]

The destruction of Sepphoris as a Jewish centre took
place soon after the establishment of the Christian Roman
Empire. It was in the fourth century that the commander
of the army of the Roman Gallus, who divided the Empire
with Constantine, provoked the Jews to fresh revolt,
ravaged the town, and wiped out the Jewish quarter and
its schools. The destruction counted with the fall of
Jerusalem and of Bittir, the stronghold of Barkokba in the
uprising of the second century, as one of the fatal blows

[1] Tractate, *Baba Bathra*, fol. 75.

against the cultural and spiritual hegemony of Palestine over the Diaspora. Thereafter the schools of Palestine were subordinated to the schools of Babylon; and the Nasi or Patriarch of Eretz Israel, who had been for two centuries the acknowledged head of the scattered people, resigned his primacy to the chief of the exile in Babylon. In the Middle Ages Seffurieh was a place of Jewish pilgrimage, and the graves of Rabbi Judah and his sons were shown there. At the neighbouring village of Kefr Kenna, the Cana of the miracle of Jesus where the water was turned into wine, medieval tradition placed the burial cave of the Prophet Jonah; and the Moslems who shared many of the Jewish " Nebiim " placed over it a mosque.

Near Seffurieh, on an isolated hill in the Plain of Acre, stands the village of Shefa-Amr that is known in Jewish records as Shefaram. When the Jewish people were excluded from Judaea in the second century, it was the seat of the Sanhedrin. It is now a very small town, the smallest municipality indeed in Palestine. It is inhabited by three communities, the Moslems, the Christians, and the Druzes; but till the war it was divided between four communities, for Jews also were there. We have record of their presence, indeed, from the fourteenth century; and they were engaged in agriculture as well as commerce. As late as 1901, the Jewish Encyclopædia recorded the settlement of seven Jewish families comprising three merchants of drygoods, a vegetable dealer, a druggist, a doctor, and a Rabbi-teacher. In 1924 the Jews departed, having been called away by the lure of Haifa. The mayor of the little town took us to see the monuments of the earlier settlement, the tower which was part of an old synagogue, and below it a cemetery with tombs bearing the emblems of the Shield of David, the Shewbread, and the doves.

It is a curious coincidence of the present-day re-settlement that the Jews have left places of earlier urban habitation and settled in new villages at their side. To-day there is rising at the side of Shefa-Amr, from what was a marshy waste, the Halutz village of Jidru; and the whole area of what is called Haifa Bay is to be one of the large blocks of the Yishuv.

On the road from Acre to Safed through the Galilean hills lies another village that had for centuries a Jewish peasant majority, and is now inhabited by Druzes, Christians, and Jews who work the soil together. It is known to the Jews as Pekiin, and to the Arabs as Bukeia; and it is identified by many with the Tekua of the Rabbis. When we were there the Druzes numbered about 300, the Christians 200, and the Jews less than 100. It is one of the rare places where an old settlement of Jewish peasants has survived to our day. In the thirteenth century a traveller Samuel ben Samson found there fifty Jewish farmers. When Lord Kitchener, at the time a lieutenant in the Royal Engineers, was carrying out a survey of Western Palestine for the Palestine Exploration Fund between 1876 and 1880, he came to Pekiin and was surprised to light upon persons talking Hebrew—a tongue he knew slightly— who seemed to him to be indistinguishable from the Arab fellaheen. He believed that they were the descendants of Sephardic Jews who were planted in Galilee in the six-teenth century when that diplomatist of the Sublime Porte and the forerunner of Zionism, Don Joseph of Naxos, obtained from the Sultan permission to redeem a corner of the land of Israel. It is certain, however, that their settlement had a much earlier origin, and the village has been celebrated in Jewish annals for nearly 2,000 years. The local Jews cherish a tradition that a cave in the hill-side was the hiding-place for thirteen years of the mystical saint, Rabbi Simon ben Jochai—of whom more anon.

The farmers of Pekiin have fallen on hard times, at the very time when their brethren are returning to the life of the soil. Cut off for centuries from any refreshing stream of immigration, they have lost their vigour, and have been compelled to sell much of their land to the Moslems and the Druzes. They still have their synagogue, in the walls of which are stones bearing the emblem of the seven-branched candle-stick and the ark of the Law; and there are columns in the village which display emblems of an older Jewish settlement. Some American friends have come to their help; and it may be hoped that this Jewish outpost in the hills of Galilee will be strengthened, and enter upon a new lease of life.

From Pekiin the way to Safed lies through country of almost dense forest. The slopes of the Jermuk, the highest mountain of Palestine proper, which rises over 4,000 feet, are covered with pine, beech, and carob; and the wild peony blooms in the spring. The leopard is reputed still to frequent these haunts. The Druzes are now the principal inhabitants of a region which was once full of Jewish settlements. The ruins of the synagogues of Kefr Birim, of Nephratein, of Irbid or Arbela, and of Meirom, all built in the Hellenistic style, survive from the epoch when the leaders of the nation, fleeing from Judaea, formed a new national home in Galilee of the Gentiles. Of these old synagogues one is still a place of pious pilgrimage, more celebrated than any other Jewish site in the land outside of Jerusalem, and constantly described in the chronicles of medieval travellers who looked to the graves of famous Rabbis as the Christian pilgrims looked to the sites of the miracles. These travellers wandered from false sepulchre to false sepulchre. And tradition, which loved to fore-shorten space, placed at Meirom the tombs of Caleb, of the Prophets Obadiah and Habakkuk and of numberless Rabbis. The Synagogue, which lies on the side of the Jermuk Mountain, some five miles to the west of Safed, is in our day annually the scene of a great assembly, particu-larly of the Kabbalists and the Hassidim, who come there to venerate the tombs of Hillel and Shammai and their thirty-two pupils, and, above all, of Rabbi Simon ben Jochai. That worthy of the mystics was the disciple of Rabbi Akiba and the reputed author of the Zohar, the holiest book of the Kabbalistic literature. The eve of the thirty-third day between Passover and Pentecost (Lag-bé-Omer) is the great occasion in the mystics' calendar. The vast crowd comes in procession from Safed, carrying decorated Scrolls of the Law; and, gathering in the court-yard of the old Synagogue, dances in a wild ecstasy around the tomb and throws offerings upon a vast blazing pyre. A feature of the ceremony is the cutting of the hair of young girls which is thrown into the flames. As they leap and dance to the music of the pipers, they cry the refrain:

> Rabbi Shimon ben Yohai,
> He will never die,
> His name is glorified on high,
> Rabbi Shimon ben Yohai.

They come from Persia and Bokhara, from Egypt and Baghdad, as well as from all parts of Palestine. They give expression to that more intense longing for a communion with God by means of ecstasy which moved a large section of the Jews, as of the Christians and Moslems, in those Dark Ages when the burden of life seemed intolerable.

" The Jewish pilgrim [wrote Oliphant fifty years ago] has the same intense faith as the Russian peasants who assemble in the Church of the Holy Sepulchre on Easter to catch the Holy Fire."

Like the Samaritan Paschal sacrifice on Mt. Gerizim,[1] the survival of the mystics' Feast at Meirom is threatened by the vulgarization and the too easy communications of our age. The crowd of onlookers to-day outnumbers the bands of devotees. And when a religious celebration is turned to a spectacle and made to serve the common purposes of camera and cinema, it is on the way to perish.

If Meirom is the Mecca of the mystics once in a year, Safed, " the city set on a hill " above it, was for centuries

------

[1] See below, p. 136.

their home and school. It is not mentioned in the Bible; but a legend of the early centuries of the civil era told that the Messiah will spring thence: it is now numbered with Jerusalem, Hebron, and Tiberias in the four Holy Towns. Doubtless its proximity to Meirom made it a favourite home of the mystics and the followers of the "mist-shrouded symbolism of the Kabbala." It owed its place as the most populous Jewish seat of learning in the later Middle Ages to Joseph of Saragossa, who, as his name indicates, was a refugee from the Spanish Peninsula. Its fame was established by the close of the fourteenth century. Isaac Chelio, writing about 1350, records that the city was people by Jews from all parts of the world.[1] And in the fifteenth and sixteenth centuries, after the expulsion of the Jews from Spain, it became a great centre of refuge for the scholars. The masters of the Kabbala, Rabbi Luria and Rabbi Caro, who, by the paradoxical combination of the mystical and the legal in Jewish tradition, were also the masters of the Rabbinical lore, founded there a home for the wandering Jewish soul. A vivid picture of their life has been painted by Dr. Schechter in his *Studies in Judaism*, and it would be presumptuous to repeat the picture.

One master of the schools in the sixteenth century, Jacob ben Rab, sought to make the Holy Land again the seat of authority for all Jewry; but the head of the Rabbinical Colleges at Jerusalem denounced the plan. The founders of the schools were Sephardim from Spain and Portugal; but in the eighteenth century, a new migration came from Poland and Russia, the followers of the Hassidic sage and wonder-worker, the Baál Shem, the Master of the Name. Early in the nineteenth century an earthquake shattered the town, and many of the scholars who survived fled to Damascus. Since that disaster the town of Safed has fallen from its proud Jewish pinnacle, and its schools and synagogues have no longer any pre-eminence.

[1] *Jewish Travellers*, Adler, p. 148.

After the British Occupation, the city was threatened, too, with economic ruin, on account of its remoteness from railways and highways. The making of new roads and the surpassing healthiness of its mountain air offered new prospects, when the murderous attack on the Jewish community and the destruction of some 200 of their houses in August, 1929, struck afresh at its well-being. The Jewish community, however, have resolved to build a new and better quarter at Safed to replace that which was burned, and to settle there younger men and women to invigorate the populace. A new era then may dawn. Certainly no city after Jerusalem has so impressive a site; clustered among the hills, more than 3,000 feet above the Lakes of Galilee and Meirom, it looks over to the majesty of Hermon and the rolling uplands of the Hauran and Bashan to the East, and to the height of Jermuk and the spurs of the Galilean hills stretching to the Mediterranean on the West. The winding ways of the town are dominated by the medieval citadel. Occupied by the Templars in the twelfth century, the citadel fell to Saladin, and finally was taken by the Mameluke Beibars, who built the present castle. The citadel marked the farthest outpost of Napoleon's invasion in 1799. The Turks failed to defend it in their rout of September 1918; and the town was governed for some weeks by an English corporal who was left there with two wounded privates as the invading cavalry swept northwards.

A large part of the hilly country between Safed and Tiberias and the Sea of Galilee is now wild and deserted, given over to Bedouin Arab tribes and to the poorest of fellaheen. It is strewn with boulders and vast dolmens which bespeak an early human settlement. An ancient tradition has placed in this scene the story of Joseph and his brethren, which is more usually assigned to the Samarian plains. An enormous rock is marked as the pit into which Joseph was thrown by his brethren; and the blackness of the stones is ascribed to the tears of Jacob as he looked for his son. The tradition goes back to the Book of Jubilees where it is written:

"Jacob crossed the Jordan [coming from the East], and dwelt around Jordan, and pastured his sheep from the sea of the Heap [*i.e.* Galilee] unto Beth Shaan [*i.e.* Baisan]."

These hills like those above Safed are strewn with the ruins of ancient synagogues marking the populousness 2,000 years ago of the then favoured land, which had its dense Jewish population and its active Jewish communities both in the towns and in the villages. The ruined synagogues have in every case the form of Greek temples. The most venerated are those at Tell-Hum, identified by some with the Capernaum where Jesus at one time lived and preached and with the Kefar Nahum of the Talmud, and at Kerazeh, which is known in the Talmud and the Gospel by the name of Chorazin. The ruins of the Synagogue at Tell-Hum lie on a promontory on the northern shore of the Sea of Galilee, some three miles west of the place where the Jordan flows into the Lake. Others identify Capernaum with Tell-Minyeh, at the head of the lake to the west, but no ruins of a synagogue have been found there. Whether or not the site is correctly identified with Capernaum, and the building of "a certain centurion who loveth our nation and hath built a synagogue," here are the remains of a splendid Jewish house of assembly, built in the classical style, and resembling a basilica without the apse. It was constructed with marble brought from afar, and decorated with ornamentation, including the representation of animals, which indicates the artist's hand. The building dates from the end of the second century; but it is likely that it was a reconstruction of an older synagogue.

The belief that this was the synagogue of Capernaum led one of the Christian Monastic Orders to acquire the site at the end of the nineteenth century; and the devoted

care of the Franciscan monk, Père Orphali, was responsible for the restoration of the broken columns and capitals,
which before covered the ground, into the form of a pillared shrine. He died in 1927, during the meeting in
Palestine of an Oriental Congress which was visiting the
place, before he could complete his labour of love; and it
remains partially reconstructed.

Chorazin is likewise concerned with the ministration of
Jesus, but has not received from the Christians the same
regard as Capernaum. Its synagogue is identified indeed
with greater certainty, because the old name lives on un-
mistakably in the modern Kerazeh, a poor village lying on
the hills some four miles to the north of Tell-Hum. It was
of this place that Jesus exclaimed when the people did not
heed his teaching:

"Woe unto thee, Chorazin! Woe unto thee, Beth-
Saida! for if the mighty works which were done in you
had been done in Tyre and Sidon, they would have
repented long ago in sackcloth and ashes. But I say
unto you, it shall be more tolerable for Tyre and Sidon
on the day of punishment than for you." (Matt., xi.
21-22.)

The synagogue lay on the crest of the hill above a narrow
gorge through which there are beautiful views down to the
silvery waters of the lake 1,500 feet below. There is reason
to believe that the congregation here and at Capernaum
faced south, looking through an open doorway towards the
Lake and Jerusalem. It was not a large building, an
oblong about eighty feet by sixty feet, with rows of columns
along the side wall. Few of the pillars now stand in their
place, but the ground is strewn with fragments of columns,
lintels, and capitals. It is remarkable that on some of the
fragments are figures not only of animals but also of men.
One of the columns too bears a remarkable ornamentation, which looks like a twisted rope but is indeed the sign

of the twisted bread that is the origin of the " Chalah " of the Sabbath-eve table. The plaited dough, said by some scholars to be a representation of the shew-bread, goes back to the days before the destruction of the Temple, and it is maintained in the Orthodox Christian church as well as in the Jewish household. At the Orthodox Easter in Palestine sweet bread in a twisted form is a part of the ceremonial.

In 1926 a striking Aramaic inscription was found on the front of a basalt cathedra, which must have been the seat of the synagogue elder, whom we would call the Parnass. It runs:

" Blessed be the memory of Judah, son of Ishmael, who made this porch and staircase. May he have a share with the righteous." [1]

The interest of the congregation of Temple Emanuel of New York in Jewish history and archaeology has secured that this synagogue shall be preserved in Jewish hands. The congregation has made a grant to the Hebrew University of Jerusalem with a view to the acquisition of the site as a permanent heritage. Amid the wealth of the ruins of the Hittite, Egyptian, Canaanite, Greek, Roman, Crusader and Arab civilization, with which Palestine is covered and undermined, the principal Jewish monuments are these ruined synagogues of Galilee. And it is right that the Jews who are now taking their full place in archaeological research in the Holy Land should have their restoration and protection as a special concern and care. It may be indeed that around the synagogue of Chorazin which has survived from the Diaspora of 2,000 years ago there will gather a village of the Return of our day.

At Tabgha, which has its name from the Arabic adaptation of the Greek Hepta-Pegai—the seven springs—

---

[1] *P.E.F. Quarterly*, 1927, p. 51.

another Franciscan father has planted by the lake a pleasance which, in the winter anyhow, is an earthly paradise. The shores of Galilee, which are rich with the memories of the life and preaching of Jesus, have been the subject of more poetry than any other lake in the world. They offer the most lovely and fertile landscape in Northern Palestine. An old Jewish proverb runs, " God made the seven seas, but the Sea of Galilee is his delight." New Jewish settlements, Migdal, corresponding with the ancient Magdala; Kinnereth, meaning the harp, which was the name the Jews gave to the harp-shaped lake; and Poria, meaning the fruitful, have been planted in a region which, according to Josephus, was the most populous in the Jewish land. There were, he says, 204 cities, each with a population of over 15,000.[1] In spite of the meticulous counting, we may suspect exaggeration; but—allowing for it—in his day the "sea" must have mirrored cities, synagogues, wharves and villas.

In the midst of the new Jewish settlement is the city of Tiberias, which, alone of the many historic towns around the Lake, has survived from the days of Herod Antipas. That king built it in c.e. 16 and named it after his Imperial patron. He designed it to be a centre of Hellenism, of which he, like his semi-barbarian father, was a great patron. Despite its equipment of Greek temples, baths, and gymnasia, it was thoroughly Hebraized in the second century, and became one of the chief homes of the Rabbinical schools. Here the Jerusalem Talmud was compiled by the famous Amoraim of the third and fourth centuries; and some five centuries later the Massorah, the Hebrew vocalized text of Scripture, was fixed. After the Roman Empire, now Christianized, was divided in the fourth century between the Western and the Eastern spheres, and Palestine fell to the Eastern or Byzantine Emperors, Jerusalem remained closed to the Jewish people and schools, and Tiberias was the religious capital. The Nasi, or

[1] *B.J.*, III. iii. 2.

Patriarch of Jewry, who, from the beginning of the third
century was the spiritual head of the scattered nation,
and maintained contact with the communities of the
Diaspora, had his home at Tiberias and received from
the Diaspora the self-imposed taxation for the upkeep of
the Jewish schools.

The Christian Emperor Theodosius abolished the
Palestine Sanhedrin in the fifth century; and Tiberias,
and indeed Palestine, ceased to be the dominant centre of
Jewish learning, which had to remove to Babylon. Yet
though shorn of her glory, she continued to be the chief
Jewish town until the seventh century, when the Jews were
allowed to live again in Jerusalem after their exclusion for
500 years. Even then the academy of Jewish learning had
its seat in the Galilean town; and its head was entitled
" Gaon of Tiberias, Head of the School of Israel." The
fragments of the archives which were recovered from the
Cairo Geniza by the epoch-making discovery of Dr.
Schechter at the end of the last century, include correspondence about the relations of the Gaon of Tiberias with
the heads of the Exile in Babylon.[1] They include also beg-
ging letters on behalf of Jews who repaired to the hot
baths of Tiberias to be cured of all mortal ills; and they
show that in that early age the Chaluka system was already
instituted, and the schools received their support from
Jewish communities abroad.

The medieval predilection for graves fostered the belief
that the tombs of Jochabed, Miriam and Ziporah, mother,
sister, and wife of Moses, were gathered here, as well as
those of 24,000 pupils of Rabbi Akiba, the hero of the
mystics. Its place in Jewish affection in the Middle Ages
is demonstrated by its choice as the burial-place of the
great Jewish philosopher Maimonides; and, if the Manuscript reading of Benjamin of Tudela is correct, also of
one of our greatest poets and sages, Jehudah Halevi. Here,
as elsewhere in the land, Jewish life suffered a partial

[1] See Mann, *op. cit.*

eclipse during the occupation of the Crusading Christians from 1099-1280; but in the fourteenth century when Moslem rule was restored it is recorded that it included thirteen synagogues and several schools.

The town had a remarkable revival in the sixteenth century through the activities of Don Joseph of Naxos—of the family of Mendes—mentioned above. That worthy was a Marrano refugee from Portugal at the court of the Ottoman Sultan, Suleiman the Magnificent; and as a reward for his diplomatic services his master gave him Tiberias and seven adjoining villages, and authorized him to rebuild the walls of the town and settle Jews therein. He restored the medieval walls that still enclose the town with their black basalt stone. And he invited Jews from the Papal States in Italy to come and redeem the land of their fathers. Some hundreds of families responded, and this modern Nehemiah was the forerunner of the Zionist re-settlement. The importance of Tiberias as a Jewish centre was furthered a century later by the activities of a famous Rabbi Abulafia. From his day the Jews have been a considerable part of the population; and they now form a majority of the citizens and of the Municipal Council. Jewish enterprise dominates in and about the town. The hot springs which made the place famous in the Roman Empire are to be turned into a modern Spa. New quarters have been built on the hills above the Old City, and a ring of agricultural villages has sprung up. It is remarkable that, of all the towns in Palestine which have a mixed population, Tiberias alone has not known serious strife between Arabs and Jews since the time of the British Occupation.

From Tiberias two roads lead to Haifa. The high road passes the Horns of Hattin, where the flower of Christian chivalry fell before Saladin and the Saracens in the twelfth century (1187), and the fate of the Latin Kingdom was decided—and it continues by Kefr Kenna to Nazareth. Then, running along the ridge of the hills of Lower

Galilee to the Kishon, it overlooks the plain of Esdraelon which is stretched like a smooth " bend " across the rugged shield of Northern Palestine. The other and more direct track leads away over the plain, passes Mount Tabor and Mount Gilboa, known as the Little Hermon, and so comes to Afuleh. Then crossing the plain of Esdraelon it reaches the southern slopes of Carmel's ridge. The way leads almost wholly through a Jewish area.

For the Plain of Jezreel, which, some twenty miles in length and six miles broad, descends from the Mediterranean to the rift of the Jordan, is the " Emek " or Valley of Valleys in the affection of the Jewish people, and the main centre of Zionist agricultural development since the War. The Plain is dotted with villages, and is teeming with memories of the history of Israel in the days of the Judges, of Saul and David, of Jeroboam and Ahab, Elijah and Josiah. It is teeming also with other historical memories, some older some younger than the Biblical story. In this Plain about 1500 B.C. the King of Egypt, Thotmes III, laid low the might of the Hittites; the Mameluke Sultan 3,000 years later hurled back into the Ghor of the Jordan the most terrible of Palestine's invaders, the Mongol hordes; and, 300 years later again, Napoleon, bursting from Acre on the Turkish army which had surrounded the small force of General Kleber, drove it in headlong rout.

Tabor, which dominates the landscape both in height and in majesty, is in the Bible and Jewish legend the symbol of beauty and strength:

" Surely, as Tabor is among the mountains and Carmel by the sea, so shall he—the Redeemer—come." (Jer., xlvi. 18.)

And the Rabbis say that the Temple would have been built on its height, but God would not give every attribute to one place. Historically it is the spot where Deborah and Barak assembled the men of Israel before the victory

over Sisera who was routed in the marshes of the Kishon
below (Jud., iv.). And from the height you see "that
ancient river," which swept away the hosts of Canaan,
meandering its way through the plain. Tabor plays a
larger part in Christian tradition than in Jewish, for it is
reputed to be the Mount of the Transfiguration, and its
summit, which commands a wonderful view even for
Palestine, is crowned with churches and monasteries. A
Christian sanctuary was built there first in the fourth
century; and though in the vicissitudes of the wars between Cross and Crescent many a shrine was built only to
be destroyed, the Franciscan monks have continuously
occupied the hill for 300 years. The most modern building,
in loveliness not unworthy of the site, is the Franciscan
basilica gleaming in its brilliant marble that was brought
from Italy.

The other mountain standing sentinel in the Plain is
Gilboa, which rises 2,000 feet. It is the site of Saul's tragic
fall in his fight with the Philistines. Beneath the two
mountains you see a smiling countryside, red-roofed
houses, green plantations, silvery irrigation channels and
a black tilth—the villages of the new Jewish settlements of
the Emek. Many of them are Kvutzoth, or communes, in
which the principle of the new social order holds—from
every man according to his capacity; to each man according to his need. By one village, which nestles under Tabor
and is called Kfar Tabor, the Jewish agricultural college
to be established by the British Government from the
bequest of the late Sir Ellis Kadoorie is beginning to rise.
Another is called Ain Harod, and lies by that copious
spring at which Gideon tested his men to see whether they
lapped or scooped up the water with their hands. Another,
nearer the Jordan Valley, is Beit Alpha, and is notable not
only for its experiment in communal farming, but also for
the mosaic floor of an ancient synagogue which was found
there in 1928. The mosaic, which proclaims its date by a
mention of the Emperor Justin (c.e. 500), has thrown a

flood of light on Jewish popular art in the land during those early centuries. The art was Byzantine in the Byzantine Age, and the picture compares with the mosaics of contemporary churches. The mosaic is trilingual; there are Hebrew inscriptions in square Hebrew character; an Aramaic record of the date in the same character, and lastly, a Greek inscription giving the names of the craftsmen who laid the mosaic. Beside the regular Jewish emblems of the Ark with the Scroll of the Law, Lulov and Esrog, Menorah and priestly hands, we see a representation of the Zodiac flanked by genii portraying the four seasons. In the centre of the design is the four-horse chariot of the sun, from which the twelve signs of the Zodiac radiate.

Another tableau pictures Abraham's sacrifice of Isaac, showing the ass with the two servants, the ram caught in a thicket, and above it a hand emerging from a cloud; while below Abraham holds a knife in his right hand, and with his left lifts up Isaac. The Jews of Palestine had at that time, it seems, no objection to the representation of animals and human figures for decoration. The art is not fine, but the mosaics indicate the participation of the Jews in the common artistic culture of the day; and the synagogues here and at Jerash demonstrate the presence of Jews in the Holy Land during the early Byzantine Empire. Their life was soon to be rudely disturbed; and the centre of Jewish culture had to be moved to Babylon. Jewish culture and learning indeed found their way back to Palestine intermittently through the centuries; but the national life was not to return to these scenes till our own day.

V

WHERE THREE MANDATES AND TWO RIVERS MEET

The land of Israel of the Bible is to-day divided between three Mandated territories, Palestine, Transjordan, and Syria. Palestine and Transjordan are together under a British Mandate: but the British Mandatory enjoys different powers on the different sides of Jordan, and the High Commissioner exercises authority under different warrants. Syria is under a French Mandate. If we consider the old tribal divisions of Biblical times, the land of the Tribes of Reuben, Gad, and Manasseh is in Transjordan; the land of Naphtali and Zebulun is in Syria; the land of the other tribes is in Palestine. By the terms of the Mandate, as it was finally settled in the later Wisdom of the Powers, the policy of facilitating the establishment of the Jewish National Home applies only to Palestine west of the Jordan. On the east side of the Jordan there is an independent Arab State in which so far Jewish influence has hardly begun to penetrate, save at the Jordan Electrical Power Station which is described below. The Ruler of the Arab State of Transjordan is the Emir Abdallah, the son of the late King Hussein of the Hedjaz and the brother of King Feisal of Iraq.

The frontier between the three mandated territories is not based on any clear geographical or strategical feature, or on historical grounds. When the mandates were allotted at the Peace Conference, Mr. Lloyd-George demanded that the new Palestine should stretch from Dan to Beersheba—its Biblical limits—and this it does. But at the north end it has length with very little breadth. The frontier with Syria is drawn close to the borders of the Sea of

Galilee, and stretches indeed only some fifty metres beyond the shore. But at the southern end of the Sea of Galilee a promontory of Palestine juts into the hills to the east of the lake, where the Yarmuk falls in rapids through a deep gorge on its way to the Jordan. South of the Yarmuk is Transjordan, while above the gorge is Syria; but the gorge itself between them is Palestine.

The gorge was the scene of one of the decisive battles of the world. Yarmuk is the Arabic corruption of the Greek name Hieromax; and it was by the banks of that stream that the Moslems, in the year C.E. 636, when in the first flush of their conquests, laid low the might of the Byzantine Empire and obtained the mastery of Syria and Asia Minor. In the following years they took Jerusalem, Caesarea, Damascus, and Antioch, established the Crescent in the centres of Eastern civilization, proved their ascendancy over Christendom in its original home, and launched the great Arab emigration which made an attempt at universal empire.

That triumph of the untrained Arab tribes over the trained armies of the Roman and Persian Empires is one of the most amazing passages in the annals of civilization. It was at the end of the life of the Prophet Mohamed, in C.E. 629, that the tribes from the Hedjaz, burning with new religious ardour, had their first clash with the Christian peoples. They raided the cultivated lands at the southern edge of the Dead Sea; and, a year or two later, they were the victors in a regular battle over the Imperial forces near Gaza. All Palestine fell into their hands, and in 635 they captured Damascus and Emesa (Homs) in Syria. Then the Emperor Heraclius, who had been engaged in campaigns with the Persian foe, realized the new menace to the Empire, and mustered a great army. But it was driven, like chaff before the wind, by the onset of the Faithful at the Battle of the Yarmuk: and for 1,000 years the Easterns were to retain the hegemony of the Near East.

The place in the gorge of the Yarmuk where the three

mandated territories meet is called El Hammeh, meaning
the hot springs. There is nothing to mark it but a station
of the Hedjaz Railway and a few huts. The station buildings were wrecked by the Arabs of Lawrence's and Feisal's
army during the thrilling days of September 1918 in their
triumphant and devastating advance on Damascus, and
have not been repaired. The Hedjaz line itself is in an
anomalous position, befitting this abnormal corner of the
earth. It is a Moslem Wakf, endowed for the benefit of the
Moslem pilgrimage to the Holy Places in Arabia. The line
is laid in the English mandated territory from Semakh at
the southern end of the Lake of Galilee, near to the ruins of
the Hellenistic city of Hippo, to El Hammeh. But it is
managed at present by the Syrian Railway Administration,
and is exterritorialized. For the Boundary Commission,
which in 1922 demarcated the frontier between Palestine
and Syria, placed the line from Semakh to Damascus under
Syrian control.

El Hammeh takes its name from the hot sulphur springs
which burst out of the ground in the hills above the
Yarmuk, and flow in a boiling sulphurous torrent to the
river. It was known in the Talmud as Hamatha—which is
the same Semitic root—and very recently the remains of
an ancient synagogue have been excavated here. The
baths of Tiberias some ten miles away are still famous, as
they were in the Roman times. The baths at El Hammeh
were even more frequented in the Roman age, and relics
of the Roman occupation are scattered about the scene.
Hard by the railway station you see the ruined walls and
the ruined gates of a Roman theatre, and a little way up
the hill, on the other side of the Yarmuk, are larger ruins
of two theatres, temples, and a forum. They lie by a rough
Arab village now known as Um-Keis, which is identified
by scholars with the Graeco-Roman Gadara, a city famous
for nearly 1,000 years as a centre of culture. The hill on
which the ruins are strewn commands a magnificent view
of Jordan and all Galilee.

The Mishna records that Joshua placed a fortress here at the time of the conquest of Canaan by the children of Israel. But the name Gadara does not occur in history till the days of Antiochus the Great, King of Syria in the third century B.C.E., who built a fortress on its commanding height above the river. Thenceforth it was one of the most important of the League of ten towns known as the Decapolis. In those ten Islands of Hellenism the Graeco-Roman civilization flourished, with the active patronage of the Greek and the Roman rulers or overlords, around the national home of the Jewish people, during the three centuries before and the first centuries of the common era. Among the other nine cities of the League were Scythopolis, the old Beth-Shaan and the modern Baisan,[1] Amman and Jerash, known by their Greek names of Philadelphia and Gerasa, in Transjordan; Damascus and Canata in Syria; Gaza, Azotus (the old Ashdod), and Dor on the western coast of Palestine. The ruins of these Hellenized cities, with their pagan apparatus of temples, baths, hippodromes, and the like, mark how closely Judaea and the Jewish nation were surrounded by cultural enemies. On the sides which were not commanded by these Greek city-states, they had the hostile and partly Hellenized kingdoms of the Idumean and the Nabatean Arabs.

At the beginning of the first century before the Christian era, the fortress of Antiochus the Great was conquered by the Maccabean, Alexander Jannaeus, who compelled the inhabitants to adopt Judaism and become " proselytes of justice." Thirty years later the town was severed from the Jewish Kingdom by the Roman Pompey, and became the capital of the Province of Peræa. The citizens expressed their gratitude by calling the city " Pompeian Gadara." It was given by the Emperor Augustus to his favoured Herod; but after Herod's death reverted to the Roman province. And it was here that the Roman General

[1] See ch. viii. p. 159.

H

Vespasian was camping in his campaign against the Jews in C.E. 68 when the news came of Nero's death, and he was hailed as Emperor of Rome by his Army.

The baths of Gadara were second only in fame during the period of the Roman Empire to those of Baiae in the Bay of Naples; and the town which grew around them was a centre of intellectual culture, and known as " the garland of the Muses." In the first century of the Christian era, Gadara produced the Epicurean philosopher Menippus, who was the creator of the satire and the short story, and the poet Meleager, who was one of the principal composers of the Greek *Anthology*. Hellenism and Hebraism rubbed shoulders in these Hellenized towns. Of his birthplace the poet says, " she is Attic but lies in Syria "; and he tells in one of his epigrams of a Jewish rival who competed even on the " cold Sabbath " for his lady-love. In the second century the satirist Oenomaus, a Voltaire of his time, flourished there; and some have identified him with Abnimos Hagardi, with whom Rabbi Meir had discussion.[1]

Gadara is famous in the New Testament for the story of the casting out of the devils into the swine which rushed down the steep slope to the sea. The Sea of Galilee lies some seven miles from the ruins; but in those times the territory of the city must have extended to the borders of the lake.

To-day the baths of El Hammeh are simple and rough indeed, shorn of their old glory. They are simpler and more modest than those in the neighbouring Tiberias; for they consist of natural pools in which the water bursts out, and a few wooden huts where the patients may rest after taking the waters. Yet, in the season between April and July, these springs are thronged by thousands of Arabs who camp around in the tents, pay three piastres a day (fifteen cents.) for the privilege, and, if they have faith, are healed. The Jews prefer the hot springs of

[1] See *Judaism*, by F. G. Moore, i. p. 45.

Tiberias; for that ancient town is more predominantly Jewish than any other in Palestine, and has hotels and the other appanages of modernity; and it is governed by a Municipality with a Jewish majority and a Jewish Mayor.

The whole area around the Sea of Galilee is indeed becoming once more a focus of agricultural and industrial development. The land is rapidly changing its face, so that soon its old condition will hardly be known. It is symbolical of its new status that the air-route from England to India has now a stopping-stage and aerodrome by Semakh. And the seaplanes come to rest in the Lake of Galilee. The place where the three Mandates meet is close to the place where the two chief rivers of Palestine meet; the Jordan that divides the two mandated territories under the British Mandatory, and the Yarmuk which descends from the Syrian Plateau of the Hauran to lose itself in the Jordan. The course of those two rivers is diverted so that they may be united and generate electric force; and the dam which turns the waters of the Yarmuk into a new channel is placed near El Hammeh. The Jordan, which is the chief river of Palestine, and well-named in Hebrew the " descender," rushes headlong in the course of its fall of nearly a thousand feet between its exit in the Sea of Galilee to its entrance into the Dead Sea, where its waters are swallowed up in the lowest pit of the earth's surface. Here it is some 100 feet broad, and enclosed by steep rugged banks. It has already fallen over 2,000 feet from its source under Hermon to the Sea of Galilee, that is itself 600 feet below the Mediterranean.

For ages the Yarmuk has fallen in cascades into the Jordan stream 300 feet below, and a Roman bridge that dates back to the time when Gadara was a flourishing city spans the falls. The bridge is called " Jisr El Majamieh," that is, " the bridge of the gathering of the waters." The bridge is now to go, and the Jewish village near which it stands has a new name, Naharayim—" the place of the two rivers." The falls, too, will be abolished, and the waters

of the Yarmuk and the Jordan together will be led tamely
and obediently in channels made by men to form a placid
lake in union; and then, tamely and obediently again,
they will pass through great tubes down a cemented slope
to work the turbines, which will in turn generate 20,000
horse-power of electricity. The hill above the present falls
and the future lake has been named " Tell Or," the Hill
of Light; and at the time of our visit was an island of
method in a sea of experiment. It was occupied by the
houses of the 400 Jewish workmen who, with some hundred
Arabs, were engaged in the enterprise, and housed, fed,
educated and doctored by the Electricity company. For
here the works of the Palestine Electric Corporation designed by Rutenberg are rising fast; and will make
possible the irrigation of the Jordan Valley and a pro-
gressive material development such as Palestine has not
known since the Graeco-Roman Age. The power-house
will generate electric current for lighting and industrial
purposes for all Palestine and Transjordan. It is to do for
the country what the National Home in Palestine is to do
for Judaism and the Jewish people—to spread illumination.

So I wrote in 1930. To-day the plan has been realized.
The dam, the lake, the canals, the power-house, are completed. The groups of workmen have gone away to other
fields; and the light and power are distributed to the
towns and villages of the land, carried on wires across
pylons that bestride the hills and the valleys.

There are those who complain of the modernization as
contrary to the holy character of the land. They would
like to keep it as an open-air museum ; but they forget
that in the Bible epoch it was a centre of civilization
with two or three times its present population ; very
different from the desolate land to which four hundred
years of Turkish neglect reduced it.

VI

THE SHORES OF THE DEAD SEA

In the spring of 1929, Palestine Jewry and the Jewish world outside Palestine were startled by the report that a party, which included the son of the first High Commissioner of Palestine and his wife and several leaders of the Zionist organization, had gone on the Dead Sea for a day's picnic in a motor-boat, had not returned, and, it was feared, had been lost. When aeroplanes and a rescue-boat brought by land from Jaffa, some sixty miles away, had returned without tidings, and distress had been aroused to the breaking-point, the party suddenly appeared in their damaged craft which they had navigated with improvised sails for three days. It would seem incredible that a boat could be lost for that time on a land-locked lake about the same size as the Lake of Geneva, and nowhere more than ten miles broad. But the Dead Sea is one of the most uncanny spots in the world, deserted alike by man and all living things, and a very pit of desolation, " a Hell with the sun shining on it." Its shores, indeed, have been the scene of some of the most poignant dramas in the history of Israel; but they have been dramas of death and destruction, fitting the death-like scene. As Sir George Adam Smith has written of it:

" The history of the Dead Sea opens with Sodom and Gomorrah: and may be said to close with the Massacre of Masada."

The sea lies 1,200 feet below the level of the Mediterranean; and in places its waters have a depth of 1,500 feet. It forms the lowest point of the deepest rift of the

world's surface, which was caused by a great convulsion
and stretches through the Red Sea, Nubia, and East
Africa. Before that convulsion what is now the desert of
Syria was a fertile plain, and the rivers ran through it and
across Palestine to the Mediterranean Sea. Its confined
and embittered waters are much heavier than those of
any other sea, because they hold in solution masses of
salts that have been brought down from the soil by the
Jordan and the other rivers which empty themselves into
the abyss. The water is evaporated, and the level of the
lake remains fairly constant, but the store of salts is constantly piled up. The Hebrews significantly called it the
Sea of Salt. When the Greeks entered Palestine with the
army of Alexander the Great, and brought their scientific
curiosity to the land, they were amazed at the floating
bitumen upon the surface of the waters and called it the
Asphalt Sea. It retained that name with Josephus and
the Roman and early Church historians. Tacitus, the
Roman, who was contemporary with the destruction of
Jerusalem by Titus, thus describes it:

" It is a lake of vast size like a sea, but its waters have
a nauseous taste, and its offensive odour is harmful to
those who live near to it. The waters are not moved by
the wind." [That is not true; and the writer cannot
have seen the sea on a stormy day when the waves are
almost mountainous.] " Neither fish nor flesh can live
there. The lifeless waves bear up whatever is thrown
upon them as on a solid surface. Swimmers, whether
skilful or not, are buoyed up by them. Not far from the
sea are places which once were fertile and sites of great
cities, but later they were devastated by lightning."

Sir John Mandeville, the medieval traveller who tells
many good tales and many tall stories, recounts, with more
imagination, that

" the sea casts out a thing called bitumen in pieces as large as a horse every day and on all sides. Iron would float on it; but if you throw on it a feather, it sinks to the bottom."

In his day the Lake had obtained its modern name because of the absence of animal life.

The Dead Sea, indeed, to-day belies its name, and, with the rest of Palestine, shows every sign of revival. It is, in fact, a reservoir of inexhaustible chemical wealth, and its depths contain almost infinite quantities of potash and bromide which may be extracted by evaporation. It has been calculated that two thousand million tons of potash, and still more astronomical figures of common salt, are held in its heavy waters. The Palestine government has granted a concession for the exploitation of these mineral resources which, if successful, may on the one hand become an important source of revenue for the State, and on the other make Palestine the centre of the greatest chemical industry in the world. If that prospect is realized, we may expect that the Sea will be covered with fleets of motor-boats, and its shores at the northern and southern ends, where the mountains do not close around it, will be covered with pipes and industrial plant, the houses of workmen and the apparatus of modern industry. And the products of this Dead Sea will be transformed into fertilizers for the soil and medicine for the body of man.

Already on the northern shore there has sprung up in the last years a busy village where some 200 Haluzim live healthily and happily. They are engaged on the work of the Company which is laying out vast pans over an area of 500 acres. The water is pumped from the lake into the pans, and allowed to evaporate, leaving the potash and magnesium and vast piles of common salt. A little way off is an Arab settlement, where the 200 Arabs engaged in the enterprise have their dwelling. What was a few years ago a picture of desolation and ruin is now a thriving hive

of industry. Yet the Sea elsewhere still wears its air of
mystical lifelessness and other-worldliness. Save at this
one point, there is scarce a sign of settled habitation along
the sixty miles of its coasts on either side. Before the potash
works were started one small motor-boat crossed the lake
for the service of another salt enterprise which was producing rock-salt from the southern end of the waste. It
was in that boat that we made a tour of the lake from its
northern end to the furthest south.

There is a peculiar majesty in the line of limestone,
basalt, and sandstone cliffs which rise straight from the
water in rugged masses to a height, on the eastern side, of
from 2,000 to 4,000 feet; and there is a unique scenic
beauty as well as sad historic association about many of
the places that border on the waste of waters. Leaving
the Dead Sea Post, our first stopping place was at the
Wady Zerka Main, which is identified by the archaeologists with the hot springs of Calirrhoe that were famous
as a pleasance in the Roman time. Pools of warm sulphurous water bubble up a few hundred yards from the
shore, and nourish palms and tropical vegetation that
break the solemn bareness of the cliff. Towering above
the springs is the height of Machaerus, which was one of
the fastnesses of the Maccabees, and was later fortified
again by Herod, and used by him as the prison of John
the Baptist. The Maccabean princes in their struggle with
the Seleucids prepared for themselves refuges on either
side of the Dead Sea where, isolated in trackless mountains, they could in case of need resist the Hellenistic
armies. And during two centuries of the fight for the life
of the Jewish nation, first against the Hellenistic and then
against the Roman tyrants, the castles of refuge received a
constant stream of desperate warriors. Of those fastnesses
Machaerus on the eastern side and Masada on the western
side are the most famous, and look out on each other, two
inscrutable guardians of the Sea; and each the scene of a
death struggle of the Jewish people in the first century.

Either Machaerus or one of the heights around the ravine, which are covered with huge dolmens and menhirs of an early cult, must have been the Beth-Peor where Balaam stood on one of his three vain attempts to curse the children of Israel camped in the Plains of Moab. And the gorge may well have been the place of Moses' burial, of which it is recorded in Deuteronomy:

"And he buried him in a valley of the land of Moab over against Beth-Peor; but no man knoweth his sepulchre." (Deut., xxxiv. 6.)

Conder indeed identifies the gorge of Zerka Main with Nahaliel, the Valley of God, mentioned in the Bible as one of the stages of Israel's march through the Land of Moab (Num., xxiv. 19), and he conjectures that this ravine was the burial-place. Certainly it is fitting by its awfulness and its isolation for the resting-place of the Prophet. The gorge, as he describes it, is some 1,700 feet deep, and yet the stream in its depths is still some 1,600 feet above the Sea.

"Tawny cliffs of limestone capped with chalk rise on the north, and are seamed with gulleys where the marl has been washed down, like the snow-streaks left in summer, beneath the cliffs. On the south is a steep brown precipice with an undercliff of marl, and a plateau stretching thence to another and yet another ridge. Beyond and above this plateau appeared the shining waters of the lake and its western cliffs, fading away into a blue mist on the south. . . . At the bottom of the gorge the scene was wonderful beyond description. On the south black basalt, brown limestone, gleaming marl. On the north, sandstone cliffs of all colours, from pale yellow to pinkish purple. In the valley itself the brilliant green of palm clumps, rejoicing in the heat and in the sandy soil. The streams, bursting from the cliffs, poured

down in rivulets between banks of crusted orange
sulphur deposits." [1]

Our next stopping-place was the mouth of the Arnon, or
River of Moab, which is called by the Arabs Wadi el
Mujib. The clear stream of the river finds its way into the
salt waters through a wonderful narrow gorge of red sandstone, with cliffs on either side rising sheer some hundreds
of feet. The colour of the cliffs is the same as in the rose-red
city of Petra, and forms a striking contrast with the silvery
stream of the river, the blue waters of the Sea, and the
patch of green vegetation which is caused by the miniature
delta at the estuary.

It was near this stream that in the middle of the nineteenth century a German discovered the Moabite stone
which records in the Moabite dialect the exploits of Mesha,
King of Moab (c. 870 B.C.E.), who fought successfully against
Israel. The interpretation of the script, which is very like
the Hebrew, by the French savant, M. Clermont-Ganneau,
marked one of the most important advances in the science
of Semitic epigraphy.[2]

Sailing on from the Arnon, we came to the curious promontory that breaks the line of the Sea for some ten miles,
called the Lisan or tongue. Its soil is a soft marl that may
contain oil, and its white hillocks have both the look and the
feel of a snow-field. A small Bedu settlement is camped on
the shore of the creek formed by the promontory; and a
road mounts up from their encampment, 4,000 feet, to
Kerak, the ancient Kir of Moab. We rounded the cape of
the promontory called Point Costigan, after an intrepid
Irish sailor who in the early part of the nineteenth century
explored the waters of the Sea that were then uncharted.

---

[1] Conder, *Heth and Moab*, p. 145.
[2] The stone itself was broken to pieces by Arabs, who feared its
magical properties, before any of the contending archaeologists, who
were bidding against each other for its purchase, could acquire it.
A squeeze of the inscription had already been taken.

He lost his life from the trials which he suffered from the sun and the lack of water. The southern point of the promontory is called Molyneux, after another sailor of the English navy who, a few years later, explored the Sea in a canoe, and also lost his life from the fever which he caught on the voyage. The two names are incongruous on the map of Palestine with its Bible associations.

We bivouacked on the southern shore of the Lisan. Bivouacking by the Dead Sea is a pleasant and easy form of camping. There is a soft beach; no insects disturb, there is no fear of rain; and everywhere is abundance of wood. Although almost the only vegetation is the deceptive Dead Sea apple which, looking so well-favoured, turns to dust and ashes when you touch it, yet the shores of the Sea are the best wooded part of a deforested country. For all along them are great logs and branches, and even whole trees, brought down by the flood of the Jordan after the winter rains. They are impregnated with all manner of salts, so that they burn fiercely with multi-coloured flames.

The next morning we sailed across to the south-western corner of the Sea where, 300 feet from the water, rises the solid mass of crystal salt which, according to a tradition, is Lot's wife. The whole Sea is called by the Arabs the Sea of Lot, and this mass is called Jebel Usdum, or the Mountain of Sodom. Having stood intact for thousands of years, in our utilitarian age the cliff is being turned into a salt quarry. Some score of miners work the salt, cutting it from the top of the face of the cliff and hurling it down to the beach below, whence the boat, in which we were travelling, carries it each week to the northern end of the Sea to be taken to the markets of Jerusalem and Hebron. It is no common salt, but a white quartz, looking like crystal; and in the face of the cliff there is a grotto receding 250 yards. Through a shaft at its far end the sunlight is let in to make a magic scene.

From Jebel Usdum we tacked to the southern-most edge

of the Sea where the waters have been slowly but steadily gaining on the low-lying land, and withered trees rise with their ghostly branches in the shallows. Here there are springs of fresh water and rough cultivation of the Bedouin at the Ghor El Safy, and here in the early and middle ages was a civilized human settlement, Zoar, of which a few Byzantine ruins remain. Beyond the cultivation the sands and limestone wilderness stretch away, rising gradually to the Araba, the cleft which runs from the Dead Sea to the Gulf of Akaba.

Professor Albright, a few years ago, discovered in this region ruins of habitation which ceased to be occupied about 1800 B.C. That exactly accords with the Bible story and chronology of the destruction of the Cities of the Plain. Some scholars, indeed, place Zoar, which was one of the Cities overwhelmed with Sodom and Gomorrah, and which Moses overlooked from Pisgah, at the northern end of the Dead Sea.[1] The weight of authority, however, for the southern site is overwhelming. Josephus says that the Dead Sea extended from Jericho as far as Zoar (*B.J.*, IV. viii. 4); and the Christian historian, Eusebius, of the fourth century, confirms that statement and adds that a Roman garrison was there. Moreover, the mosaic map found in a Christian church of Madeba, which is dated from the fifth or sixth century, places Zoar at the south-east corner of the Sea. The medieval Arab chroniclers refer to it frequently as an important commercial centre on the trade route between Akaba and Jerusalem, so important that the Sea itself is called the Lake of Zughar. It was then populated by Jews; and a Karaite historian, Sahel ben Mazliah of the tenth century, records that, after Jerusalem was destroyed (by the Romans) the Jews of the Negeb, *i.e.*, Southern Palestine, dwelt in Zoar.[2] There Jews must have played their part in the trade which went overland from

---

[1] See Mallon, *J.P.O.S.*, xi. 55: and Conder, *op. cit.*, p. 148.
[2] Mann, *op. cit.*, p. 43.

Egypt to Syria and the Middle East. They were already becoming, perforce, the most international of peoples.

In the middle of the nineteenth century a scheme was put forward in England for a canal which should pass through the Dead Sea and link the Mediterranean and the Red Sea. It was an alternative plan to the Suez Canal, which was then regarded as a French enterprise. The canal was to start at Haifa, and would involve cutting a channel through the Plain of Esdraelon so as to let the waters of the Sea into the Jordan depression, and, again, a cutting from the southern end of the Dead Sea to Akaba. The level of the Jordan Valley would be raised to sea-level; and it was realized that this would involve the submerging of Tiberias and the shore of the Lake of Galilee, as well as a large area around the river. But it was said blithely that the territory was useless for the most part and incapable of cultivation; and that Tiberias, though holy to the Jews, was inhabited by foreign Jewish immigrants whose objections to a great commercial enterprise should not prevail. It was overlooked, however, that the cutting from the southern end of the Dead Sea would have to remove a relatively lofty plateau, since the highest part of the Arabah which runs from Zoar to Akaba is some 1,000 feet above the level of the Red Sea, and over 2,000 feet above the present level of the Dead Sea. The scheme did not survive expert examination; and the feeling of the Biblical people of England rebelled against the idea of eliminating the Sea of Galilee and the Jordan for the sake of commerce.

We sailed back along the western coast of the Sea until we came to the beach that lies before Masada, the most romantic of all the spots around the Sea and the Gibraltar, as it were, of Palestine. Masada is a square precipitous hill rising 1,500 feet sheer above the scarred and desolate waste. It was chosen for its inaccessibility as a fortress of the Maccabees, and two centuries later of the Zealots; and it was chosen by Herod as his retreat from Jewish rebellion or Roman caprice. It looks worthy of its history. The

Zealots who have made it famous were that section of the Jewish people who were the implacable enemies of Rome, and died in literally the last ditch after Titus had destroyed the City and the Temple of Jerusalem. They have been compared with the Montagnards of the French Revolution, " driven by their own indomitable passion to assert the truth that possessed them with a ferocity that no possession would justify." After the fall of Jerusalem the remnants of their bands threw themselves into Masada, and there withstood a siege for two years.

The camps of Flavius Silva, the Roman commander who was appointed to war them down or starve them out, the lines of circumvallation around the mountain, the Roman road running straight from the sea to the camps, and the ramp, or " agger," by which the Romans fought their way up the sheer mountain side and brought up their siege-engines—all these remain almost intact in the rainless desert area. The ramp, indeed, has been shattered in part by the earthquake which occurred in Palestine in the summer of 1927, so that the top of the mountain, always difficult of approach, is now almost inaccessible. But the scene recalls with incredible vividness the inflexible might of Rome and the desperate heroism of the Jews. On the top of the hill one may see the walls behind which they defended themselves and the rocks hurled by the Roman catapults against them. When they could resist no more, they put an end to their own lives rather than that they or their wives or children should fall into the hands of the Romans.

In one of the most moving passages in the story of the Jewish Wars, Josephus, who had himself betrayed his command in Galilee and made his peace with the Romans, puts into the mouth of Eleazar, the leader of the Zealots at Masada, a speech on the theme that death is to be chosen before servitude to the Romans:

" And as for those who have died in the war, we should

deem them blessed, for they are dead in defending, and
not in betraying, their liberty: but as to the multitude
of those that have submitted to the Romans, who would
not pity their condition? And who would not make
haste to die before he would suffer the same miseries?
Where is now that great city, the metropolis of the Jewish
nation, which was fortified by so many walls round about,
which had so many fortresses and large towers to defend
it, which could hardly contain the instruments prepared
for the war, and which had so many myriads of men to
fight for it? Where is this city that God Himself inhabited? It is now demolished to the very foundations.
And I cannot but wish that we had all died before we
had seen that holy city demolished by the hands of our
enemies, or the foundations of our holy Temple dug up
after so profane a manner. But since we had a generous
hope that deluded us, as if we might perhaps have been
able to avenge ourselves on our enemies, on that account,
though it be now become vanity, and hath left us alone
in this distress, let us make haste to die bravely. Let us
pity ourselves, our children, and our wives, while it is in
our power to show pity to them. For we are born to die,
as well as those whom we have begotten; nor is it in the
power of the most happy of our race to avoid it. But for
abuses and slavery and the sight of our wives led away
after an ignominious manner with their children, these
are not such evils as are natural and necessary among
men; although such as do not prefer death before those
miseries, when it is in their power to do so, must undergo
even them on account of their own cowardice."

Of the garrison only two women and five children survived the self-massacre.

Leaving Masada, we landed at one more place before we
returned to the Dead Sea Post. It was at the oasis of Ein
Gedi, the Spring of the Goat, which is marked by very
different memories from those that hover around Masada.

The caves in the wilderness by Engedi were a scene in the drama of David and Saul when David caught unawares the King who, with 3,000 men, was pursuing him, and spared his life (1 Sam., xxiv). A thousand years later it was one of the principal habitations of that mysterious and mystic Jewish sect, the Essenes, who pointed the extreme contrast of attitude with the Zealots, eschewing all political life and the use of arms. Extremes meet in this abnormal region. The Essenes must have been there in those days of the death-struggle with Rome, living their monastic life while some ten miles away the tragic story of the hopeless resistance of Masada was enacted.

It is a gentile writer who tells of their settlement by Engedi. The Roman Pliny, who composed at the end of the first century a Natural History, in describing the Dead Sea, says:

> " The Hessenes live on the West side, away from the shores, out of reach of their baneful influence . . . a solitary sect and strange above all things in the entire world. They live without women, they eschew money, and dwell among the palm trees. Yet the number of their society is maintained, for there flock to them from afar many who, wearied with battling against the rough sea of life, adopt their system. . . . Below them lay Engedi, a town once second only to Jerusalem in its fertility and groves of palms. Now it is but one more tomb."

He must be referring to the destruction which overtook all the villages of Judaea after the Jewish revolt was put down with Roman ruthlessness. Perhaps his estimate of the fertility was exaggerated; yet in the Song of Solomon the vines of Engedi are an image of fruitfulness.

Of the Essenes, we are told by Philo, who affected himself for a time that ascetic kind of life, that they were a sect some 4,000 in number, and so-called because of their saintliness. In Hebrew their name was probably Hassidim; and they were an extreme branch of the larger religious body whom we know as Pharisees. Their Greek name is associated with the Greek root, Hosios, which means saintly.

" They lived [says Philo] in villages and avoided cities, in order to escape the contagion of evils rife therein. They pursued agriculture and other peaceful arts. . . . No slave was found among them, for they saw in slavery a violation of the law of nature which made all men free brothers. . . . Moral philosophy was their chief pre-occupation, and their conduct was regulated by their national laws. These laws they studied on the Seventh Day, which they held holy."

The Essenes were the models and predecessors of those ascetic societies who, when the Roman Empire became Christian, filled the wilderness of Judaea and the desert lands around Palestine with their monasteries, and in their austerest development inhabited the caves that abound in this country of limestone hills and precipitous cliffs. Of the monasteries that they founded in the wilderness some still remain, such as Mar Saba in the combes of the hills a few miles west of the Sea, and Hoglah and Mar Hanna in the Jordan Valley, to the north of the Sea. Others are ruined and abandoned, and marked only by fragments of wall that seem to belong nowhere.

Engedi itself must have recovered in some measure from the destruction at which Pliny hints. It is referred to in several places in the Talmud, particularly as a place where they made wine. And in the fourth century, Eusebius, the Christian historian, speaks of a Jewish village in that spot. But now only a wretched settlement of the Bedu surrounds the spring which, rising copiously from the barren hills, produces a sudden burst of trees and vegetation in the midst of the desolate land.

I

The view over the waters of the Dead Sea, and to the hills of Ammon and Moab beyond it, which one gets from the hill on which the spring rises, is often of a mystical beauty. " The hazy shimmer of the air in the catastrophic pit of the world " affords its peculiar character. But on the day of our coming the air was thick with locusts which flew around like snowflakes and covered every bush and tree. The score of Bedouin, who form the whole population to-day of Engedi, rushed out to meet them with wild cries, brandishing sticks and clubs in a desperate effort to drive the pest from their patches of barley and vegetation. Remarkable to say, their primitive methods seemed to be successful. At least the locusts changed their course and, as we heard afterwards, flew back to Transjordan whence they had come. It would have been a disaster, indeed, if the one green and fertile spot on the long barren shore should be eaten up by the winged hordes.

From Engedi we sailed, passing the black cliff of Feshker, to the Dead Sea Post, our starting-point three days before. We climbed in the moonlight to Jerusalem, enjoying at the end of our journey a view that is incomparable even in Palestine, the Holy City " all compact together," and the Temple area seen in the solemn stillness under the light of the moon from the shoulder of the Mount of Olives.

> Dull would he be of heart who could pass by
> A sight so touching in its majesty.

VII

THE HIGHLANDS OF EPHRAIM
AND THE SAMARITANS

The struggle between the southern and the northern kingdoms of the House of Israel is regularly pictured in the Bible as the conflict between Judah and Ephraim, the favoured son of Jacob and the favoured son of Joseph. The lands of these two tribes almost adjoin; they are separated only by the narrow and bare strip of Benjamin, but physically they are very different. The land of Judah is for the most part an arid and stony plateau, broken by deep valleys and ravines, and passing gradually to the stark wilderness of Tekoa before the steep drop to the abyss of the Dead Sea. The land of Ephraim which includes the land of Manasseh, is indeed, also, a hilly plateau, but more fertile. It is a land of rich pastures, well covered with olives and figs, broken by wider valleys where water is abundant and the soil is bountiful, and descending more gradually on the eastern side by cultivated valleys to the fruitfulness of the Jordan plain.[1] The history of the two lands was as different as their physical character. Ephraim was always in close touch with the materially richer lands to the north, Syria and Phoenicia. Her people borrowed the gods, the pagan ceremonies, and the luxurious manners of their powerful and richer neighbours, the worship of Ashtoreth and Baal and their attendant cruelties. Judah was cut off, isolated on the one side by her wilderness and

---

[1] The blessing which Moses gave to Joseph was, "Blessed be the Lord for his land; for the precious things of heaven, for the dew, and for the deep that coucheth beneath; and for the precious fruits brought forth by the sun, and the precious things put forth by the moon." (Deut., xxxiii. 13.)

on the other by her steep hills. Though from time to time the pagan penetration contaminated her kings and people and caused backslidings, yet her leaders and her people maintained more steadfastly the austere worship and the higher morality of the God of Israel.

No marked geographical feature divides the two lands. They are both parts of the central mountain system which runs through Palestine from the Lebanon spurs to the desert of Sinai, and is broken only by the plain of Esdraelon, that runs from the Bay of Acre to the Sea of Galilee. And when you pass some twelve miles north of Jerusalem from Bireh and Rama of Benjamin, that were included in the kingdom of Judah, to Bethel (now Beitin) that was included in the kingdom of Israel, nothing dramatic marks the change. It is one of the frequent wonders of the history of antiquity that a small, and now negligible, barrier has been momentous in the development of civilization. Thus, in ancient Hellas the people who lived on the bare rocky promontory of Attica, which is still smaller and barer than Judaea, and who gave to the world the art, the science, the philosophy and the political freedom of Athens, were the immediate neighbours of the people who occupied the more fruitful hills and valleys of Boeotia and were a byword for boorishness and rusticity.

There is a hill just over the borders of Ephraim, a few miles north-east of Bethel, which gives one of these wide-embracing vistas peculiar to Palestine, and enables us to take a bird's-eye view over the two ancient kingdoms of Judah and Ephraim. It is Tell-Azur, the highest spot in southern Palestine where the range rises to a height of some 3,500 feet. The extra elevation of 500 feet above the surrounding hills of the central backbone makes a vast difference in the width of the prospect. The hill is identified as " Baal-Hazor which is beside Ephraim ": mentioned in the Book of Samuel as the place where Absalom the son of David revenged his sister's shame by killing Amnon at the feast of the sheep shearers (2 Sam., xiii. 23). Those who have seen the " Crown of David " played by the Habima Company will have a vivid picture of the scene. The Hebrew name in the Bible must refer to a Canaanite deity, Hazor, that was worshipped on these high places. And, to this day, the hill-top is crowned with a clump of sacred trees that are still revered by the local Arabs and tended with oil lamps.[1] The present name, Azur, is a modification of the old Hebrew; and one can understand that survival of primeval cults on the summit of the hills whence the Holy Land is seen stretched in all its variety and majesty. Looking northwards, Hermon, ninety miles away, may be seen beneath its white mantle; and the hills of Galilee are discerned above the nearer mountains of Ephraim, Gerizim, and Ebal. To the west you look over the crinkled hills to the Shefela, and then over the plain to the coastal dunes rolling from Jaffa to Caesarea, and beyond them to the point of Carmel with the shimmering sea on the horizon. To the east the Dead Sea gleams with its steely blue waters, like a cut filled with quicksilver in the world's surface; and, beyond, the mystical wall of Gilead and Moab rises steeply from the Ghor, or hollow of the Jordan. To the south, you look over the whole land of Judah. Jerusalem itself is hidden; but the two towers on the Mount of Olives which dominate it are prominent; the slender Russian belfry and the overpowering castle-like tower of the German Hospice that was lately Government House. On the western side, the mosque which is placed over the grave of the prophet Samuel on the hill that bears his name, Nebi Samwil, strikes the eye. It has been rebuilt since it was shattered during the defence of Jerusalem in 1917. Bounding this southern landscape the hills of Judah and Bethlehem roll away, and the conical mounds that lie between their inhabited slopes and the Dead Sea; and the purple haziness of the hills of Hebron closes the horizon.

[1] See " Tell Azur," by Dr. Orr-Ewing, *P.E.F. Quarterly*, 1927, p. 15.

Some ten miles to the north of Tell Azur, after passing through a succession of hills and valleys, you debouch on a high plateau in which is a small undistinguished Arab village. By the side of the village are outwardly unimpressive ruins, some Byzantine, some older. The Arabs know them as Khirbet Seilun, that is, " the ruin of Seilun," and modern scholars have identified them, with some certainty, as Shiloh, the first sanctuary of Israel in Canaan. The excavations of recent years conducted by a Danish expedition have confirmed the judgment.[1] The Biblical indications of the shrine are exceptionally distinct:

> " There was a yearly feast of the Lord in Shiloh which is on the North side of Bethel, on the East side of the highway that goeth up from Bethel to Shekem, and on the South of Lebonah." (Jud., xxi. 19.)

The village of Seilun lies to the east of the highway—now asphalted—which runs from Bethel—(Beitin, still a large village)—to Shechem (Nablus), and on the south of Lubban (Lebonah).

Shiloh is first mentioned in the Book of Joshua as the place where the leader of Israel divided the land of Canaan between the tribes after the conquest (Josh., xviii. 8). There the Ark of the Covenant and the Tabernacle rested till the days of Saul; there the father of Samuel came up to worship and sacrifice to the House of the Lord; and there the prophet Samuel himself ministered to Eli the High Priest, and the Lord revealed himself (2 Sam., i. 3; iii. 21). It played no important part in the history of Israel —after that revelation; and the Ark and the Tabernacle, which were for a time captured by the Philistines, were moved in the later days of Samuel to Nob—a more defensible sanctuary and Kirjath Jearim near Jerusalem (*ib.*, xxii. 19). The place must have been destroyed by the Philistines who were constantly fighting with Israel for the

---

[1] *J.P.O.S.*, vol. x. 1930: and *P.E.F. Quarterly*, April 1931.

possession of these hills and valleys in the days of Samuel. The recent excavation has revealed destruction by fire of the old city-wall which is dated at about 1050 B.C.E. The fall of Shiloh was taken by the prophets of Jerusalem as a symbol of destruction, like the fall of Ascalon and Tyre. Thus Jeremiah says:

> " Go ye now unto my place which was in Shiloh, where I set my name at the first, and see what I did to it for the wickedness of my people Israel." (Jer., vii. 12.)

Shiloh was not far from Jeremiah's own village of Anathoth, the modern Anata; and he must often have passed the scene of desolation. That prophet indeed records that in his day, after the fall of Gedaliah, men came from Shiloh and Shechem in mourning to bring offerings to the Temple, and were slain (*ib.*, xli. 5).

From the finding of Hellenistic and Maccabean coins during the excavations, it is surmised that the city was restored in the Hellenistic epoch, when Palestine assumed a fresh importance as a Mediterranean land in touch with other Mediterranean countries. Like its neighbours, Nablus, the old Shechem, and Sebastia, the old Samaria, Shiloh was rebuilt; but of its history at this period we have no record, and it cannot have regained any special religious significance. It blossomed out again as a Christian settlement in the early centuries of the Common Era, when the religious sites of the Old Testament acquired a new reverence. There are among the ruins of this epoch a basilica and a pilgrim church, which is believed to have been originally a synagogue. A mosaic floor, the constant feature of Byzantine places of worship, was uncovered, and revealed figures of stags round a pomegranate tree and water, that illustrate perhaps the verse in the Psalms, " As the hart panteth after brooks, so panteth my heart after Thee."

The Jewish traveller, Isaac Chelio, of the fourteenth century, records that he saw at Seilun a

" tomb of the High Priest Eli and his two sons Hophni and Phineas, where lights are kept perpetually burning by both Jews and Moslems."

He adds that there was living near these monuments an old Kabbalist from Germany who made his livelihood by writing copies of sacred books, and particularly of the mystical literature.[1] Chelio settled in Palestine; and described all the routes and the principal places of the country. His testimony is therefore reliable, and goes to show that Shiloh was still in that day an inhabited village or holy site. Two centuries earlier another Jewish traveller, Samuel ben Samson, who visited the Holy Land when it was still under Christian rule, and was the forerunner of a famous pilgrimage of 300 Rabbis from England and France, recounts that he went from Bethel to Shiloh. " We saw the tomb of Joseph the Just. We slept there and kept a joyous Sabbath." [2] Joseph the Just (who is the Patriarch Joseph), was buried outside Shechem, and his tomb was a place of pilgrimage for the children of the three faiths. Another Jewish traveller who is usually more accurate, Benjamin of Tudela, confuses again Shiloh with Mizpah, the hill to the North-West of Jerusalem which was the burial place of the prophet Samuel and is to-day dominated by the mosque in his honour. He must be reproducing a current false identification such as was almost invariable in the days of the Crusades when pilgrims were gullible and their guides were greedy—and lazy.

Continuing from Shiloh some twenty miles along the highroad to the North, you come to the chief town of the Land of Ephraim which has an older and more unbroken history than Shiloh. The city is now called Nablus but in the Old Testament was Shechem, and in the New Testa-

---

[1] See *Jewish Travellers*, ed. Adler, p. 141.
[2] *Ibid.*, p. 105.

ment was Sychar.[1] It is mentioned in the Tel-el-Amarna letters as Sakmi, and some explain this older name as meaning the two shoulders of Gerizim and Ebal, on which the town has always reposed. The Hebrew Shechem more certainly means the shoulder. It is curious to reflect that " Nablus " is the same as Naples; both are local modifications of the Greek Neapolis, or " new city," and the full name of the Palestine foundation during the Christian Era was Flavia Neapolis. A Hellenistic city-state with the name Sychar was erected by the side of the ancient Shechem that was destroyed when the Assyrians led away the captives of Israel; and Neapolis was a restoration after the later destruction in the struggle of the first century between Jews and Romans.

Recent excavations have shown that the original city lay two miles to the East of the present Arab town, at what is now the village of Balata. Under the remains of a strong Canaanite fortress a Hyksos stronghold, dated about 2000 B.C. was found. The city was surrounded by massive Cyclopean walls in which two gates have been identified. It stood grim and forbidding in the centre of the narrow pass, commanding the road from the Jordan Valley to the fertile coastal plain. This must have been the fortress which Abimelech laid waste, as is recorded in the Book of Judges (ix.). A further confirmation of that story has come to light in the finding of a ruined temple at the foot of Mount Gerizim that is identified with the shrine of the Baal Brith. Objects of Canaanite worship and a bronze sword with two spears, symbols of war, were found buried by the altar in the temple—an offering to the deity of peace. Two cuneiform tablets of Babylonian script came to light in the excavation, one being a business contract and the other a letter.

Nature has designed the plain between the two ranges

[1] Some commentators have suggested that Sychar mentioned in the Gospel of John was a separate place a few miles from Shechem; but the probabilities are against this theory.

of Gerizim and Ebal for a centre of population. She has given bountifully of her treasures of water, so that the place is known to the Arabs as " The Little Damascus." A level plateau stretches on the Eastern side between the two mountains, and descends on the West in a narrower valley to the coastal plain. It is raised some 2,000 feet above the sea, and is fanned at all seasons by breezes from the sea and from the mountains. By its position at the water-shed between the Mediterranean and the Dead Sea, where the Great North Road crosses the main road from West to East, it was bound to be an important place of commerce and culture; and it maintained that importance from the dawn of Jewish history.

Shechem is bound up closely with the story of the Patriarchs. When Abraham departed from " Haran " and entered the land which God showed him, he passed into the plain of Shekem and by the same oak he received God's promise.

> " The Lord appeared unto Abraham and said, ' Unto thy seed will I give this land '; and there builded he an altar unto the Lord who appeared unto him." (Gen., xii. 6.)

When Jacob after serving Laban returned from Haran with his wives and family, he too came to the city of Shekem and bought a portion of the field where he had spread his tent, and he erected there an altar and called it after the God of Israel (Gen. xxxiii. 13-20). The plain of Dothan where Joseph was sold by his brethren is generally located some twenty miles to the North of Shekem; and the bones of Joseph, which the children of Israel brought up from Egypt, were buried after Joshua's conquest of Canaan in that field which Jacob had bought (Josh., xxiv. 32). Needless to say, the tomb of Joseph has been located here and there. A firmer tradition held alike by Jews and Christians, Samaritans and Moslems, has placed the well of Jacob on the outskirts of the town as you approach it from Jerusalem.

The well had a special sanctity in the eyes of the Christian Church because, according to the Gospel of John, Jesus, on his way from Judaea to Galilee, rested there. And here he had a meeting with the Samaritan woman from whom he asked water to drink, and revealed himself as saviour. She was amazed that a Jew should have dealings with a Samaritan; and when she asked him how he would draw living water, he answered:

> "Whoever drinketh of this water shall thirst again, but whoever drinketh of the Word that I shall give him shall never thirst: the water that I shall give shall be in him a well of water springing up into everlasting life."
> (John, iv. 5-13.)

A Christian Church was built by the well, and on the site there are ruins of a Church from the time of the Crusades. The Greek Orthodox community, which acquired the site at the beginning of this century, began to build a large edifice over the well, but the work was stayed and has never been completed. It is a stony excrescence on one of the most pregnant scenes of religious history.

Shechem, or rather Mount Gerizim and Mount Ebal opposite to it, furnish the theatre designed by nature in which took place the inaugural service of Israel on taking possession of the land of Israel. Half the congregation stood over against Gerizim, and half over against Ebal; " and Joshua read out all the words of the Law, the blessings and the cursings " (Josh., viii. 33). Here, too, when the conquest was complete

> "Joshua made a covenant with the people and set them a statute and an ordinance in Shechem. And he took a great stone and set it up under an oak that was by the sanctuary." (*Ib.*, xxiv. 25.)

Though David and Solomon made Jerusalem the capital of their kingdom, Shechem, as the physical centre of the whole land of Canaan, was the place where the people assembled when a new king was to be chosen after Solomon's death (1 Ki., xii. 1). And when Judah and Israel separated, it became at first the capital of the kingdom of Israel. It was not, however, easily defensible, and the capital was soon removed to a fortress-site some ten miles to the north-west—Samaria. The religious shrine of the new kingdom was, too, placed not at Shechem but at Bethel, the original holy place associated with Jacob (*Ib.*, xii. 25).

Shechem declined in importance during the rest of the history of Israel, and its inhabitants, with those of Samaria, were taken away captive to Assyria by Tiglath-Pileser in 738 B.C.E. In place of the Israelites the Assyrian king planted in the land of Ephraim men of his northern empire from Hamath and Babylon and Cutha. They were pagans and feared not the Lord, and therefore He sent lions among them which slew some of them. When that was reported to the King, he ordered that some of the priests that had been taken captive should be sent back to their old home to teach them the manners of the God of that land. The God of Israel, he surmised, could be correctly worshipped only by his own people. One of the priests who had been carried away from Samaria came and dwelt in Bethel, the old shrine of Israel, and taught the people. But each group of the colonists still made gods of their own; " the men of Cutha made Nergal, and the men of Babylon made Succoth, and the men of Hamath made Ashima."

" They feared the Lord and served their own gods after the manner of the nations whom they carried away from thence." (2 Ki., xvii. 24 *ff.*)

Thus does the Bible record the resettlement of the land of Israel with the mixed multitude, whom we know later as the Samaritans, and expounds their estrangement. In Rabbinical literature they are known indeed as Cutheans, after the name of one of the Assyrian towns from which they were drawn. They called, and still call themselves, " Samerim," which corresponds with the Hebrew Shomerim, *i.e.* the Observers. Their implied claim to be the true keepers of the Law may have been the reason for the Rabbinic choice of another name. Be this as it may, the Cutheans or Samaritans were bitterly opposed to the returned Judaeans when Cyrus allowed the Captives of Babylon to lead back a remnant to what had been the southern kingdom. Tribalism was dead in Israel after the intermingling of the Captivities of Assyria and Babylon. The God of Israel and Judah had become universal; and the prophecy of Isaiah should have been fulfilled that " Ephraim shall not envy Judah, and Judah shall not vex Ephraim " (Is., xi. 13). It was not, however, so to be. The remnant of Israel and the strangers who had adopted a half-Judaism mingled with the older paganism continued the old hostility, and hampered the rebuilding of the Walls of Jerusalem and the rebuilding of the Temple by Zerubbabel and Ezra (Neh., iv).

Throughout the succeeding centuries, while the Jewish nation had its home in Palestine, there were not indeed two kingdoms as before, but there were two Hebraic religions, one with its centre at Jerusalem and the other with its centre at Shechem. The original national home of the Hebrew people when they entered the Land of Promise became again a religious capital. A temple was erected on Mount Gerizim which the Samaritans, by a bold alteration of Scripture, claimed to be the place where the Law was recorded on the Twelve Stones (Deut., xxvii. 14). Our Hebrew text makes Mount Ebal the place on which those stones were to be set up, although the height of Gerizim, which is opposite to it, was the place from which the blessings were recited. The Samaritans were distinguished from the Jews also by their acceptance of the Pentateuch alone as Holy Writ. The books of the Prophets and the later historical books and the oral tradition were not acknowledged by them. Moses was the one prophet of God, even as was Mohamed in the eyes of the later religion which sprang from Judaism. They claimed too to have the true descendants of Aaron as the high priests of the cult on Gerizim. Their relations with the Jews were of intermittent hostility, like those of the Scots and the English before the Union of the two Kingdoms of Britain.

When the Macedonians conquered the East and occupied Palestine about 330 B.C.E., they marked Shechem for one of the Hellenistic settlements in which, following the principles of Alexander, Hebraism and Hellenism were to be fused. The Samaritans were more pliant than the Jews, just as Israel had been more easily subjugated to paganism than Judah. They accepted the Hellenization of their cult, and according to Josephus they themselves invited Antiochus Epiphanes to erect a temple on Mount Gerizim to Zeus Xenios, the Hospitable (Jos., *Ant.*, XII. v. 5). They were naturally favoured by the Seleucids and the Ptolemies; and colonies were taken to Syria and Egypt, and constituted a separate element in those countries for many centuries. As naturally, they were not loved by the Jews. Ben Sira, writing at the beginning of the second century B.C.E., speaks of

" the two races my soul abhors, and the third which is no nation; those that dwell in Seir and Philistia, and the foolish people which sojourn in Shechem." (Ecclus., l. 25.)

Folly is the characteristic which other Jewish writers ascribe to the sect. One of the Apocryphal books known as the Testament of Levi speaks of Shechem as the City of Fools.

In the flush of the Maccabean conquests Shechem fell to John Hyrcanus 132 B.C.; and the Temple on Mount

Gerizim, which had existed for over 200 years, was destroyed. Its fall was celebrated by a new feast-day in the Jewish calendar, the day of Gerizim, that is parallel with the days of Hanucah. The Jewish triumph over the Samaritans as over the Hellenistic cities of Palestine was short-lived. Pompey constituted Shechem as an independent city, and the Samaritan temple was restored. In the great Jewish rebellion of the next century, town and temple were again destroyed. But Vespasian, doubtless to mark the subjugation of the Jewish people and of their exclusive religion, rebuilt and renamed Shechem. Henceforth it was " Flavia Neapolis," named after the Imperial house and enjoying the Imperial favour, endowed with a Roman municipal organization and using Latin as an official language. Again, after the crushing of the still more desperate Jewish revolt in the days of Hadrian, that Emperor erected on Mount Gerizim a splendid temple to Jupiter of which the foundations may be still seen: and while the sacrifices and pilgrimages ceased at Jerusalem, they remained at Shechem.

The Samaritans were, however, too closely alike to the Jews, religiously, to be favoured by the last of the pagan emperors in the third century when the struggle of dying paganism with the growing power of Judaism and Christianity took on a fiercer colour. And their traditions tell of persecutions. The oppression became more intense for Samaritans as for Jews when the Empire became Christian. As Graetz wrote, " Golgotha, when raised to the height of the Capitol [of Rome] oppressed with double might Zion and Gerizim." Oppressive laws were decreed by the fervent Theodosius and by the supreme codifier Justinian against their worship; and many adopted the dominant faith. The Christians had already appropriated their holy places which, as we have seen, bore a special sanctity for the now victorious creed; and an octagonal Church of the Virgin, built by Justinian, crowned Gerizim in place of Samaritan and pagan shrines.

It was in these times of adversity that a reformer of their religious teaching and organization appeared among the Samaritans.[1] He is known in their Midrash as Baba Rabba, and seems to have been another Ezra. He formed a Council of seven wise men, three priests and four laymen, to take the place of the old priestly hierarchy. Of the same period is the principal Samaritan theologian, Marka, the Aramaic Targum of the Bible, and the Midrashic literature. Their literary and cultural development follows closely that of the Jews.

Perhaps it was the effect of the religious reform to make the Samaritans more assertive of their religious independence. Certain it is that in the reign of Zeno in the fifth century they burst into a desperate outbreak against the Christianized Roman Empire, and were crushed, as the Jews had been crushed 300 years before by Titus and by Hadrian. Their temporal power never recovered from that blow, though they were not driven altogether from their ancestral home.

Before this epoch they had been cut off from the Jewish community, which was drawing in the cords of its tent to resist the perils of sectarianism and contamination with strange doctrine. It was in the same period that the Hellenistic development was repudiated. The attitude of the earlier heads of the Jewish schools towards the Cutheans was generally tolerant. In the second century Rabbi Simon ben Gamaliel declared that the Samaritans observed more scrupulously than the Jews the laws which they accepted.[2] Their devotion to the Law of Moses was generally acknowledged; and the points of heresy were limited to the worship on Mount Gerizim and the denial of resurrection. They shared in the latter particular the standpoint of the Sadducees. In that more tolerant epoch they were treated rather as a schism than as a heresy; but intermarriage with Jews was forbidden. At the end of

---

[1] See Montgomery, *The Samaritans*, Philadelphia, 1907.
[2] Talmud. Kidd 76a, and Ber. 47b.

the third century, however, a sharper division was made, which is ascribed to some degeneration of the Samaritans. We may suspect that Gnostic teaching had made its way into the sect, for we know that heresies such as that of the Dositheans sprang up in Shechem. The Rabbi said to one who asked why the ban was intensified: " Your fathers did not corrupt their ways, but you have corrupted your ways." A Talmudic tractate, Masseketh Cuthim, sets out in detail the disabilities of the rejected branch. And they have remained outside the community to this day, and steadily declined.[1]

They survived as a considerable sect through the Byzantine and the Arab dominion in Palestine, and retained always their centre at Shechem. They were persecuted by the Abbassid Caliphs who ruled the east from Bagdad in the eighth and ninth centuries, and favoured by the heretical Fatimid rulers of Egypt and Palestine in the tenth. A Samaritan governor ruled the country from Sepphoris at the end of that century. The Crusader Chroniclers indeed do not mention them, presumably because they hid their distinction from the common Moslems during that foreign domination. But Arab historians give us tidings of the community both in Palestine and in Egypt and Damascus where their colonies subsisted. At the end of the twelfth century, a chronicler of Damascus records that outside Nablus they mustered only about a thousand families. A Samaritan inscription from a village near Nablus, which has been recently unearthed and is dated C.E. 1214, indicated their presence in the villages of Samaria [2] But their communities suffered massacre during the invasion of Palestine in the thirteenth century by the wild Tartars. From this time Jewish travellers began to give attention to the sect and to provide an account of their doctrine; Benjamin of Tudela found in Nablus no Jews, but a thousand Cuthean families—who

---

[1] See Montgomery, *op. cit.*, chs. x. and xi.
[2] *J.P.O.S.*, x. 222.

K

observed the Mosaic law without the Rabbinical tradition.
Their priests, called Aaronites, would not marry with any
other family. He found also 200 at Caesarea, 300 at
Ascalon, and 400 at Damascus.

> " On Passover and the other festivals they offer up
> burnt offerings on the altar which they have built on
> Mount Gerizim, as it is written in their law; Ye shall
> set up the stones on Mount Gerizim. . . . Their alphabet
> [he says] lacks three letters of the Hebrew alphabet, He,
> Heth, and Ayin. In their place they use the Aleph, by
> which we can tell that they are not of the seed of
> Israel." [1]

The legend of the three missing letters is repeated by later
travellers, but is entirely baseless. The Samaritans have
preserved, in fact, the older Hebrew script and alphabet:
and the Talmud recognized the priority of their writing.
" The Hebrew script was left after the Captivity to the
Idiots " (*Tr. Sanh.*, 216); while the Jews adopted the
Assyrian characters, which we still use.

Benjamin's account of their sacrificial worship on
Mount Gerizim is true so far as the Paschal offering is concerned; but on the other festivals, though they go up the
mountain, they do not sacrifice. The slab of rock on which
they kill the animals is known to them as Sakhra, corresponding with the sacred rock at Jerusalem over which the
Moslems built the " Dome of the Rock." And the Samaritans claim that their mountain was the place of Abraham's
sacrifice, the true Moriah. Two Jewish travellers of the
fifteenth century, Meshullam ben Menahem and Obadiah
de Bertinoro, repeat the testimony about their pilgrimages
to the Mountain of Nablus at the festivals; and the latter
recounts that he was accompanied from Cairo by a number
of the sect who were making the " Regel." They add two
new legends which have no foundation in fact, that the

---

[1] Benjamin. Ed. Adler, pp. 20-21.

Samaritans worshipped a dove, and that they observed the Sabbath only till mid-day.[1] In their day the number of Samaritan families was estimated at 500; but that may well be an under-estimate. And Obadiah declares that in Egypt the members of the sect held high administrative posts in the State. They were, like the Copts in Egypt to-day, distinguished in commerce and administration.

Scaliger, reputed the greatest scholar of modern times, acquired in 1584 from Cairo two Samaritan calendars and a copy of their Book of Joshua, and from Gaza letters about their tenets. With this material he initiated a scientific study of their doctrines and history. Twenty-five years later an Italian scholar obtained from Damascus copies of their text of the scripture. When the texts were published they gave an impulse to the critical study of the Hebrew text of the Pentateuch and Hebrew epigraphy. In the last hundred years Samaritan manuscripts have been a favourite quarry of the Semitic scholar, and Samaritan inscriptions are found in comparative wealth in Palestine. That is to be expected since the sect has maintained a religious and a cultural independence of a sort for more than 2,000 years, and lived all that time in one land. A famous Codex of the Pentateuch which is ascribed by them boldly to the grandson of Aaron is yet in their hands, though it has been mortgaged to American helpers. It may be 2,000 years younger than its reputed date: but it is very old.

The Samaritans have remained at Nablus to this day, but are now reduced to some fifty families, eking out a poor existence in petty trade and the sale of manuscripts, genuine and spurious. Elsewhere they have altogether disappeared. They are more like museum specimens than a living community. They were the first sect among the Jews, and sects have not flourished in Judaism. The " catholic conscience " of the people developing from age to age has been too strong for any section or party which

[1] See Adler, *Jewish Travellers*, pp. 171 and 225.

broke away from the main body, as witness also the disappearances of the Sadducees and the Karaites. The Samaritans still celebrate the Passover on Gerizim, when the community goes up for the seven days of the Feast to camp on the Mountain, and the High Priest sacrifices the Paschal Lamb and each head of a family makes the offering. Later all the company eat the roasted flesh. But even this religious survival tends to become a commercialized performance. The number of onlookers increases as the number of celebrants diminishes. Yet, if spiritually the Samaritans are a dying community, ethnologically they offer a most interesting field of research. For they are the survivors of the Semitic Judaized people who have lived in Palestine continuously for 2,500 years.

The town of Nablus has maintained a reputation for extreme Arab nationalism and fanaticism. It is a strange reflection that the two towns of Palestine, Nablus and Hebron, which are particularly connected with the common ancestor of the Arabs and the Jews, Father Abraham, are the hearths to-day of Arab intolerance. Alone of the chief towns of Palestine, Nablus has effectively resisted any Jewish penetration. Its population to-day is composed of about 25,000 Moslems, 700 Christians, and 150 Samaritans; and one single Jew, a teacher of the Samaritans. It is the home of great feudal land-owning families, and still has a reputation for Moslem learning. The Old City, which contained picturesque, if unhealthy, bazaars and quarters, was badly shattered by the earthquake of 1927, as it had been in earlier earthquakes in the eleventh and thirteenth centuries, and the larger part of the older Arab quarters was laid low. It is curious to read in Hebrew manuscripts from the Geniza of Cairo descriptions of the earthquake in the town in the eleventh century, which are apposite to the catastrophe of 1927. One of the Rabbis describing it, said that the verse was fulfilled, " Behold, the Lord empties out the land and lays it waste, distorts its face and scatters its inhabitants." And one is reminded of the special prayer in the Atonement ritual, that " the homes of the inhabitants of Sharon may not become their graves."

We have mentioned that Nablus lost its capital prerogatives in the days of the Kings of Israel, first to Tirzeh, which has been identified with an Arab hamlet Teiasin between the highlands and the Jordan Valley, and then to the town which is called in our English Bible Samaria. Its Hebrew name is Shomron, or the watch-tower, which indicates probably the fortress character of Omri's city, though it is ascribed in the Bible to the name of the owner of the hill on which the King built it (1 Ki., xvi. 24). It stood at the head of the chief pass to the coast.[1] The prophet indicates the beauty of its site when he writes

" the glorious beauty which is on the head of the fat valley shall be a fading flower and as the hasty fruit before the summer." (Is., xxviii. 4.) [2]

Perched on a rocky spur that breaks off from the ridge of Ebal to the north-west of Nablus, the ruins and the Arab village by their side command a wonderful view over the mountains of central Palestine, and the smiling valley which leads to the coastal plain of Sharon and the sea. The green fields broken by the golden inroad of sand dunes, seen at sunrise or sunset from the hill-top which is covered with silvery olives and fig-trees, afford a vista of singular beauty.

The site has been excavated twice in recent years; by an expedition of Harvard University before the War; and in 1931 and 1932 by a joint expedition of Harvard, the Hebrew University of Jerusalem, and the British School of Archaeology. The excavations have revealed some striking

[1] See Sir G. A. Smith, *Jerusalem*, vol. ii. p. 93.
[2] The intermediate capital of Tirzeh is also a synonym of beauty in the Song of Solomon.

marks of its royal past, more than have remained in any other town on the west side of the Jordan. In 1931 the diggers unearthed a corner of the old city wall, and large parts of the palace of the Kings of Israel which are in three sections: of Omri, of Ahab, and of Jeroboam son of Joash. The masonry of the wall laid in a cutting of the solid rock is amazingly strong and of fine workmanship. The palace is comparable in size with those of the Assyrian Kings in Chaldea, and bespeaks the military power of Israel's ruler. Outwardly Samaria must have been far more magnificent than Jerusalem. There were columns faced with white marble, which must have been part of the " ivory house " of Ahab and Jezebel (1 Ki., xxii. 39). In 1932 more relics of the " ivory house " were unearthed, panels with bands of lotus flowers and designs of lions and celestial beings taken from the Egyptian Pantheon, but significantly without hieroglyphs. Part of the panels had been covered with gold, and inlaid with green and blue enamel. They show both the wealth of the palace; and also the close connection of the Kings of Israel and Egypt.

The excavations of an earlier period gave up a remarkable collection of potsherds or " ostraca," on which records are written in ink with reed pens. The writing is in the old Hebrew script which is said to be similar to that of the Siloam inscription of the days of Hezekiah.[1] They are dockets belonging to the payment of taxes in kind by towns and districts, and record the payment of oil and wine. From their association with a dated Egyptian jar of the reign of the Pharaoh contemporary with Ahab, they are attributed to the time of that king of Israel. Many of the names of the payers are familiar from the Bible, Elisha, Baalath, Avibaal and Aviezer; but the language differs from the Biblical Hebrew which was the dialect of Jerusalem.

---

[1] See " The Oldest City of Jerusalem," ch. ii. p. 32.

The city was the principal fortress of the kingdom of Israel, and was destroyed by Sargon the Assyrian king when the kingdom came to an end. It was the seat of the heathen worships of Phoenicia and Syria, of the calf of gold; and was denounced fiercely by the prophets as the source of wickedness. "Where are the gods of Hamath and Arphad? have they delivered Samaria out of my hand?" (Is., xxxvi. 19). "The prophets of Samaria prophesied in Baal, and caused the people of Israel to sin" (Jer., xiii. 13). The book of Hosea indeed is one continuous indictment of the wickedness of Samaria.

When the Macedonian Greeks conquered Palestine and Syria in the campaigns of Alexander the Great, they chose Samaria as their seat of government. It looked towards the Mediterranean Sea, and commanded the pass from the centre of the country to the Sea. The town was re-settled with Greek veteran colonists as well as with Samari-tans. During the Maccabean struggles for national inde-pendence it was captured by John Hyrcanus, and so com-pletely destroyed that, as Josephus records, it was not possible to say that a town had been there. Modern ex-cavations has shown this to be a Josephine exaggeration; but the winter floods were allowed to play havoc with the old city so that it was called "the city of graves." It received fresh glory in the first century B.C.E. when Herod became King of Judaea and Galilee and rebuilt it in honour of his wife Mariamne, and his patron, the Emperor Augustus. He renamed it Sebaste—the Greek rendering of Augusta—whence comes its modern name Sebastiyeh. Always striving for magnificence and a display of Hellen-istic culture, he erected a great temple on the crest of the hill and a hippodrome and a theatre, and settled the town with his veterans and mercenaries who were largely bar-barians. There, too, he killed Mariamne and his sons. The excavations of 1932 unearthed a vast structure rising in tiers from the bottom of the hill to the ruins of the great temple on the summit, which is in design, if not in form or

beauty, comparable with the Propylea of the Acropolis of
Athens, the most spectacular monument of Hellenistic art
on this side Jordan, and the best evidence which has
survived to the outward splendour of the Herodian
period.

Philip preached the Christian Gospel at Samaria in the
first century, and a late Christian tradition, recorded by
Jerome, made it the burial-place of John the Baptist; and
that was enough to render the place important in the
Byzantine Empire. Palestine was not indeed Christianized
till the fourth or fifth centuries; save where the Jews persisted, it remained pagan. But from the fifth century,
churches were multiplied; and the churches and basilicas
which have been revealed on the hill of Samaria are of
that date. The most remarkable of them includes paintings
of scenes in the life of John the Baptist, who was, as it were,
the Patron-saint. The painting shows his execution and
burial.

Jewish medieval tradition on the other hand, placed
there the graves of Elisha and Obadiah—who hid the
faithful prophets—and accordingly made it a place of
pilgrimage. Benjamin of Tudela visiting it found no Jews,
but saw the ruins of the Palace of Omri and marked the
fertility of the hill. It was a place of gardens, orchards,
and vineyards. Its history as a place of culture came to an
end after the fifth century when it was destroyed in one of the
invasions of Palestine. And now it is the site of a small
village; though the village mosque, built in the ruin of a
Crusader church, displays the beauty of Gothic arches;
and for a circuit of two miles columns, erect and fallen,
stand out from the cornfields and olive groves, witnesses of
the past glory.

To-day the mountains of Ephraim are almost innocent
of Jewish settlement: though the coastal plain and the
Valley of Jezreel below those mountains are populated by
the Halutzim. The prophecy of Jeremiah, " Thou shalt
yet plant vines on the mountains of Samaria," is not yet

realized; for the so-called colonies of Samaria, Zichron-Jacob and the surrounding villages, are in Sharon and not in Shomron, in the plain which was possessed by Phoenicians and Philistines, and not in the highland of Ephraim.

VIII

EGYPT IN PALESTINE

It has been the fate of Palestine, from the beginning of history down to the present day, to be the bone of contention between the power which holds the rich valley of the Nile to the south-west, and the power which rules over the rich plains of Syria and Assyria to the north-east. For Palestine, geographically, is the thin strip of cultivable land between the desert and the sea that links, or separates, these two fruitful regions—the cradles of human civilization. And the rulers have fought for mastery in her plains, and marched against each other through her coastal road. Palestinian archaeology and Egyptology are establishing more abundantly each year that Egypt bore rule for long periods in the land of Canaan, and that the early civilization of the people of Canaan was largely Egyptian. In the Bible the relationship is symbolized by making Canaan and Mizraim (that is, Egypt), brothers.

Circumstances in the Palestine campaign of the Great War, 1916-1918, gave me the opportunity of following in its stages the Egyptian penetration of the Palestine marches. For between January 1916 and January 1918, we proceeded slowly from the delta of the Nile to the Promised Land and Jerusalem, by the route the armies of Egypt had traversed century after century; [1] and it is that experience and the knowledge gleaned from visits to the sites since excavated which have induced me to set out again the oft-told tale.

In ancient days, indeed, the two countries were more

---

[1] It is of interest to note that the Sinai military railway was laid by the British Army in the track of the chariots of the Pharaohs.

closely connected geographically than they are to-day. The delta of the Nile, which is now terminated some fifteen miles west of the Suez Canal, extended then some fifteen or twenty miles to the east of Lake Tina through which that Canal is carried. At the mouth of the Pelusiac branch of the great river stood the important city known in the Graeco-Roman period as Pelusium, which was one of the chief seats of power of the Pharaohs and their principal fortress against the enemy from the east. Some scholars have identified it with the town of Raamses which the children of Israel were forced to build for the Pharaoh of the Oppression. Be this as it may, here it was that Ramases III in the twelfth century B.C. crushed the attack of the wild tribes of Scythians and other northern peoples who had passed through Syria and the coastal plain. And here, 500 years later, Cambyses, the Persian King of Kings, laid low finally the might of Egypt, so that never again has it been governed by a dynasty of Egyptian, or even African, origin.

Seti, the warrior king of the eighteenth dynasty, in the fourteenth century B.C. started to build a wall from Pelusium to the edge of the Gulf of Sinai, following the line of the present Suez Canal. He designed in this way to keep off the peril to the civilization of the Nile valley from the east, just as the Romans sought by their walls in Britain and Germany to keep off the barbarians of the north; but the plan was not completed. Centuries later, one of the last native kings of Egypt, Psammetichus, built the frontier fortress of Tahpanhes south of Pelusium, in the region of the present Kantara on the Suez canal. The fortress became a city of refuge for the Jews at the time of the Babylonian Captivity, and the prophet Jeremiah himself went down to it (Jer., xliii. 7); and the ruin is still called by the Egyptians the Castle of the Jew's Daughter.

Pelusium, under the name of Farama, was an important place of maritime trade throughout the Middle Ages. The European traveller bound for the East landed here and began his overland journey; it is mentioned in this regard in the Arabic Book of Ways of the ninth century describing the routes of Jewish merchants. Our word " blouse " is derived from the place through the French " Pelouse "; because its flax, from which the article of dress was made, was famous in Europe. When the British Army in 1916 started to make its way across the desert, they placed a station of the military railway by the site of the Tell that covers Pelusium; and some of us who were encamped there dug up Roman pottery and coins, and bared fragments of ancient walls.

When the army advanced, we encamped for some weeks in the summer of 1916 by the sea at a place called Mahamdia, some thirty miles east of Port Said. Our military maps marked a second name, the Fort of Chabrias. And along the shore, a few miles east of our camp, was the imposing ruin of a fortress built of solid Roman brick like the ruins of the Roman castle of Richboro' in Kent. The walls came down to the edge of the sea, and there were huge fragments of masonry in the sea. We had only to scratch below the surface to find pots and coins of the Byzantine age. The fortress took its name from the Athenian general who, in the early days of the fourth century B.C., entered the service of the Egyptian King and fought for him against the Persian invader. Here, later, was one of the Roman fortresses of the early centuries of the Common Era, which were placed at intervals of fourteen miles to guard the high road from Egypt to Palestine against hordes from Arabia. The latest historian of Sinai, Major Jarvis, identifies the ruins with the Roman port of Gercha.[1] Fourteen miles further east was another Roman fortress, Celsus, where Pompey was murdered as he landed after the flight from the disastrous battle of Pharsala.

Another stage on our march brought us to the ruin of a

[1] Jarvis, *Yesterday and To-day in Sinai.*

Byzantine monastery now almost buried, in the desolate region of the lagoon which lies ten feet below the level of the sea. The salt lagoon is the " Serbonian Bog " of our poet; but by the Arabs is called Sabket Bardawil. Here was another fortress of the Roman road, Ost-racine, which received the Arab name of " Filusiat," because, it is said, of the great finds of coins—Arabic, " Filuz "—that were found amid its ruins. The Arabic name of the lagoon itself recalls another epoch in the history of the relations of Palestine and Egypt. It is a transformation of Baldwin, the first and greatest Latin King of Jerusalem of that name, who died on the march from Jerusalem to attack the Saracens in Cairo. The dying King was taken back to El Arish, the town at the north of the River of Egypt, which is mentioned in the Bible (Gen., xv. 18) as the boundary of the Promised Land. Some medieval Jewish travellers identify El Arish with the Succoth of the Exodus. The place was celebrated in early Church history for its monasteries and holy men: and is to-day the head-quarters of the governorate of Sinai. It is inhabited by some 7,000 Arabs of the most mixed breeds, sprung from the stragglers of countless armies. In Hellenistic and Church history it is known under the name of Rhino-colura, meaning the cutting of the nose. The strange name was derived from its use as a penal settlement by the rulers of Egypt, who cut off the noses of the convicts when they were sent to penal servitude.

Advancing on the road through the Negeb, or parched land, we encamped by Rafa, the Rapu or Raphia of anti-quity. Here stood the terminal fortress of the military road across the desert; and here two decisive battles were fought for the dominion of Palestine between Empires of the old world. Sargon of Assyria, in the eighth century B.C.E., met the hosts of Shabak of Egypt and worsted them. The Kings patched up their quarrel, but the power of the Pharaohs reeled from the blow, and in less than fifty years it collapsed before the renewed attacks of the

Assyrians under Ezar-haddon. The words of Jeremiah were fulfilled:

> " Egypt riseth up like a flood and its waters are moved like the rivers. . . . This is the day of the Lord of Hosts, the day of vengeance that he may avenge him of his adversaries; and the sword shall devour, and it shall be satiate and made drunk with their blood. For the Lord of Hosts hath a sacrifice in the north country by the river Euphrates. . . ." (Jer., xlvi. 8, 10.)

And at this spot at the beginning of the second century B.C.E. the Seleucid Antiochus defeated Ptolemy Philopator of Egypt, and changed the destiny of Palestine. His victory brought Judaea under the more vigorous Hellenizing activity of Antioch in place of the more tolerant sway of Alexandria. Without that impulse of persecution the Maccabees' revolt might never have been provoked, and the history of humanity might have been different.

A few days more, and we were in Khan Yunis, the southern-most village along the Palestine coast, which is dominated by a ruined but noble mosque of the Egyptian Mameluke Sultan Beibars. It seems strangely out of place amid the mud-huts of the half-Bedu Arabs who form the present population of the village, and it bears witness to the time when both Egypt and southern Palestine were seats of Moslem culture. It was in this village that Napoleon Bonaparte, having crossed the Desert of Sinai with 10,000 Frenchmen, in as many days as we had taken months, was nearly captured as he rode ahead of his advance-guard with his personal staff into a Turkish outpost.

In March 1917 came the first attack of the British Army on Gaza—the strong city, as its name signifies—which resisted our invasion as it had often resisted invasion from Egypt. For six months we sat down in trenches and dug-outs by the Wadi Ghuzzeh, the river of Gaza. The river was not, indeed, a full stream like a river of the Western

Front, but for the most part a dry river-bed, hollowed between steep banks. In the summer a thin silvery streak of water runs between the stones, and here and there widens to a pool fringed with reeds and oleanders. In the winter, when the rains pour down from the hills, it can be for a few days a rushing torrent which overflows its banks and tears through the sandy soil to the sea. The relics of war and civilization are imprinted on its banks. Tracing its career backwards from the sea, we found at its mouth deep caves now inhabited by owls, but once a dug-out of warriors. Then we came to a towering earthwork, where man's hand has improved on nature. At Shellal, a few miles beyond, a squadron of Anzac cavalry alighted on a mosaic pavement of a design and inscription which proclaimed it Byzantine of the early centuries of the Christian Era. Beyond Shellal, again, rose another of those dominating mounds, which was ascribed to—wrongly— Crusaders and provided a providential place for an observation post. Thence the Wadi ran eastwards and was known as Wadi Khalassa, after the ruins of another Byzantine city above it.

Our knowledge of the history of Gaza and this region, and of the relations of Egypt and Palestine, has been amazingly increased since those fairly recent days. We associate Gaza with the Philistines because of the exploits of Samson. But it is also a city of constant record in the Egyptian monuments from the earliest time, and it was for a period the capital of the Egyptian rulers of Palestine. To-day the British School of Egyptian Archaeology, under the direction of its ageless head, Sir Flinders Petrie—who has passed his jubilee year of excavation—is engaged on the exploration of the vast Tell which lies a few miles south of the present city, and is revealing its wealth of primitive and Egyptian treasures. It was a fortunate ill-wind of the Egyptian authorities towards foreign expeditions which blew the English school in Egypt to Palestine. The excavations of three years have established that below this Tell, known as the hill of the Calf (Tel Ajjul), which rises some fifty feet above the Wadi, there was a city of over fifty acres, many times as big as ancient Troy or ancient Jerusalem. Its development seems to have come to an end at the time of the eighteenth Egyptian dynasty, about 1500 B.C.E. It is surmised that malaria spreading from the pools of the Wadi was the cause of the sudden abandonment of the fortress-town, and the removal of Gaza to the north. There are remains of habitation from the Copper Age (3000 B.C.E.); but the main city was of the Hyksos, the Semitic people which came either from the north or from the desert on the east, and ruled Palestine and Egypt from the middle of the third to the middle of the second millennium B.C.E.

The streets of the city have been preserved beneath the soil and the sand as perfectly as those of Pompeii; and no later civilization was imposed on the remains of the first occupation. It is a thrilling experience to wander through these streets made nearly 5,000 years ago, and into the houses opening to it on each side, to scale the walls of the palace of the Hyksos kings, whose scarabs have been found within, to wander into their bathrooms and find the water jars perfectly preserved, to stand at the fire-place or possibly the altar, on which the burnt lime is still visible, to examine the platters and jars and vases of pottery, some beautiful with pictures of birds and cattle, others decorated with geometrical design, to gaze down on the ditch or moat some forty feet below the ground level, which must have run around the city and been its defence, and lastly to see in the courtyard of the palace the burials of the Hyksos princes with their horses. The human body is placed in a curiously arranged position at the bottom of a circular pit some six feet deep; while a perfect skeleton of the horse is found on the ground level at the door of the pit. The consecration of the horse and its association with the princes is a distinctive feature of the Hyksos culture. The horse was the source of their martial strength; and it was by the power which the new war-animal gave them that they mastered Egypt. They are known in history as the shepherd-kings; and Sir Flinders Petrie has compared them with the Turks of modern times, who likewise brought terror to the more civilized peoples by the power of their cavalry.

In the middle of the advanced line of the British Expeditionary Force in the summer of 1917—the line which stretched from the sea at the outlet of the river of Gaza twenty miles to the east—was a sugar-loaf hill proclaiming its artificiality by its square sides. To the Arabs it was known as Tell-el Djemmi: to the Army it was "Jimmy's Hill." That Tell, too, has since been excavated by Flinders Petrie, and proved with scarce a doubt, even among archaeologists, to be the Gerar of the Bible where Abraham pitched his tent and made a covenant with the King or Sheikh Abimelech (Gen., xx. 1). Gerar commanded the road from Egypt direct to Jerusalem, and was a place of importance on the caravan route from Egypt to Syria. As Flinders Petrie has said, it seems to have been what Gaza is now, a centre for trade and business, for weapons and clothing of the Arabs. Two miles away were ruins named on our maps Umm el Jerar, or the Mother of Gerar. There, under cover of the night, we took a convoy of 4,000 camels, each loaded with fantasses containing thirty gallons of water, which we poured into ancient rock-hewn cisterns in preparation for an attack on Gaza. Unfortunately the cisterns no longer held water; and that expedition had to be repeated. But the cisterns may have been there from the time of Abraham.

The Tell covers a city which must have been a strong place of importance on the frontier. For it is mentioned among the places which the Egyptians held when their power was threatened, and as the limit of the Jewish pursuit when King Asa routed the Egyptian army (2 Chr., xiv. 11). The hill is some 600 feet long and 200 feet high; and of that 200 feet half is represented by the debris of successive towns and settlements. The spade revealed first a series of granaries which could hold corn sufficient to feed 100,000 men for two months. They were like the granaries which lie to-day below the streets and the squares of Valetta in Malta. Their date is put at the fifth century B.C.E., and they are ascribed to the period of the Persian Empire when they were designed presumably as a preparation for the reconquest of Egypt. It is a striking illustration of the mingling of peoples and cultures that a beautiful Greek vase of the same period was found in the granary, probably left there by a Greek mercenary of the Great King. Below the granaries were walls ten feet thick ascribed to Psammetichus the king of Egypt who fought the terrible Scythians from the north. Below this again a slighter building which is ascribed to the town built by King Amaziah of Judah who conquered Edom. And under that the more solid foundations of an Egyptian town said to be of the period of Shishak who, as we know from the Bible and the pictorial record of a palace at Karnak, occupied Palestine about 930 B.C. Below that layer, again, were rough stone walls of the period of Thothmes who was the conquering Egyptian monarch. No walls were found below that level, but many flint sickles bespeaking a neolithic culture. The Egyptian dominion brought art and craft; before it and after it the Canaanite peoples lived in a more primitive condition.

A few miles east of Tell-el Djemmi rose another half-artificial hill, Tell-el-Farah, of similar construction, which was also a place of our army's encampment and was scarred by the trenches and the dug-outs of the Australian troops. It too has been thoroughly excavated by the skilled hand, and interpreted by the ingenious mind, of Flinders Petrie, who has disclosed another Egyptian fortress. He conjectures that it is the Beth Peleth mentioned in Nehemiah (xi. 26).[1] The hill like the other is composed

---

[1] He has not yet convinced the learned world of this identification. See Albright, *The Archaeology of Palestine and the Bible*, 1931.

of the ruin of successive settlements. It was a fort rather
than a city; and the similarity of its plan to that of the
fort in the Eastern Delta of Egypt known as Tell el Yehudi-
yeh, the Jew's Hill, has led the excavator to attribute its
construction to the Hyksos or Shepherd Kings. Those
rulers of Lower Egypt in the seventeenth and the sixteenth
centuries B.C. were a Semitic people coming from the
desert, like the Hebrews, or perhaps from Canaan. Some
scholars, ancient and modern, associate the Hebrew settlement in Goshen and the Exodus with the rise and decline
of the other Semitic intruders into the land of the Nile.
Josephus, in his reply to the Egyptian anti-Semitic writer
Apio, already adopted that idea 1,900 years ago. It is
likely that, when they were driven out of the Delta about
1550 B.C., the Semitic warriors kept their hold on the
Eastern frontier of Egypt and " Egypt over the border "
before their final expulsion. The place where they made
one of their stands against Egypt in the sixteenth century
B.C.E., was Sharuhen, mentioned as a city of Simeon
(Josh., xix. 6); and it has been identified with Tel el
Sheria which lay opposite our lines and was the central
point of the Turkish trenches on the Beersheba-Gaza
front. We were to enter it a few months later, in November
1917, when the army, after the occupation of Beersheba,
rolled up the Turkish flank; and we could appreciate its
natural strength.

Again exploration disclosed several strata of Egyptian
occupation at Tell Farah. Above the Hyksos walls a
block of brick marked the residence of an Egyptian
governor of the eighteenth century, and revealed the
luxury of a bedroom with a bathroom attached, as well
as a wine-store. Another block is ascribed to the invasion
of Shishak in the days of Rehoboam. The objects found
in the fort give evidence of that mingling of civilizations
which is characteristic of the " bridge-country." The
scarabs are partly Egyptian, and partly Palestinian modifications. And an ivory band of a box inscribed with a

picture of rural life is declared to show traces of Cretan work. We know that the Philistines coming from the West and probably from Crete itself—(see 1 Sam., xxx. 14, which speaks of the Negeb of the Cretans)—occupied the coast lands and the hill country of the south of Canaan from about 1300 B.C., and gradually supplanted Egyptian rule and influence.[1] The relics of the Philistine era are mixed with or imposed on the Egyptian strata of the Tells, and are distinguished by their different masonry and pottery, and their inferior art and craftsmanship.

Recent excavation at Beth-Zur, the Maccabean fortress of Southern Judaea, has unearthed a head carved on a piece of stone, which is ascribed to the later period of the Hyksos (*c.* 1600 B.C.). And Hebron was one of their strong places. It is remarkable that the Bible, in recording the journey of the twelve Spies to Canaan, mentions that Hebron was built seven years before Zoan in Egypt (Num., xiii. 22). Zoan is identified with Tanis where a famous Temple was built in the seventeenth century. Some vague memory lingered of the Egyptian origin of the burial-place of the Patriarchs. Hyksos remains have been found also in another Tell of Southern Palestine near Hebron, Beit Mirsim, which was recently excavated by Professor Albright and identified by him with Kiryat Sefer.[2]

Palestine has been not only the bridge between Africa and Asia, but also, as Sir Martin Conway has called it, " A land of the over-lap, where the Aegean or Mediterranean civilization has constantly fused with the civilization of the east." Its strip of fertile land and cultivable hills looks on the one side to the east and the south, and is part of Arabia, the land of the wandering Semite; and on the other to the sea and the home of the roving Aryans, and

---

[1] Some scholars now think that the Philistines came from Cappadocia in Asia Minor.

[2] See Albright, *The Archaeology of Palestine and the Bible*, New York, 1931: and *J.P.O.S.*, iv. p. 131 and xii. p. 54.

is a part of the Levant. The civilization of Palestine is formed by the meeting of these two streams. The Philistines were the first of a succession of invaders from over the seas who mingled with the native population and brought to them new arts. They were followed by the Greeks who were planted by Alexander the Great and his successors, the Romans who came with their soldiers and governors, the Franks who came to recover the land for Christianity in the Middle Ages and for 200 years bore rule over part or all of it; the monks and religious orders who settled there after the temporal power of Christianity was broken; and lastly, the Jews who are to-day bringing their acquired Western civilization to fertilize again, both physically and spiritually, their Eastern motherland.

That mingling of civilizations is remarkably illustrated in the ruins of Ascalon in southern Palestine which I visited during the autumn campaign of 1917 after the fall of Gaza. As we advanced up the coast we were encamped at Esdud, a poor Arab village, the old Ashdod of the Philistines, and from there I rode the few miles to the coast to look at the picturesque mass of ruins peeping up from fertile fields and sandy dunes which remained of a once famous city. Ascalon was, for more than 2,000 years, from 1400 B.C.E. to C.E. 1300, a city of renown, celebrated in Egyptian monuments, in Bible prophecy, in Greek and Roman and Byzantine literature, and in the chronicles of the Crusaders and Saracens.

When we were there, the columns and fragments of the wall lay undisturbed; but some years later, when the Civil Government was established, their exploration was among the first objects of the archaeological zeal which during the last decade has revealed the treasures of the ancient world. The former Deputy Director of Antiquities, the Rev. Phythian-Adams, has written a sketch of the history of the town, to which I am indebted; and I will linger a little over the story which has been partly revealed by the spade and partly filled in through literature. For it illustrates admirably the age-long connection of Egypt and Palestine.

The name " Ascalon " occurs in the Tell Amarna tablets—of which more anon—in a cuneiform letter from her king Yetia to his master in Egypt. " He is frantic in his professions of loyalty, he kisses his feet, he throws himself seven times to the ground, he sends tribute." But the vassal king of Jerusalem accuses him of having made league with Gezer and Lachish to give help to the Khabiri invaders.[1] The name occurs, also, in the still more famous hieroglyphic stele of the Egyptian king Merenptah which contains the first mention of Israel.

> " Canaan is taken with all his tribes: Ascalon is carried off: Gaza is seized: Israel is desolate without seed."

Between the fourteenth and twelfth centuries B.C.E. when the children of Israel coming out of Egypt were conquering the hill country of Canaan, Ascalon, and Gaza and other towns of the coast were invaded by people arriving in ships from over the water. These were the people who gave Palestine her name among the Gentiles, and who contended with Phoenicia for the coast towns, and with Israel for the fertile plains and the low hills of the Shefela. The Philistines wore down the waning might of Egypt in her province; and they remained the dominant cultural people of the coast till the time of the Captivity, except during the short period of Israel's supremacy under David and Solomon.

Ascalon was overwhelmed by Sennacherib in the Syrian invasion about 700, and it is recorded in the monument of the monarch that he carried off her king to Assyria. Some seventy years later, as we learn from the Greek historian Herodotus who came to Syria to learn about the " bar-

[1] *P.E.F. Quarterly*, April 1921.

barian " peoples, she was threatened by a horde of Scythians but was saved by a pestilence which fell on them. Egypt asserted her sway again for a time with Assyria weakening; but not for long. Philistia and Judaea were to fall before the overwhelming might of Babylon. And the Philistines never recovered from that " scourge of God." When the more tolerant Persians succeeded to world empire, the coast land of Syria and Palestine was delivered to the Phoenicians, and the Philistines are lost as a people, merged partly in the Hellenistic mass, partly in the proselytizing Jewish nation.[1]

A ruler of Egypt reappeared in Ascalon 300 years later, but now in the guise of a Greek King. The Ptolemies encouraged the interchange of gods, peoples, and cultures; and Ascalon became a Hellenistic city-state and a centre of philosophy. Egypt lost once more to Syria her hold over Palestine at the beginning of the second century B.C.E., and Ascalon received a Seleucid over-lord. But when the Maccabees won the independence of the Jews, she soon came to an understanding with them. Yet her citizens had little love for that Jewish puritanism; and when Rome interfered in the affairs of Syria, they obtained again their tutored independence. Herod, who was born there, endowed his native city with imposing buildings in his lavish way, baths and costly fountains and cloisters. And though she suffered from Jewish inroads in the course of the long Jewish struggle with Rome, she thereafter enjoyed the comfortable, if deadening, " Pax Romana " for some 600 years, till the Arab invasion shattered the illusion of almost perpetual security.

Egypt was again to dominate her destiny. Two hundred

---

[1] See " What Has Become of the Philistines," by R. N. Salaman, *P.E.F. Quarterly*, 1923. The last record in the Bible of the enemies of Israel occurs in the Book of Nehemiah, where the rebuilder of Jerusalem reproaches the Jews who had married wives of Ashdod: " and their children spoke half in the speech of Ashdod and could not speak in the Jews' language " (Neh., xiii. 23).

years after the Arab conquest of the East, in C.E. 878, the
Moslem Governor of Egypt, Ibn Tulun, made himself
master of Palestine. Another 200 years, and the greater
part of the Holy Land was in the hands of the Christian
knights coming from over the seas. But Ascalon, " the
bride of Syria," remained under the Crescent and subject
to the heretical Caliph of Egypt for another half-century;
and the Jews remained in the town under their more
tolerant sway.

The fragments of the Cairo Geniza contain correspondence about the congregation in Ascalon. In the twelfth
century Benjamin of Tudela found there 200 Jews, 40
Karaites and 300 Samaritans; which indicates its commercial importance. And it is recorded in Arab chronicles
that Jews helped the Moslems in the destruction of the
Green Church, when Ascalon which had passed to Christian
Knights was recaptured.[1]   Saladin, fearing that she
might fall into the hands of Richard of the Lion-heart and
become a Frank base against Egypt, caused her forts to be
razed and her city to be destroyed. She never recovered
from that blow, for though Richard occupied the site and
set his army to rebuild the forts, the strength was gone.
In 1270 the Iconoclast Sultan Baibars demolished the city,
and she has been uninhabited to our day. The doom of
Ascalon and of other cities of Philistia was a constant
burden of the Hebrew Prophets. Jeremiah exclaimed:

" Baldness is come upon Gaza, Ashkalon is cut off
with the remnant of their valley." (xlvii. 5.)

The Prophet Zephaniah amplifies the doom of Philistia:

" Gaza shall be forsaken and Ascalon a desolation . . .
and the sea coast shall be the dwelling place for shepherds and folds for flocks."

[1] See Mann, *op. cit.*, p. 199.

And the doom has been fulfilled. Perhaps the more comforting message will also be fulfilled:

"And the coast shall be for the remnant of the House of Judah: In the houses of Ascalon shall they lie down in the evening; for the Lord their God shall visit them and turn away their captivity." (Zeph., ii. 4 and 7.)

For nearly 250 years from the time of Baibars, Egypt maintained her rule over Palestine; but then for three centuries Egypt and Palestine were alike under the government of a foreign power which held sway from Europe, the Ottoman Empire. As that power began to decline, the semi-independent Viceroy of Egypt again sought to absorb the country over the border. Ibrahim Pasha was stayed in his course at the beginning of the nineteenth century by the European Powers; and so Turkey continued her unprogressive and wasteful sway till Allenby came and again opened the gate to civilization.

We must return from this diversion, and summarize the history of ancient Egypt in Palestine, as it is revealed by the excavations and the monuments, the tablets and papyri, the learning and the ingenious interpretations of scholars. It was the invasion of the Hyksos from the desert that opened the eyes of the Kings of Egypt, hitherto secure and isolated in their bountiful river valley which is protected by the desert on either side, to the danger from the East. They determined to establish a Greater Egypt over the border and to advance against Asia. Palestine was to Egypt what Wales was to England after the Norman conquest, a dangerous base for an enemy. And she was brought under the rule of the Egyptian dynasties from the time of the warrior king Thothmes I, about 1600 B.C.E., who initiated Asiatic conquests, to the days of Ramases III about 1200 B.C.E. whose epoch was once believed to coincide with the Exodus of Israel. The country was first

invaded and overrun in campaigns against the Hittites,
whose centre of power was in the valleys of the Orontes
and Euphrates, to the north of Syria. But then it was
subdued or brought under overlordship. Throughout
these centuries, Egypt held the intervening land either
under direct rule or under a kind of suzerainty much as,
to-day, England holds India. As the late Dr. Hall said of
this period:

"Canaan is the Egyptian king's land, its people are
his subjects. He is responsible if the caravans of Babylon
are attacked by it. . . . Egypt's resident governors and
travelling inspectors uphold his authority. The Canaanite kings receive their unction as anointed kings from
their Egyptian overlord. The sons of Canaanite chiefs
are sent to Egypt for their education. It is not a land
simply terrorized by a series of raids, but it is Egyptian
territory ruled by Egypt, loosely here, more closely
there, but still ruled." (*P.E.F. Quarterly*, July 1923.)

Egypt's hold was fastened by a ring of forts guarding
the " way of the sea," from Pelusium to the Jordan crossings
on the road to Damascus. The principal stations on the
road whose names are recorded on the monuments or
tablets include Gaza, Ascalon, Lachish and Jaffa in the
south, Dor, Megiddo, Taanach, and Bethshaan, the famous
quadrilateral which guarded the plain of Esdraelon, in
the north.

There were other strong places off the main road in
which a stratum of Egyptian civilization has been revealed,
such as Ain Shems in the Judaean hills, and Gezer in the
Shefela, which was later given by the King of Egypt as a
dowry to his daughter when she married Solomon. The
most recent excavation of Jericho by Professor Garstang
has revealed that the king of that fortress town of the
Jordan valley was a vassal of Egypt in the reign of
Thothmes.

Of all the places mentioned on the monuments, Baisan, the old Beth-Shan, one of the fortresses which guarded the Jordan end of the Plain of Esdraelon on the road to Syria, has disclosed to the excavator the clearest and fullest picture of Egyptian penetration during the period of the eighteenth dynasty.[1] Between the present town and the River Jalud, a tributary of the Jordan, which lies in the pit some ten miles to the East, rises a vast Tell that commands the approach to the Jordan. It is named by the Arabs " El Hosn," " The Mound of the Fortress," and it consists of a series of superimposed citadels ranging in date from the early Bronze Age to the Arab conquest. The Tell is being thoroughly explored by an expedition of the University of Pennsylvania; and five separate strata of Egyptian civilization, dating from 1500-1000 B.C. have already been exposed.[2]

The most striking of the finds hitherto have been a series of Egyptian-Canaanite temples dating from the time of the Middle Empire from Thothmes III, 1500 B.C.E., to Ramases III, 1200. Within the temples were several Stelae, monumental tablets recording the exploits of the conquering Pharaohs. Two are of Seti I, and proclaim his victory over the Asiatics from across the Jordan, and refer to the Apeiru, whom some have identified with the Hebrews. A stele of Ramases records how he pacified the fighting that had occurred among all the peoples, and those who fomented it came bowing before him at his city of Ramases. Another remarkable monument bears the name and figure of an Egyptian officer who held the posi-

[1] The place was known in the Hellenistic period as Scythopolis. The name is generally interpreted as " The City of the Scythians," and is said to commemorate the invasion by the wild north-men who raided Syria and Palestine shortly after the time of the Babylonian Captivity. But an ingenious modern scholar has conjectured that the Hellenic name was an adaptation of the Semitic Beth-Seket, which is a synonym of Beth-Shan. (Tscherikower, *Hellenistiche Stadt-Grundungen*, p. 71.)

[2] See *P.E.F. Quarterly*, 1927-1931.

tion of overseer of the granaries of Pharaoh and steward of the castle. A man of his name occurs in a papyrus of the epoch, and is addressed thus by a scribe with regard to the country around Baisan.

" Oh scribe, to whom nothing is unknown: [suppose] thou art sent on an expedition at the head of a victorious army. You do not know how to ration them. The army wants to start but there is no bread. Teach me about Beth-Shan and Tarquel. How is the Jordan crossed? Tell me about the crossing of the waters of Megiddo? "

The passage calls up a vivid picture of an officer in Egypt obtaining information from his predecessor in office about the distant country to which he expects to be sent, or on which he is to furnish a report for the Staff College of the time.

It is remarkable that the temples are not erected to Egyptian but to Canaanite deities; and the many finds concerned with worship indicate an early syncretism of Egyptian with local cults. In paganism there was always free-trade in gods and goddesses. Thus the largest and oldest of the temples, built by Thothmes, is a combination of a covered temple having a stepped altar, as was regular in Egypt, with a high-place in the open, such as the Canaanites used. The high-place generally contained sacred stone columns (Mazzevoth) for the god, and sacred trees or poles (Asheroth) for the goddess. Here a Mazzevah was found in the middle of the sanctuary; and by its side an Egyptian representation of a deity named Mekal " the Lord of Beth-Shaan," with a prayer that the god may grant life and prosperity for the Ka of the favourite of the god, the builder. Mekal is known later as a Phoenician deity, worshipped in Cyprus.

A collar-bone of a young bull with a dagger by its side was also found in this temple floor. In the same temple Mr. Rowe found a basalt panel bearing the figure of a

lion and a dog below, and a lion alone above. It is the
finest work of art from the Canaanite period. The lion
has been interpreted as Nergal, the lion-God of Assyria,
and the dog as the guardian of the sanctuary keeping off
the intruder. In the Book of Kings we read that the men
of Cuth made Nergal a god when they were planted by the
Assyrian conqueror in the Land of Israel (2 Ki., xvii 30).
Nergal is said also to represent the scorching heat of the
sun and the pestilence—(maybe, of malaria); and the
men of the garrison of Baisan dwelling below the level of
the sea may well have equated the spirit of evil with that
god as they were afflicted by the torrid heat. The temples
of Amenophis and Seti appear to have been dedicated to
Ashtoreth, the goddess of fertility. She is shown in
Egyptian Hieroglyphs as Ashtoreth of the Two Horns,
and also as the warrior goddess. It is another notable
indication of the juxtaposition of Egyptian and Syrian
civilization at the time, that in these temples were discovered amulets and rings bearing the name of the Egyptian
King, together with many Syro-Hittite cylinder seals.

One of the two temples of Ramases II is also dedicated
to Ashtoreth; but in the other the excavators unearthed a
cylinder seal bearing the name of the king, and facing him
the figure of the warrior god Resheph, which suggests that
the temple was erected in his honour. Resheph is identified
with Dagon the Philistine deity who was worshipped here
200 years later (1 Chr., x. 10). The cult objects, the
jewellery, the vases, and the furniture of burial, if it may
be so-called, in the cemetery manifest the same combination of Egyptian and Canaanite motives. And in the later
votive objects a third element appears of Aegean character, which is found in other remains of the Philistines.
At Baisan, as in the southern Tells, we find Egyptian and
Philistine religion and art mingling with each other. For
some centuries the two foreign influences must have competed; but finally the Philistines, who may be compared
with the Danes in England, took up their settlement in the

land and prevailed over the Egyptian military and official caste.

If we may carry the analogy of the settlement of England further, the Canaanites were as the original Britons, the Egyptians as the Roman Conquerors who held the land for some centuries, the Hebrews, who overran the country and possessed most of it, as the Anglo-Saxons, the Philistines, who coming in ships occupied the coast, as the Danes, and lastly, the Assyrians and Babylonians were as the Norman conquerors.

The Book of Judges records that the Tribe of Manasseh who settled in this part of Canaan failed to drive out the inhabitants of Baisan, Megiddo, and Dor, the other frontier fortress. Two hundred years after the date of the latest of the Egyptian monuments at Beisan, the Philistines were the lords of the town; and when they defeated King Saul at Mount Gilboa hard by, they placed his armour in the house of Ashteroth, and fastened his head to the wall of the temple of their deity Dagon.

By the side of the picture which the spade at Baisan has given to us of the domination in Canaan of the earlier Pharaohs of the eighteenth dynasty, we may put the picture of the decline of Egyptian power in the land under others of that dynasty. We gain a vivid idea of this set-back from the documentary records of the " Tel-el-Amarna letters," which were found during the latter part of the nineteenth century in the ruins of the royal Egyptian town, the capital of the religious reformer Akhen-Aton, who was originally called Amenhotep IV. The letters are in the form of over 300 clay tablets, in cuneiform Babylonian script, addressed to the King of Egypt or his scribes by the Egyptian officers and princes in Palestine and Syria. They are part of the Foreign Office correspondence, " the oldest body of international correspondence in the world," and were deposited " in the place of the records of the palace of the King." The Babylonian script is significant of the previous rule of Assyria in Palestine and of the establishment of Egyptian hegemony over the former Assyrian provinces.

Akhen-Aton was the puritan head of the eighteenth dynasty who reigned about 1350 B.C.E. and sought to institute a syncretistic universal religion—in vain. He reversed the imperial policy of his predecessors and resigned all idea of Eastern domination; and his reign marks the beginning of the Egyptian decline in Syria and Palestine.

The tablets have been divided by Sir Flinders Petrie into three classes or periods; the first, of the epoch of Amenhotep III (1370), when the Egyptian power and protectorate over the native chiefs along the Syrian coast was still maintained; the second of some years later, when the rulers of Northern Syria were threatened by the enemy from without and rebellion from within; and the third, of a few years later, when Southern Syria as well as Northern was falling a prey to internal rebellion as the Egyptian will to rule declined. It is in this third series that we find the letters from the King of Gezer to his royal suzerain, and the more famous letters from the Governor of Urusalim imploring for help to be sent. At the end of one epistle he thus addresses the scribe who will receive it:

"Bring aloud before my lord the King the words: 'the whole land of my lord the King is going to ruin, the Khabiri occupy the cities, even to Gazri.'"

Urusalim is almost indubitably Jerusalem of the Bible, and these events occurred before the Jebusites—who were probably a branch of the Hittite race—had become masters of the city. Many have thought that the Khabiri represent the Hebrews, although the date of these tablets is before that long ascribed to the Exodus, and the name Khabiri has no direct relation with the Hebrew name of the Hebrews, "Ivri." A distinguished French scholar of Jerusalem, Père Dhorme,[1] has argued that the name

[1] See *J.P.O.S.*, "Les Habiru et les Hebreux," vol. iv. p. 163.

Khabiri is connected with the Hebrew root " Haber," which means both companion and ally. The name would then be given naturally to a number of confederate peoples who leagued themselves against the might of Egypt. It would be generic rather than particular. According to this interpretation the Khabiri would be a band of Hittite and Canaanite peoples who threw off the yoke of the Pharaohs, and so prepared the way for the conquests of the children of Israel when, a little later, they entered the Land of Promise from the Wilderness.

While the majority of scholars till the latest years allotted the Exodus of the children of Israel from Egypt to the thirteenth or twelfth century B.C., the latest digging in Palestine is inducing an acceptance of an earlier date which accords better with the Bible chronology. Professor Garstang's excavations at Jericho, Ai, and Hazor, a Canaanite fortress mentioned in the Book of Joshua, have gone far to establish the accuracy of the figure in the Book of Kings of 480 years between the Exodus and the foundation of the Temple by King Solomon (1 Ki., vi. 1). The date of King Solomon lies between 1000 and 960 B.C.E.; and on that reckoning the Exodus would have taken place about 1450, and the destruction of Jericho and the other Canaanite fortress about 1400. That tallies with the evidence of the excavator. Professor Garstang discovered on the outskirts of Old Jericho a cemetery of the late Bronze Age, full of objects, jars and pots, jewellery and scarabs, which give a certain date because they mention the Egyptian Pharaohs by name. The latest burial was of the end of the Bronze Age about 1400 B.C. He then went on to explore parts of the fortress Tell itself, and disclosed chambers which were filled with pots and jars of the same design and character as those of the tombs. There were, too, clear marks of sudden destruction by fire, and also of earthquake which had twisted the courses of brick in the two chambers. The evidence of the tombs and the chambers together, the charred remains of pots and grain, the

twisted courses of wall and rampart—have brought home
the certainty of the identification. Jericho was overthrown
by the children of Israel as the Book of Joshua tells us;
" when they burnt the city with fire and all that was
therein " (Josh., vi. 24); and that event is placed by
Professor Garstang at about 1400 B.C. A later Jericho of
the early Iron Age was rebuilt, as the Book of Kings tells
us, in the time of King Omri of Israel; and was superimposed on the ruins of the Canaanite city. A cobbled
street of that city leading from the spring to the citadel
has been unearthed. But the Egyptian hand in all the
remains is to be found only in the city of the Bronze Age.
If Professor Garstang's deductions are correct, the children
of Israel would have been entering Canaan at the period
of the Tel-el-Amarna letters; and the case is strengthened
for identifying them with the Habiri, who threatened the
Egyptian underlings.

The Egyptian hold over the country appears to have
been lost for several generations. There was later a re-
covery, or rather a series of recoveries, after this evacuation.
Seti, Merenptah (or Amenophis), Ramases II and
Ramases III, as we know from the excavations at Baisan
and from the walls of their temples at Karnak and Thebes,
drove out the Asiatic hordes and reasserted Egyptian
supremacy. Seti indeed extended his conquests as far as
Aleppo to the heart of the Hittite power. And it was not
till the end of the reign of Merenptah IV (1200 B.C.) that
Egypt weakened again.

The Egyptian overlordship was not destroyed for some
centuries after the children of Israel captured the hill
country of the Canaanites; and it survived in some vary-
ing degree through the period of Joshua and the Judges
till the election of a King of Israel. But the measure of
Egyptian control varied according to the strength or weakness of the central power in Egypt. The corresponding
Egyptian epoch is between the reign of Ramases II and
the end of the nineteenth dynasty. The coast-land was not

M

governed as a province or incorporated in the kingdom, but divided up among a number of tributary princes. To take a modern analogy, Canaan was a buffer state, such as Afghanistan in the last century was between England and Russia.

An ingenious theory has been propounded by Professor Garstang and Phythian-Adams that the oppression of the Tribes of Israel by one or other of the Canaanite peoples occurred in those periods when the control of Egypt was relaxed. Egypt was " the hornet " referred to in Joshua (xxiv. 12) which God sent before Israel to drive out the peoples of Canaan; and the periods when " the land had rest " correspond with the epoch of firm Egyptian control. The judges rose to protect Israel when the Egyptian suzerain could not preserve order. This at least seems certain, that the menace of the Philistines occurred between the twelfth and tenth centuries, as the sovereignty of the Pharaohs was more limited to the land of the Nile.[1]

According to this theory, the oppression by the Moabites which is recorded in chapter iii. of the Book of Judges occurred before Seti I had established his sway in Egypt, and ended with his invasion of Palestine and Syria which, as we have seen, is commemorated in one of the Baisan temples. The eighty years of " rest " which followed the subjugation of Moab (Jud., iii. 30) cover the reign of Seti and of his strong successor, Ramases II (1292-1225). This conjecture of dates is supported by a remarkable identification of the Biblical Shamgar Ben Anath, who laid low the Philistines (*ib.*, iii. 31), with the Syrian Ben Anath, a sea-captain who, as we know from documents, was in the service of Ramases. The next attack came from the north during the anarchy at the end of Merenptah's reign, when a Syrian usurped the throne of Egypt. This was the time when the Syrian Sisera oppressed Israel, and Deborah rescued her people. The period of " rest " of forty years (Jud., v. 31) which followed synchronises with the strong

---

[1] See Garstang, *Joshua and Judges*, Constable, 1931.

rule in Egypt of Setnekht (1200-1198), the founder of the Twentieth Dynasty, and his son Ramases III, whose statue also was found at Baisan. The successors of this Pharaoh were weaklings, and their statues are not found in any of the Palestine fortresses. And there is a period of oppression by Midian (Jud., vi.) from which the people of Israel were saved by the might of Gideon. The Ammonite oppression which produced the saviour Jephthah (*ib.*, ix. and x.), and the short rest of six years which followed, are associated with the final breakdown of Egyptian authority in Palestine, when the country was overrun by the Assyrian Tiglath Pileser I (1133-1107). By this time the Philistine invaders were established as the paramount power on the coastal plain; and so it is the Philistines who are the oppressors of Israel in the last section of the Book of Judges which records the exploits of Samson.

The position of Israel in Canaan was indeed changed during the heyday of the early Jewish Kingdom. David and Solomon built up a powerful independent state, ruling over peoples who had long recognized foreign overlords, the Syrians of Damascus, the peoples of Ammon and Edom, and the Phoenicians of Tyre and Sidon. The kings of Israel took an attitude of equality with the lords of Egypt. Solomon, in particular, appears to have maintained close relations with Egypt, and to have dealt in horses and chariots with his richer neighbours (1 Ki., x. 28). The independence of Judaea, however, did not remain undisturbed for long. When the kingdom was split into two on the death of Solomon, Jeroboam the usurper invited Shishak the Libyan Pharaoh to attack his rival, and Jerusalem suffered one of her many sieges and sackings. This Pharaoh, as we have seen, left his mark on many places in the country, and his triumph is recorded on the wall of a temple of Karnak which shows a gigantic figure of the God Amon leading captive the hundred cities of Judaea.

The military strength of Egypt, however, was on the

wane: and King Asa of Judah some fifty years later went
out to battle against it. In fair fight " the Ethiopians and
the Lubim, a huge host with many chariots and horses,
fled before Judah and were destroyed before Jehovah "
(2 Chr., xiv. 13). It has indeed been suggested that the
Jewish King worsted not the Army of Egypt itself, but
the Nubian garrison of Sinai and the Negeb, which was
under Egyptian suzerainty.[1] After this victory the overlordship of Egypt over Judah and Israel was destroyed;
and the children of Israel had to defend themselves
against the menacing forces of Assyria from the north which
grew strong as the other Empire grew weak. Israel in vain
called on Egypt to help her against Shalmaneser and succumbed. Judaea was saved for a time by the miracle of
the destruction of Sennacherib's host outside the walls of
Jerusalem. Her rulers indeed still looked in times of peril
to the great power of the West. But Rabshekeh, the emis-
sary of Sennacherib, warned the Jewish people against
trusting the bruised reed, " on which if a man lean it will
go into his hand and pierce it." For another century
Egypt eschewed Northern adventure; and when she resumed it, Judah was no longer subservient to her. The
battle of Megiddo (c. 600 B.C.) between Josiah King of
Judah and Neco King of Egypt at which Josiah met his
death, was fought, perhaps, by him as the vassal-ally of
Assyria in a vain attempt to check the Egyptian invasion
of the Northern territory of the overlord. The waters of
the Euphrates passed through Judah, overflowing and
going over, reaching even to the neck (Is., viii. 8). The
pendulum of power was swinging steadily to the North and
East; and though Assyria fell, Babylon immediately took
her place and was still more ruthless. As it is written in the
Book of Kings:

" The King of Egypt came not any more out of his
land, for the King of Babylon had taken from the River

---

[1] See Albright, *J.P.O.S.*, iv. p. 147.

of Egypt to the river Euphrates all that pertained to the king of Egypt."

The prophet Jeremiah preached the truth in and out of season to his people before the fatal attempt of King Zedekiah to throw off the Babylonian suzerainty. He saw, what the Court party failed to see, that Egypt could no longer help; and after the doom fell he had to go down to the land of Egypt which was henceforth to be a refuge for Jew and Judaism when the northern oppressors afflicted Palestine.

Egypt did not enter Palestine again as conqueror till after the period of Empires of Babylon and Persia was over. By that time the Jewish people had been fortified in their religion and national individuality by the Captivity and the Synagogue, and had realized with intense conviction the superiority of their universal creed and moral law over the licentiousness, the cruelty, and the tyranny of the pagan empires. When Egyptian culture, now arrayed in the seductive Hellenistic garb, again sought to penetrate Palestine, the Jews in their moral armour were proof against any allurements. And the Macedonian sovereigns of Egypt, the Ptolemies, had the wisdom to realize and respect their religious strength and their national solidarity.

The moral position of the two peoples was now reversed from what it had been at the time of the Exodus and of Bible history. Whereas then Egypt was the proud and all-powerful leader of thought and religion, and the Jews were serfs or underlings, now the Jews, though a subject people, were conscious of a religious mission to the world and were recognized everywhere as having a doctrine and a message. They were respected by the Greek conquerors of the East both as warriors and as the possessors of a special philosophy and ethics; they were given a definite place in the cosmopolitan cities which the conquerors founded to unify East and West. They were encouraged to settle in the land of Egypt, even as far as Assuan, and when a less wise Hellenistic power coming from the North, the inheritors of the Assyrian Empire, oppressed them in their national home, to remove and carry on in Egypt their traditional Temple worship. The Pharaoh of the second century B.C., unlike his predecessor of 1,000 years, was willing to let the children of Israel go out and worship their god as they listed; and in the land of Goshen, some twenty miles from Cairo, you may still see at the "Tell of the Jews," the foundations of the sanctuary which the exiled High Priest, Onias, built to be a religious centre of Israel in dispersion while the Temple at Jerusalem was defiled. At the beginning of the Common Era Philo records that a million Jews were living in Egypt, and at Alexandria they were an element in the population and civilization of the capital of the East comparable with their position in our day in the population and life of New York. It is significant that the Roman Emperor Vespasian dismantled the Temple of Onias and prohibited Jewish worship in it at the same time as Titus destroyed the Temple of Jerusalem. So closely were the Jewish civilizations of Palestine and Egypt bound up while the Jewish nation was independent.

Through the centuries the Jews remained an important part of the population of Alexandria; and at the time of the Arab conquest in the seventh century they still numbered 40,000. The treaty of peace by which the Arabs were confirmed in the possession of Egypt stipulated their right to remain in the city. But the settlement of the Jews in Egypt is another story.

IX

AKABA, PETRA, AND THE OTHER-SIDE OF JORDAN

Akaba, " the very name is like a bell " to call to romance, to the fleets of King Solomon and of the Crusader Renaud de Chatillon, and to the more recent deeds of Lawrence of Arabia. And the scene is worthy of its romantic association. Our first sight of the Gulf of the Red Sea which bears that name was from the rocky crags of Sinai, whence we overlooked the mystic Sea of deepest blue framed between its walls of pristine, bare brown mountains stretching away as far as eye can see, and, beyond, to the East was the inaccessible " island of the Arabs." We had driven from Palestine across Sinai and the Wilderness of Zin where the children of Israel spent forty years till the generation that came out of Egypt had passed away. We had gazed wonderingly at the little trickle of water flowing from Ain Kades, the Kadesh of the wanderings, which now gives drink and pasturage to a few goats. Thence we drove across the northern plateau of the peninsula, halted at the Egyptian frontier station of Kuntilla, and sped over one of the highways of commerce and history, the pilgrimage road from Egypt, along which for 1,200 years bands of the faithful bearing the annual gift of the Holy Carpet passed to the Holy Cities, and the merchandise of the East passed to the countries of the Mediterranean.

That road is marked to-day not by any army of pilgrims, but by telegraph posts which suddenly end on the top of the pass, the Nagab of Akaba. Here Egypt ends, and Palestine, which we had left the day before, again begins. The pass, which descends some 2,500 feet in three miles, through a wonderful gorge of many-coloured rocks to the shore of the Gulf, is in Palestine; and a strip of the Gulf at its mouth gives Palestine its outlet to the Red Sea. It is one of the minor ironies of the modern history of the Middle East that in 1904 England and Turkey nearly came to war over an attempt of the Sultan Abdul Hamid to advance the Turkish frontier further into Sinai, and to cut off Egypt's access to the Gulf. The Turks seized an Egyptian fort and an oasis a few miles south of the pass; and it required the firmness of Lord Cromer and a demonstration of the British fleet to make them retire and restore the eastern shore of the Peninsula to the Khedive. It is recorded by Lord Cromer in his *Modern Egypt*,[1] that one of the motives of the Turkish usurpation was a scheme mooted, but never accomplished, to settle Russian Jews in and around the village of Akaba. That made the Sultan apprehensive that the Jewish people would make that place the basis of operations for recovering the Jewish State. Had the British Proconsul not persisted, half the Sinai Peninsula might now be within the British mandated sphere.

There was a time when the pass and the village of Akaba itself were included in the Egyptian province of the Sultan. The road through the defile, which now tumbles over rocks and boulders, shows here and there the masonry of the highway which Ibrahim Pasha built in 1830 to carry his guns in the campaign against the Wahabis, the modern Puritans of Arabia and the ancestors of the subjects of King Ibn Saud. The approach at the end of the defile spanning the Wadi bears witness to the thoroughness of his work. An inscription 500 years older records the cutting of " the blessed road " by " our master, the Sultan el Malik el Ashraf Khunsuh el Ghuri."

From the bottom of the pass to the village of Akaba is a run of half an hour; and in the middle of the way, crossing the vast sandy Wadi of the Araba which stretches from the Dead Sea to the Gulf, we passed from Palestine to Trans-

---

[1] Vol. ii. p. 287.

jordania. There is no frontier barrier; but in the village the red, black, green and white flag of the Emirate of Transjordan flies from the Serai—the Government office—which stands gleaming white on the seashore.

Continuing our way along the shell-strewn seashore for another three miles, we were in the Kingdom of the Hejaz, and within the jurisdiction of King Ibn Saud. Again there is no visible frontier between the States, though " Hejaz " means simply barrier, and the land is barred to the infidel. The frontier is marked only by a ruined Turkish block-house perched high on the cliff. We should not have known that we had entered another kingdom had not the Kaimmakam (governor) of Akaba sent out two police mounted on camels to bring us back, lest we be molested for trespass into the sacred land. Within one hour we had driven along the shore of the Gulf through four territories, Egypt, Palestine, Transjordan, and Arabia; and we were thankful that the Orient does not yet rival Central Europe in its consecration of Customs Houses.

Akaba itself seemed, at first sight, an ordinary mud-village set by the sea and fringed by palm groves. To-day it has some six or seven hundred inhabitants. Before the war, and indeed until recently, the population was larger, but commerce has now fixed its centre at Maan, some seventy miles to the north-east, where the Hejaz Railway has its temporary terminus. But Akaba, though lowly in its present state, has its insignia of history, so that the traveller feels that he is surveying one of the scenes in which human destiny has been forged. Here is the head of the Yamsuph, the Red Sea, which the children of Israel crossed when they went out of Egypt. Here, or hereabouts, was Ezion Geber—meaning Spine of the Giant, and so-called perhaps from the rocky crags that come down almost to the water's edge—from which King Solomon and King Jehoshaphat sent forth their ships down the Red Sea to Ophir, the land of the Queen of Sheba, and to Tarshish to fetch gold (1 Ki., ix). Here, or hereabouts, was the Elath of the Bible, called from the terebinths (Hebrew, Elah) which still flourish on these shores. Indeed the Arab name Akaba, which means simply " descent " is an abbreviated form of Akabat Elath—" the Descent of Elath." Here was the Roman Aila, in their province of Arabia Petrea, where the Tenth Legion was stationed to impose peace on the tribes of the desert. Bits of Roman columns are still strewn on the plain to the north of the village. Here, in the days of the Byzantine Empire and the Middle Ages, a great castle was built on the trade route which passed from Europe to the East; and the traveller may yet see fragments of Byzantine sculpture in some of the rude houses of the village.

Here the Jews maintained their hold and plied their commerce vigorously until the days of Mohamed. The Prophet of Islam made a covenant with the Governor, one Jocanan ben Reuben, who was almost certainly a Jew, for the payment of tribute. And an Arab legend that occurs twice in the Koran tells that the Jews of the place were turned into apes as a punishment for fishing on the Sabbath Day. Here the Crusaders had one of their amazing footholds, where European feudalism entrenched itself against the Saracen. You gaze at the towers of the fortress which was disputed between the Cross and the Crescent. Here Renaud de Chatillon, a great pirate baron, sailing ships across the Dead Sea and then carrying them across the waste of the Arabah, fitted out a fleet which sailed the gulf and brought terror to the coasts of Araby. From the shore you see the little Island of Graye, or, as the Arabs call it, Pharaoh's Island, which according to an historian of the sixth century, was inhabited to his day by an independent community of Jews and later was an invincible fortress of the Frankish barons.[1] And here, in more

---

[1] It is interesting that another island on the Red Sea was said by an Arab geographer, Idrissi of the twelfth century, to be inhabited by Samaritan Jews: " They descend from the Jews who worshipped the golden calf in the days of Moses." (Montgomery, *The Samaritans*, p. 161.)

modern times, Lawrence drove the Turks in rout, and
established a base from which in two years of devastating
guerilla warfare he broke once for all the connection of the
Ottoman Empire and Arabia. Of his army some trace still
remains in the iron bands of the bales of forage for the
camels which are scattered along the beach to the south
of the village. And the jetty, built for fun by the men
of H.M.S. Euryalus, though half ruined, may still be
seen.

A new jetty has taken its place as a shelter for the few
fishing vessels which go out when it is calm to catch the
flying-fish and the tunny that swarm in the landlocked
waters. It was built by the late King Hussein of the
Hejaz during the days when he held his final Court at
Akaba, while his son Ali tried to defend Jedda against the
Wahabi invader. There are other survivals of the royal
residence in Akaba. The Serai itself, in which the Transjordan Government has its offices, was the palace, and a
fountain opposite bears an inscription recording the piety
of the King. And the portal of the Saracen-Crusader
castle is strangely decorated with a coat-of-arms indicating
a fortress set on a field of swords, guns, and flags, which
likewise records the generosity of His Hashamite Majesty.
That castle, which bears also the record of the Turkish
Sultan Selim who rebuilt it in the sixteenth century is
now the barracks of the Arab Legion who represent
the forces of law and order of the Transjordan Government.

We had thought to find Akaba isolated from material
civilization and modernity. But as we sat on the jetty
sipping coffee with the Kaimmakam and watching the
flying-fish at play, we were not a little surprised to have a
message from an officer in the Arab Legion asking if we
would like to hear a concert at Paris. Returning to the
Serai we found that there was, indeed, a wireless receiver of
which the instrument could be manipulated to connect us
with Moscow or Paris, or, still more frequently, atmo-

spherics, which the young operator apparently understood to be another, and that the most popular, capital.

One other touch of modernity was disclosed that evening when our host, the Kaimmakam, told us that his two sons and his daughter were students at the American University of Beirut, and the daughter was training for a medical degree. The cause of equal rights for women is making headway even in the " Isle of Arabia."

From Akaba we made our way to Petra. The road lies through the stark and arid country to which Moses fled from Egypt when he had killed the oppressor of his brethren. Here he saw the wonder of the Burning Bush, and here he found his wife. The road climbs over 3,000 feet; and from a spot at the head of the pass you may view the whole land of Midian, sandstone and limestone hills rising in weird and fantastic array and no sign of habitation, not even the black-haired tents of Bedu. The country looks as if it were just created and were cut off from common use.

We passed Maan, which is still, as it has been for 4,000 years, a fenced city, the strong place and the market-town of this inhospitable land. The Turks had a garrison here; and to-day it is occupied by a detachment of the Transjordan Frontier force, camelmen and cavalry. It has, too, a quarantine station where the returning pilgrims, the Hajis, are detained when they return from the Holy Cities. It rises with its grey fortress walls from the desert of black flint, the last outpost of civilization before the desert which stretches to the south through Arabia, and the desert which stretches to the east, to Bagdad. Doughty records that strangers count the inhabitants of Jewish blood and point to the name Harun (Aaron) which is common among them.

Petra itself, which the Arabs call Wadi Moussa, the River of Moses, is wonderfully set in an amphitheatre of red sandhills. Its " High-Place " towers 700 feet above the ruined city, and 3,700 feet above the sea-level. A learned school of our day would place here the revelation of the Torah,[1] and like the traditional Mountain of Moses, the scene is fitting for a great drama. Two lines from an Oxford prize-poem are quoted to weariness about Petra:

> Match me such marvel save in Eastern clime:
> A rose-red city half as old as time.

The less-known lines that precede that couplet are more descriptive of the scene:

> It seems no work of man's creative hand,
> By labour wrought or wavering fancy planned;
> But from the rock, as if by magic, grown
> Eternal, silent, beautiful, alone.

The allurement of the place lies in part in its isolation. You gaze at the varied display of a Hellenistic city, theatres, forums, temples, and, above all, ornate tombs cut mysteriously in the heart of the rocky mountains; and you see scarce an inhabitant save a few rude shepherds who use the tombs as steadings for their sheep. The great Doughty had no love for its florid monuments. " Strange and horrible as a pit, in the inhuman deadness of Nature, is this site of the Nabateans' metropolis. The eye recoils from the mountainous close of iron cliffs in which the ghastly waste monuments of a sumptuous barbaric art are from the first glance an eyesore." But perchance he visited the spot on some inauspicious day. Others have regarded the Sik, the narrow gorge between the cliffs of red granite which was the entrance to the city, as one of the marvels of the world in majesty and dramatic setting.

The High-place preserves with extraordinary reality of vividness the traces of the old cults; the sunken court, the two obelisks cut out of the solid rock, perhaps the Mazzevat

---

[1] See ch. x. p. 204.

or pillars which were the object of early Semitic worship, the altar for sacrifice, and another altar on which it is conjectured that the burnt offering was laid. All these are open on the mountain top. Below them and around the primitive sanctuary rise the columns, porticoes and peristyles of the temples of Zeus and Heracles, cut also out of the red rock in a kind of Baroque-Hellenistic architecture. The kings of the Nabatean Arabs, like the princes of Edom from whom Herod was sprung, were Hellenizers in those centuries when all the civilized world, save the Jews, syncretized their religion. Looking on the remains of this borrowed civilization, one is the more impressed with the moral strength of the Jewish nation at that period when, alone of the Oriental peoples, they resisted the blandishments of the Hellenes and the overwhelming might of Rome.

Petra, though not on the high-road between Egypt and the East, lay at the meeting-place of two great caravan routes, one leading from Palestine and Syria to southern Arabia, whence merchants brought the spices and frankincense, the gold and precious stones, the apes and the peacocks which were the luxuries of the ancient world: the other leading from Egypt and Africa across the desert to Mesopotamia and Persia and the further East.

It was then a principal emporium of trade, where caravans met and exchanged their goods. It had the supreme wealth of abundance of pure water from gushing springs, and the supreme defence of inaccessibility. On three sides it was impregnable; only on the north, where it can be approached from the Araba, was it exposed to attack; and it required a determined and hardy foe to advance from that barren valley of desolation, which stretches from the southern end of the Dead Sea to the Gulf of Akaba. Hence Petra remained a secure place of commerce from the time of Alexander's conquest of the East to the time of the Arab destruction of the Byzantine Empire, nearly a thousand years. It lost some of its com-

mercial importance when the main highway from west to
east moved northwards in the second century, and remained there through the Middle Ages.

If Petra, which is the Greek for rock, is correctly identified with the Hebrew Selah—which is its equivalent—it
was the capital of Edom. The town was captured by the
Jewish king Amaziah (2 Ki., xiv. 7); and its neighbour,
Maan, was captured by his son King Uzziah (2 Chr., xxvi.
7). In a later epoch, from the third century B.C.E., it was
ruled by its Nabatean dynasty, till the Emperor Trajan, at
the beginning of the second century C.E., subdued it and
made it the centre of a Roman province. In the days of the
Apostle Paul its king Aretas IV ruled as far as Damascus.

The Nabateans were a mystery people to the Roman
historians and writers of those times. Diodorus describes
their waterless country and the Dead Sea which was in
their borders, and declares that they cannot be subdued
and will maintain their freedom for ever. And Strabo, the
geographer who wrote in the latter part of the first century
B.C.E., describes their happy political state of which he had
heard from his friend, a Stoic philosopher and a native of
Petra:

" It is exceedingly well-governed. Many Romans and
other foreigners live there; and they are occasionally
engaged in lawsuits. But none of the natives litigate
with each other, and in every way they keep the peace." [1]

In the days of the struggle between Cross and Crescent
Petra ceased to be a place of trade and was a place of arms.
The Crusaders, after the establishment of the Latin Kingdom of Jerusalem, perched themselves on an inaccessible
pinnacle of the mountain, which the Arabs to-day call the
Citadel (El-Habis), and they stood their ground for 200
years. Their principal stronghold in these parts, indeed,
was some fifteen miles to the East, at the castle of Mons

[1] Bk. XVI. ch. ii. p. 26.

Regalis or Montreal, which has now resumed its Arab name Shobek. The splendour and the strength of the medieval château may still be seen; and the Arab village, celebrated in the exploits of Lawrence, nestles securely within its ancient walls.

When the Latins were driven out of Oultre-Jourdan by Saladin in the twelfth century, Petra was deserted and almost passed out of knowledge. The Mameluke Baibars visited its ruins in the thirteenth century and recorded the marvels which he saw. Then came silence for 600 years, till the early days of the nineteenth century, when the intrepid Anglo-Swiss traveller, Burckhardt, came, saw, and described. Since then it has been a standing theme for the picturesque travel writer. It was a place difficult to penetrate till the British Occupation of Palestine and Transjordan; for the Arabs around, "perilous fellows" as Doughty calls them, were suspicious of any foreign visitor. In recent years this "sarcophagus of ancient civilization" has been more thoroughly surveyed and excavated, and has gradually given up its secrets and treasures.

Our route from Petra to Palestine followed the route of the children of Israel as they approached the Land of Promise from the Wilderness of Edom, through the lands of Moab and Ammon. It is known to-day as the Darb el Haj, the way of the Pilgrimage. For along its course the Moslem pilgrims from Turkey and Syria for centuries have wound their slow caravans to Mecca and Medina. The road runs through, or on the edge of, desolation. For all the country "on the other side of Jordan" is on the rim of the Syrian desert, and its civilization has been and will be conditioned by the desert. It is not an ordinary road but a series of tracks "beaten hollow by the camel's tread," and stretching half a mile or so in width. Once a year the army of the Faithful used to set out from Damascus for the Haj, attended by a motley array of shopkeepers, thieves, vagabonds and soldiers, and led by an

Emir of the pilgrimage who wielded supreme authority.
And along it a smaller army, which had survived the perils
of the way and of their companions, returned to Syria and
beyond. Here and there you pass a Roman milestone and
the traces of the Roman rampart, the " *limes* " which, like
Hadrian's wall in Northumbria, protected and marked off
the ordered and civilized land under the Pax Romana from
the uncharted region of the barbarians. Of this land the
famous historian of Rome, Mommsen, has well said:

> " There is hardly any region in the world in which so
> much as here civilization has not grown up spontane-
> ously, but could only be called into existence by the
> ascendancy of conquest from without." [1]

The road is marked at distances of twenty miles by a castle
guarding the " Birket " or vast cistern of water, to which
the pilgrim army came for its halts and for the burial of
those who had died on the last stage.

At the beginning of the twentieth century the sandy road
was accompanied, and almost replaced, by an iron road,
the Hedjaz railway. That enterprise was built by the
Turkish Sultan Abdul-Hamid from the freewill offerings
of the Faithful, as a means of linking the Holy Cities of
Arabia with the rest of the Ottoman Empire. It is a signal
example in modern history of the vanity of human plans.
It was barely completed from Damascus as far as Medina
—it has never been extended to Mecca—when the Great
War broke out. And during the war it proved to be the
Achilles' Heel of the Ottoman position in the Near East;
for it offered a most inviting means of cutting communications which had otherwise been invulnerable. The railway followed with scarce any diversion the line of the
Darb el Haj; and its station-buildings with their zinc
tanks and their common huts arose by the side of the
castellated forts and the monumental walls of the birkets.

Roman Provinces, Bk. II. ch. x.

N

It was designed and planned by Meissner Pasha and German engineers, and built by Turkish soldiers; but from the station of Medain Saleh southwards, which is the holy land of the Hejaz, none but a Moslem was allowed to pass, whether to plan or to build or to visit—unless he were a fearless prince of adventure like Doughty.

In the Great War what was designed as a link became a void. Lawrence and his merry tribesmen in 1916 established their base at Akaba, derailed trains, almost for sport, and blew up bridges and viaducts; and the airmen above bombed stations and depots, so that there was " no wholeness " anywhere on the line south of Jordan. By the end of the war the railway, indeed, had ceased to be such. Every station between Damascus and Maan was derelict, and nearly every bridge and viaduct was broken down; beyond Maan to the south the railway lines were torn up from the embankment. Even where the railway runs again, everything recalls destruction. At each station ruined buildings, broken tanks, roofless guard-houses, deserted gun-carriages, shattered wagons; and around it vast shell-holes and half-filled trenches. There is little likelihood that the line will serve again its original purpose; for the Haj to-day goes principally by sea to Jedda, and thence by motor-car, quickly and fairly securely, to Mecca. But what was built for religion and strategy may survive for the uses of commerce. Transjordan is a country of returning prosperity and boundless promise; and the railway is the link between its corn-land and the Mediterranean at Haifa; and it may, indeed, become a link between the Mediterranean and the Red Sea if some time a branch is laid to Akaba. A train runs once a week from Amman to Maan; but goes no further on the line. Some years back the line was restored by the ex-king Hussein as far as Medina; but the trains which passed beyond Transjordan territory had a habit of not returning, and the rolling-stock could not stand that one-way traffic.

The old road has been restored in our day when rushing

motor-cars take the place of the slow " shuffle-footed " caravans. The country is for the most part deserted and given over to the wandering Bedu tribes. Going north, through the land that was Moab, no town or large village is in sight. But the old capital of Moab where Balak must have ruled, Kir Moab (which in the Middle Ages was Characmoaba and is now called Kerak), lies some twenty miles to the west. It is dominated by a noble fortress of the Middle Ages, towering on a high peak over 4,000 feet sheer above the Dead Sea, and commanding the country for miles around. The Crusaders, of course, marked the site for one of their strongholds in the land " Outre Mer," to guard the Marches; and King Fulco of Jerusalem in 1181 built the castle which is still amazingly strong. The Franks identified Kerak with Petra of the Bible; and the Orthodox Bishop, titularly of Petra, has his seat here.

Till the middle of the last century the Arabs of Moab maintained a virtual independence of the Turkish rulers. But then the Sultan Abdul-Hamid in his centralizing policy sent troops to subdue them; and the guide shows the place where the rebels were hurled from the rock. The Jews have hardly begun to penetrate into this region; but the road from Kerak to the Dead Sea was built some years ago by Jewish engineers, and the principal Khan for travellers is conducted by a Jew.

Proceeding again from the land of Moab, you enter what was the land of the Amorites. Hesbon, Madaba, and Amman itself preserve the Bible names. Hesbon, the city of Sihon, has the imposing ruins of an Israelite fortress; Madaba, which was for centuries a mound of debris, is again a Christian centre, and famous through the world for its sixth-century Mosaic Map of the Holy Land and the surrounding countries, that is portrayed on the floor of its principal Church.

Betwixt Madaba and Amman, in a deep and romantic valley called the Wady es Sir, we visited the ruins of a fortress which dates from that obscure period of Jewish

history between the times of Nehemiah and the Maccabees. Here was the stronghold of the adventurous priest
Hyrcanus, a member of the powerful house of the Tobiads
who contended with the high-priestly family of Onias in
the third and second centuries B.C.E. Josephus tells the
story how Hyrcanus quarrelled with his brethren, and
being worsted retired to Tyrus beyond Jordan. Hence he
made war against the Arabs, and erected a fortress surrounded by a lake, and having on its walls " representations of animals of a prodigious magnitude." [1] He ruled
for seven years as a border chieftain (*c.* 180 B.C.E.); but
when Antiochus Epiphanes came to the Syrian throne, he
foresaw his downfall, and fell by his own hand.

While the other members of his family were loyal supporters of the Seleucids who were then the sovereigns of
Palestine, he intrigued on behalf of the Ptolemies who set
covetous eyes on the land which bordered on the Egyptian
Empire, and had for a century been included in their
dominions. Palestine was in those days, much as Belgium
in the seventeenth and eighteenth centuries, a battle-
ground and an object of contention between the two
powerful States to the North and South that were carved
out of Alexander the Great's Empire and were both
dominated by Hellenistic civilization.

Remarkable new light has been thrown in recent years
on the conditions of Palestine and on the family of Hyrcanus
by the publication of a store of Egyptian papyrus discovered
in the Fayum (in Egypt). They are the papers of a finan-
cial official of the Ptolemies named Zeno; and they include documents about the Tobiadae. Zeno, it appears,
had served in Transjordan in the middle of the third
century when it was under the rule of the Ptolemies; and
one contract records the sale to him of a slave woman by
a colonist who was on the staff of Tobias. In another, a
letter to Ptolemy, Tobias states that he is sending his Lord
and Master two horses, six hunting dogs and two mules.

---

[1] Jos., *Ant.*, Bk. XII. chs. iv and v.

We gather that Tobias was the governor of the Trans-jordan territory of which the capital, formerly called Rabat-Ammon, had changed its name in honour of the Ptolemies to Philadelphia. As the Palestine scholar, Père Vincent, has pointed out, it is likely that the Jewish governor had a family retreat in this castle near the capital, and that Josephus was embroidering the story, as was his habit, when he made Hyrcanus the builder of the fort-ress.[1]

The ruins show an earlier stage of the Greek architec-tural and artistic influence which characterizes the ruins of the Greek city-states in Transjordan. Corinthian capitals adorn the northern gate, and the walls within are decorated by a frieze with triglyphs.[2] They are known by the Arabs under the name of " Arak el Emir," the Prince's Cliff, and correspond closely with the description of Josephus. Then, as in the centuries nearer to our own day, the country beyond Jordan was an Alsatia of the adven-turers. It knew no firm rule of the Central power till the later Maccabean kings, and after them the Romans, established their sway, and held it down by a chain of fortresses.

Another deeply impressive ruin in this region is the Castle of Meshetta, which lies derelict on the outskirts of the desert—a few miles east of the Haj road and east of the station of Ziza, which was formerly a stage on that road and is now the site of an aerodrome on the route to India. Here, until about twenty years ago, stood a beauti-fully decorated Persian palace which is ascribed to Chosroes II, the monarch who, at the beginning of the seventh century, overran the Holy Land. Most of the lovely façade was carried off bodily by a German scientific expedition to grace the Museum of Antiquities in Berlin; and it is to-day one of the glories of that museum. The skeleton of the building was left on its site, and just enough

[1] See *Revue Biblique*, 1920, p. 161 *ff.*
[2] See Sir G. A. Smith, *Jerusalem*, ii. p. 425.

of ornamentation in a few corners and scattered ruins to give an idea of the glory that is gone.

Amman, which, as Rabbat-Ammon, was the principal town of the Amorites in the days of Moses and Joshua, is again a capital, the chief city of the Emirate of Transjordan. The city lies in a cleft made by the Jabbok river in the stark plateau. Its relics of the past are partly Hellenistic and partly Arabic. From the day when it was Philadelphia—named after Ptolemy Philadelphus, and one of the famous league of the Decapolis—it preserves a theatre for 7,000 spectators. The tiers of seats rise commandingly above the stream that runs through the main street, and a Roman bridge with one span rides the river. From the seventh century it retains the ruins of a Sassanian or Persian citadel on a hill above the present town. Till after the Great War Amman was a village, settled principally by Circassian Moslems, refugees from Russian Turkestan, whom the Turks after the Russo-Turkish War of 1877 planted there and in several places by the line of the Darb el Haj to stem the incursions of the desert tribes. It is interesting, however, to note that it appears with Jerusalem, Aleppo, and Tripoli among the places in which a British Consul was to exercise jurisdiction in the sixteenth century. There is record of a Jewish congregation five centuries earlier: and one Aaron Al Ammani, of the town, is praised by Jehuda Hallevi. Its population has grown during the last ten years from 5,000 to 15,000! and it is a larger place than it has been since the Hellenistic epoch. It has assumed the stature of a capital, and boasts a royal palace crowning with its rather incongruous Swiss architecture the hill of the citadel, a British residence which looks like a castle, government buildings, a museum, several new mosques, an English and an Italian hospital, boys' and girls' schools: and at a distance of a mile from the town a railway junction, the headquarters camp of the Transjordan police force, and the camp of the Royal Air Force.

The most imposing Graeco-Roman ruins in Trans-jordan, indeed, in the whole of Syria and Palestine, save for Baalbek, are to be found not at Amman but at Jerash, which was another of the ten cities of the Decapolis. It lies some thirty miles to the south-west of Amman and has been surely identified with Gerasa. Unknown in the Bible and mentioned first in the books of the Maccabees as a place taken by Alexander Jannaeus, it was for some 700 years the capital of Gilead and a centre of Greek and Byzantine civilization. When Arabia Petraea was a Roman province it was a garrison town. It was released from Jewish rule by Pompey during the campaign in which he dissolved the Maccabean Empire, if it may be so-called. Josephus records that it contained a Jewish community, and during the Jewish revolt against Rome its citizens treated the Jews with more humanity than did those of the other towns across Jordan.

When in the fourth century C.E. Christianity became the State Church of the Roman Empire, Gerasa was the seat of a bishopric. It had the good fortune to be the scene of an annual miracle; on the day of the Epiphany the water of the fountain of its oldest Church was turned to wine. In consequence it was enriched and glorified with a cluster of churches and religious buildings, and became also a centre of commerce. A contemporary writer describes it as " full of the most plenteous variety of merchandise."

When I saw Gerasa first, in 1911, the ruins rose from the plain chaotically but in vast extent. The hilly slopes on both sides of the stream, a tributary of the Jabbok or Zerka, whose waters fed by springs were the source of the town, were covered with remains mostly hidden beneath masses of debris. The ruins had been half excavated by a German expedition; but the Circassians placed there by the Turks were making havoc of columns and capitals that strewed the fields. After the British mandate was given, the exploration of the site became one of the chief cares of the Antiquities department of Transjordan. First

Professor Garstang and Mr. Horsfield, and later Dr.
Crowfoot of the British Archaeological School, have revealed layer after layer of civilization. The Via Sacra,
flanked by temples and forums mostly of the second century C.E., and a series of Byzantine churches decorated
with mosaics, that throw a flood of light on ancient
geography and ancient art, have been impressively restored to view. Excavation has disclosed thirteen Byzantine sanctuaries built between the third and sixth centuries. In one church the mosaics give a vivid picture of
the cities of Egypt in the form of a pictorial map. Beneath
the level of another church the excavator descried fragments of a synagogue which is dated of the fourth or fifth
century. It was somewhat older than the synagogue uncovered on the other side of the Jordan at Beit Alpha [1]
and contemporary with a synagogue discovered in 1921
at Ain Duk, north of Jericho. There the mosaic floor included a picture of Daniel in the lions' den and representations of the signs of the Zodiac, which an iconoclast had
attempted to destroy.

The mosaic of the Jerash Synagogue depicts a scene of
the Flood with the figures of Shem and Japhet and a dove
carrying a twig. In the centre are representations of Lulab
and Ethrog and an ark of the Scrolls, as at Beit Alpha.
Animals moving into the ark form the frieze around these
objects. There is an incomplete inscription in Greek of
which the end is clear. "Amen, Selah, Peace to the
Synagogue." On a panel is another inscription in Hebrew
character to the honour of the benefactors of the synagogue: " Phineas, son of Baruch, Jose, son of Samuel, and
Judas, son of Hezekiah." So late then as the fifth century,
the Jews in the Diaspora of the Roman Empire wrote
Hebrew and Greek, and were in fact bilingual.

The physical suppression of the synagogue by the church
took place apparently in the reign of Justinian (c. 530),
the codifier of the Roman law and also the author of a

[1] See " The Bay of Acre," etc., p. 96.

resolute anti-Jewish policy. Christianity was already a jealous church. But it too had not much longer rule in the land. The Arabs, 100 years later, destroyed the churches and basilicas or converted them into mosques. Jerash remained an important place under the Ommayad caliphs whose capital was at Damascus; but an earthquake in the eighth century which, according to chroniclers, killed myriads and destroyed churches and monasteries throughout Palestine, and the shifting of the caliphate to Bagdad ended its career, and it sank away to nothingness.

A theory has been put forward that the climate of Palestine and Transjordan has changed since the period of the Roman Empire, on the ground that, with the present rainfall and water-supply, it would be impossible for a large population to live at Jerash, while the ruins of the old city suggest that it must have been inhabited by about 50,000. It is alleged that the deforestation of the country has led to the diminishing of the rainfall. But against this it is pointed out that Jerash was a garrison town, and the water for its people may have been brought from without. If at some future time the town of Aden should fall into ruin, it would be fallacious to argue, it is said, that the climate of the region has changed because it appeared from the area of the ruins that the town once accommodated a population of 50,000, and the rainfall could not possibly supply water for that number.

Jerash is the clearest and easiest-read epitome of post-Biblical civilization in the Bible lands; Hellenism and Judaism side by side, Jewish synagogue giving place to Christian Church, and Christian devotion swept away by Moslem iconoclasm; then stagnation for centuries till our own day, when the quickening of national life and the firmer hand of the Administration have combined to give a fresh start to the life of the people and to disclose the treasures of the past. As you look down on the excavated fields in the early morning from the roof of the Circassian hostelry, you have a striking picture of resurrection, golden columns arising on the green sward, temples and churches shaking themselves free from the debris of ages, and a modern village built upon the relics of antiquity.

The country to the north of Jerash is a fair rolling plateau sparsely populated with Circassians and settled Arabs. Jewish penetration has not advanced so far east. Yet it is notable that one of the first projects for Jewish agricultural colonization two generations ago contemplated the settlement of Gilead, the country of the two and a half tribes who preferred to remain on the east side of Jordan. It is now, as then, a delectable land, better wooded and better watered than the uplands of Palestine: a land, as Doughty describes it, " of noble aspect in these bald countries." Laurence Oliphant, the English mystic enthusiast for the Jewish return, put forward to the Sublime Porte in the 'eighties of the last century a scheme for placing on its highlands thousands of Russian and Rumanian Jews who would restore its fertility. Unfortunately Disraeli, who was Premier of England when the scheme was conceived and favoured it, had been thrown from power before anything was done. The idea was barren of direct result. It had to be modified to the less ambitious planting of scattered Jewish villages on the Plain of Sharon. Years later the Father of the Yishub, Baron Edmond de Rothschild, acquired a large area in these parts for Jewish settlement, and the Chovevi Zion, the forerunners of the Zionists, supported a colony that was established in it. But the scheme did not prosper, and the area is now leased to Arabs. Yet one day the peoples of Palestine, Jews as well as Arabs, will take their part in filling the spaces of Gilead, and reclaiming its soil to the old fruitfulness.

Some twenty miles north of Jerash is another relic of past civilization, the Saracen castle of Ajlun. You come to it through wooded rolling country, with the sight of Hermon in its snows, suspended as it were between heaven and earth, along the horizon. Ajlun is in the south of the land of Bashan but is not a Biblical site. The castle which rises from the rocky cliff above the Jordan valley overlooks the whole of Palestine from Dan to Beersheba. That is one of the special features of the land of serried mountains and valleys, that you survey its length and breadth from some favoured eminence, far-seen and far-seeing. Saladin, whose seal is set in the walls, built the castle to hold the Christian barons in check. It was the direct retort to the Christian castle, Belvoir, or Kaukab el Hawa (Star of the which is perched on the escarpment of the opposite the Jordan valley between Tiberias and Baisan. was designed to hold in check particularly the bold ald of Kerak who had sought to raid from Kerak the Holy Cities of Arabia and created dismay in the Moslem councils. Though shaken by the earthquakes of 1837 and 1927 which laid low so many places, the castle still has a look of impregnability.

Going northwards again from Ajlun, you come to an Arab village of Fahil; which name conceals the sometime famous city of Pella. Here was another of the league of Hellenized cities, renamed after the birthplace of Alexander the Great, probably by some popular corruption of its Semitic name.[1] It was famous as a city of one of the earliest communities of Christians who were Jews and retained their Jewish observances but not their national feeling. When the Jews rose against the Romans, these Ebionite Christians, who were the pacifist Quakers of that day, retired across the Jordan to Pella and dissociated themselves from the national struggle. Eastwards is a region which is full of early Christian ruins, conspicuous among them the Cathedral of Bosra, built of the volcanic basalt that is the formation of the land throughout the marches of the Hauran. If you turn westwards, you may descend by the branch of the Hedjaz Railway from

[1] So in our day the Arabic Deir el Belah became to the soldiers " Dear old Bella."

Deraa to Haifa, and you come to the Jordan Valley and the place where the three Mandated Territories meet, as described in another paper.

From Amman, on the other side Jordan, the direct way to Palestine is the route by which the children of Israel under Joshua entered the Promised Land across the river near Jericho. The high road leads from Amman to Es-Salt, named from the "Saltus Hieraticus" of t^h Crusaders and famous for its raisins. The little tow on the spur of Jebel Osha, a commanding peak mountains of Gilead. The summit is venerated Moslems as the grave of the Prophet Hosea, and is fied by some scholars with the Pisgah of the Bible Moses looked over the land into which he was not t his people. From that peak, as from Ajlun, you may see the whole land, from snowy Hermon to the sullen steely waters of the Dead Sea, and the howling wilderness around it, " And the south, and the plain of the valley of Jericho, the city of palm trees, unto Zoar " (Deut., xxxiv. 3). In the foreground the great rift of the Jordan is bounded on both sides by bare mountainous slopes. From Es-Salt the road descends steeply to the Ghor or chasm of the Jordan, a rushing stream bounding over the rocks by its side. For years after the war it showed traces of the Turkish rout of September 1918, when the army that had held their left flank in the foothills was thrown in headlong flight, after the destruction of the centre and the right flank in Lord Allenby's " Battle of a Dream." A German howitzer, named by our men Jericho Jane, was abandoned in a corner of the highway, and looked like a monstrous beast hiding in the oleanders. Now it has been moved away, and all that remains of war is a fragment of barbed-wire entanglement.

A little way from the road, where it enters the salt-encrusted plain that is 1,000 feet below the level of the sea, you may see the recent excavations of several Tells, known as Teleilat Ghassul, or the Mounds of Soda, which have been claimed to be Sodom or Gomorrah. Here a city which has relics of Chaldean pottery otherwise unknown in Palestine, and so seems to indicate a link with the civilization of Ur, the home of Abraham and Lot, was suddenly overwhelmed by some calamity of fire and was never built upon again. In this plain the children of Israel must have pitched their tents when Balaam, standing on the heights above, came to curse them and remained to bless. And here was the Vale of Acacias (Shittim) where they were camped when Moses ascended Mount Pisgah to die.

We return to the road to complete the circuit to Jerusalem, and cross the Jordan by the bridge which bears the name of the conqueror of Palestine, Lord Allenby. We pass through Jericho; and on the last lap of our journey we mount the Roman road to Jerusalem, which is suddenly disclosed at the turn of the way beyond Bethany, " beautiful in elevation, and the joy of the whole earth."

X

A JOURNEY ACROSS SINAI

It is becoming increasingly more difficult to travel well than to arrive. The motor-car is the great leveller of places. It has invaded the most secluded regions; it has made the desert noisy as the road; and it is pushing its way irresistibly to the most sacred of mountains. A motor-road, or at least a track passable by motors, runs from Suez to Mount Sinai; and the journey can now be done in as many hours as it formerly required days.

When we decided to visit Mount Sinai from Jerusalem, we were informed that the car track from Suez was impassable after the heavy rains; and we made the journey by camel caravan, the method in which the desert has been crossed for thousands of years. The ordinary route of visitors from Egypt to the Monastery is by boat from Suez to Tor on the Red Sea, which is distant three days' easy camel-stages from the Monastery. We were to take a more ancient way, and, reversing the traditional, though probably the fictitious, course of the Exodus, we trekked over the centre of the Peninsula of Sinai, across the desert of the wanderings of the children of Israel. Some of the distinguished travellers of the nineteenth century who have written of Sinai, among them Dean Stanley and Pierre Loti, have described glowingly the land route that runs south down the western side of the Peninsula from Suez, and then north up the eastern side to Akaba; but there is no modern record of the journey through the heart of the limestone desert, although it is well known to the officials of the Sinai Administration.

We made the first stages from Jerusalem by the banal

motor-car through Beersheba to Kossaima, and thence through Kuntilla, a frontier outpost of Egypt, to Bir el Themed, a station on the old Moslem pilgrim route to Medina and Mecca that runs from Suez to Akaba. From Jerusalem to Kossaima we were passing along the historic way between Asia and Africa, known as the Darb el Shur. It is the way by which the patriarchs moved from Canaan to Egypt, the Egyptian armies went out to meet Hittites, Syrians, and Babylonians, and the Ptolemies marched against the Seleucids. When the Roman conqueror brought the East under his sway, with his consolidating genius he turned the road into a continuous line of fortified outposts. Towns grew up in what had been a wilderness and a desert. Later, when the Empire became Christian, the towns and the spaces between them were filled with churches, monasteries and pilgrims' hostels.

Beersheba, indeed, has been a meeting-place of tribes from the time of Abraham to our day, because of its copious wells. It was modernized according to the best principles of German town-planning during the Great War, when it was an advanced Turkish base. To the south of Beersheba, the cities of Khalassa, Asluj, Esbeita, Birein and Kossaima, which are to-day mere names on the map, or the sites of some police post or poor village, were, in the early centuries of the Christian era, cities with important monasteries and populations of thousands. The relics of the churches and monasteries may still be traced in or amid the squalid huts of the present settlers. The story of those places has been written by Colonel Lawrence and Mr. Woolley in their book, *The Wilderness of Zin*, published by the Palestine Exploration Fund during the alarums of the Great War in 1915. The future leader of the Arab campaign and the future excavator of Ur of the Chaldees spent some months in the winter preceding the outbreak of the War in studying the remains of Byzantine civilization in the country in which the children of Israel had sojourned for forty years, and in studying also to good

purpose the life of the modern tribes that wander in the region.

Seeing it after the first winter rain, it is difficult to believe that this spacious part of Palestine which stretches south of Beersheba for some sixty miles, should be derelict. The strip of herbage " which just divides the desert from the sown " is then so green and alluring that one can imagine it turned into rich pastures or cultivation, and bearing again a settled and industrious population. One place which we passed on the way bears testimony to a striking effort of the Turkish Government in that direction. It is the ruin of Auja-Hafir, where, imposed upon the customary Byzantine relics, a town stands with a regular town-plan, like that of Beersheba, large railway sheds, a market, a public garden and a monumental column, shops and government buildings, a hospital and a school. All is gaunt and derelict, and nearly all the buildings are roofless. One single Bedouin appeared as we lunched in the treeless garden. Yet before the War the Turks had sought to establish a centre of local government, and here during the War they placed their headquarters of the Army of invasion of Egypt which made the extraordinary incursions upon the Suez Canal in 1915 and 1916. The monumental column commemorates those exploits. A railway was laid from Beersheba through Auja to the Egyptian frontier and beyond; and while the rails within Palestine have now been removed and put to other uses, the embankment and the bridges, half destroyed by British bombers, bear witness to that desperate enterprise, and on the Egyptian side of the frontier the line itself still reposes—leading nowhere.

We found at Kossaima further evidence of that outburst of Ottoman energy which, with German method to guide it, sought to harness the desert to civilization more thoroughly than any effort made since the decay of the Byzantine Empire. The Police post and the guest-house in which we lodged were substantial buildings, erected by that same army of invasion whose deeds were recorded on the pillar in the garden of Auja. Kossaima is a fruitful oasis; for a pellucid spring bursts out there, and its waters are led away to irrigate a garden of palms and a forest plantation. Lawrence and Woolley identify it with the " Kadesh Barneia " where the children of Israel rebelled against Moses; and in this region the generation which came out of Egypt was condemned to stay till it had passed away. Some few miles, indeed, from Kossaima there is another spring still known as Ain Kades, which older scholars, encouraged by the name, have declared to be the Kadesh of the Bible. If they are right, this is the place where the ideas were nourished that were to guide the moral development of humanity. We drove to it over a bare limestone plateau, and then clambered over boulders till we came to a circle of hills. From the lee of the hills a small stream winds its way between a thin edging of green. Our Arab guide told us that the place is reputed to be a " Turbah " (a holy shrine); and all the tribesmen gather there once a year, at the fast of Ramadan, in honour of the holy saint who is buried there. The stream of Kades is much less bounteous than the waters of Kossaima; and modern scholars are unanimous that, if here is the Kadesh Barneia of the Bible, the children of Israel must have occupied the whole region around, including the oasis of Kossaima and the neighbouring spring of Guderat of which the waters flow into a vast stone reservoir from ancient days. The region was their basis of operations, their sally-port to the land of Canaan, just as it was, in a reverse direction, to the Turks during the Great War, when they were preparing their attack on the Suez Canal and Egypt. There are scholars and critics who would even place Mount Horeb and the revelation of Sinai on the limestone Mountain of Hillal which rises commandingly above the desert hills in this neighbourhood. That theory is noted later.

At Kossaima we left the Darb el Shur that runs on to Suez, and, turning eastward, passed along a stony plateau, through country that became more utterly desert, to the frontier outpost of Kuntilla. From the crest of the hills the mountains of Moab and Midian stood out on the other side of the Gulf of Akaba, through the purple haze that always covers the bastion of Arabia. Had we continued the track to the east some twenty miles, we should have come to the edge of the cliff which overlooks the Gulf, and could have descended the rocky way to the port where King Solomon's fleet had its station. But our road lay south and inland to Themed, a copious spring and a halting-place for caravans, where we found the camels that had come from El-Arish to carry us to southern Sinai.

For four and a half days we trekked through the desert of the Wanderings, known to the Arabs as El Tih—which means wandering. We travelled about twenty-three miles a day, at a pace which never exceeded three miles an hour, save when we alighted from our camels and walked. After the first dozen miles across the flat desert we were proceeding through " *wadis*," that is, dry beds of streams, that once or twice in the year become raging torrents. The signs of a recent flood were apparent over the course in the wet sand and the bent scrub, but no rain came to make our way difficult. We were gradually ascending the whole time from a level of about 2,000 feet above the sea to 5,000 feet; and, as we went, the cliffs that border the wadis became higher, and we passed from the drab limestone to sandstone with its purple, black and green streaks, and in the end to deep red granite. Water was scarce, but each day we passed one place where animals and men could drink. On the second day a spring that burst out from the mountains fed a palm oasis, hard by the grave of a venerated Sheikh of the Arabs. The tomb of Atiya is a place of pilgrimage for the Arab tribes of Sinai, and we were told that they come in their hundreds on the anniversary of his death. In the tomb-chamber we saw a mass of votive offerings, baskets, pitchers, and even wooden beams; and around the place slabs of stone with rough inscriptions,

which the antiquarian of our party would fain have believed to be ancient records, but our expert knew to be the
unmeaning scratchings of the Bedouin of to-day.

Ancient writing has indeed been found on the rocks of
Sinai and has not yet been interpreted. But those inscribed rocks are at Serabit, by the workings of the copper
mines of the Pharaohs, near the western shore of the
Peninsula.[1]

On the third day we came to a larger oasis with palms
and fig-trees and gardens, under the impressive mass of
Jebel Ahmed, a mountain of Nubian sandstone which
dominated the landscape for over a day with its rounded
dome, recalling that of the Mosque of Sultan Ahmed at
Constantinople. Our camel-men, indeed, had declared in-
sistently that we were approaching the Mountain of
Moses itself; but it was only the king of the sandstone
range, and we were to travel two days more before we
entered the region of the eternal granite.

On the fourth day we were guided by some Bedouin
charcoal burners to water in a hollow of the rock at the
end of the Wadi Zallaka. They were the first human beings
whom we had met since we left Themed; for the sparse-
ness of the population in the wide spaces of the Peninsula
is extraordinary. Some 25,000 nomads are indeed scattered over it; but most of them live near the coast in the
palm oases and 7,000 are at El-Arish. The principal signs
of man's settlement, indeed, are graveyards, which here
and there are strewn around the tomb of a Sheikh or a
sacred tree, and circular tomb-chambers, *Nawamis*,
" due," so our Sinai frontiersman said scornfully, " to
ignorance," meaning that they were relics of pagan ideas.
The Bedouin whom we met at this small encampment
eked out a hard existence by burning brushwood for charcoal and carrying it to Suez, where, after a trek of some
six or seven days, they sold it for a pittance.

---

[1] Sir Flinders Petrie, however, considers that these signs, too, are
only a " local barbarism."

On the fourth day, too, peaks of the granite mountains came in sight, in particular, the trident forks of Jebl Medusus; but it was on the morning of the fifth day that, having scrambled up a pass of rough boulders between the red cliffs, we suddenly debouched on a plateau and saw before us a range of rocky mountains, jagged, bare, and brilliantly coloured. It was the range of Sinai, from Serbal in the north to Ras Mohammed in the south, with the sacred peaks of St. Catherine and of Moses in the centre. The range is in colour and configuration like the Dolomites; but the absence of snow on the tops and of vegetation at the base of the hills gives it a more austere and impressive grandeur. It has the naked beauty of the pristine rock undisturbed by geological changes and untouched by human civilization. The plateau to which we had come is traditionally the place in the land of Midian where Moses pastured the flocks of his father-in-law, Jethro, in the days when he fled from Egypt after killing the taskmaster of his brethren, and before he led the children of Israel out of Egypt. We had reached the end of the uncharted part of our journey; and we were now in the midst of traditional sites, in the country described and discussed to excess by generations of Biblical scholars.

Medieval tradition has foreshortened the lands of Moses' exploits before and after the Exodus, even as it foreshortened the scenes of the Passion, the Crucifixion, and burial of Jesus in Jerusalem. The land of Midian, without a doubt, is to be found in the region to the east of the Gulf of Akaba, and not to the south of the Sinai Peninsula where we were wandering. And, moreover, there is reason to believe that the land of Midian may contain the scenes of the greatest event in Israel's history; for modern scholars have made out an impressive case for placing there the Mountain of God and the Revelation. The spell of the name " Sinai," which in the Byzantine and Middle Ages was ascribed only to this mountainous pear-shaped peninsula, has for long exercised a numbing influence; but it has been broken by the fuller historical and geographical knowledge of our own day. Sinai, meaning the Island of the Moon-god,[1] was the name given by the Egyptians to a vast undefined area to the east of the Nile basin, and not simply to the land that lies between the Gulf of Suez and the Gulf of Akaba. The tradition which places the Revelation at what is now called Jebel Moussa, in the granite range in the south, is of comparatively late Christian origin, certainly not earlier than the third century. It was cultivated by the monks who built a chapel, in honour of St. Catherine, in those wild parts in order to attract pilgrims. If it had aesthetic fitness—and the scene around the mountain was worthy of a great theophany—it has on the other hand little historical or geographical probability.

There seems no reason why the children of Israel, after crossing the Red Sea, should have been diverted to the South by Moses; and we now know that this part of Sinai was strongly garrisoned by the Pharaohs who worked the copper and turquoise mines of Serabit; and it was therefore not likely to invite a people who were fleeing from the might of the Pharaohs. The opinion of the learned is divided between the claims of Petra and of a volcanic region to the south-east of Akaba to be the Mount Horeb and Sinai of the Bible. A Danish scholar, D. Nielson, has put the case for Petra. He relies not only on the physical features of that remote and naturally sanctified amphitheatre, but also on a strong Arab tradition and the evidence of the place-names.[2] The name Petra is the Greek for the Hebrew " selah," the rock. The Arabic name is Wadi Moussa, " The Stream of Moses "; and Jebel Harun, the mountain which commands the solemn scene, celebrates the High Priest Aaron who died, as the Bible tells, on Mount Hor in the same region. The

[1] The Sinai Arabs still call their home simply El Gezira, which means " The Island."

[2] See " The Site of the Biblical Sinai," *J.P.O.S.*, vii. p. 187.

fame and name of Pharaoh are still attached to several of
the monuments.

The Rev. Phythian-Adams (who was for some years the
Deputy-Director of Antiquities in Palestine), has written
a more convincing argument to prove that the place of the
revelation was a volcanic mountain, and finds the mountain in the lava field which lies to the south-east of Maan
and Akaba beyond " a great and terrible wilderness." He
lays stress on the Bible record of the pillar of cloud and the
pillar of fire which accompanied the children of Israel in
their Exodus from Egypt, and explains them as the emission
of vapour from the volcanic mountain in Midian to which
Moses was leading his people. He urges that the story of
the revelation of Sinai is a vivid account of a volcanic
eruption, as it is said:

> " And Mount Sinai was altogether in smoke, because
> the Lord descended on it in fire; and the smoke thereof
> ascended as the smoke of a furnace, and the whole mount
> quaked greatly." (Ex., xix. 18.)

It lends support to the identification of the particular
range with the Mountain of God that an Arab historian
of the thirteenth century records that the flames of an
eruption from these very mountains in the region east of
Medina could be seen as far as Bosra in the Hauran, that
is, a town remote twice the distance of the place from which
the children of Israel were guided by the pillars of fire
and cloud. So it was " from the mouth of the mountain
itself that the beacon of smoke and flame lifted its towering
head." The writer finds further support for his theory of a
volcanic scene in the story of the two tables of stone, which
he interprets as meteorites.[1]

There are two volcanic fields in the land of Midian, one

[1] He returns to the charge in a later article, wherein he argues that
the plagues of Egypt which preceded the Exodus, particularly the
plagues of the river and of darkness, may be due to the same seismic
disturbance. *J.P.O.S.*, xii. 86.

in the north near Maan on the borders of the land of
Edom: the other forming the barrier of the northern
Hejaz to the south-east of the Gulf of Akaba. Phythian-
Adams rejects the former as the scene, since its proximity
to a region so well known to Israel deprives it of a claim to
the mysterious remoteness of Horeb-Sinai, nor is there any
such " great and terrible wilderness " as must be pre-
sumed to separate the Mount of God from the Promised
Land. The other volcanic area fits precisely the conditions
of the Israelite tradition. So he is moved to identify a
particular mountain in the volcanic region of Northern
Hejaz with the Biblical Mount of God. Arab folk-lore
associates either region with Moses and the children of
Israel. Though that local legend is not of much weight
since it is found in many places, the presence at the mountain chosen of an encampment for a great host, the traces
of a spring on its lower slopes, the existence of a place of
sacrifice still venerable and surmounted with twelve stones,
which accords with the Bible narrative of building an altar
under the mount with twelve pillars, and, lastly, the approach to the mount through a huge wind-eroded and
uninhabitable tract—all these features combined form " a
two-fold strand of evidence which is decisively in favour
of the site."

It is remarkable that the theory was anticipated nearly
sixty years ago by a Biblical scholar, Dr. Beke, who wrote
in 1874 [1] to prove that he had found the Mountain of God
in the land to the east of the Gulf of Akaba. And the
Oriental traveller, Richard Burton, accepted that theory
and by his own travels located Midian in a region of the
Hedjaz to the east of the Red Sea. The Arab geographers
of the Middle Ages made the same identification: and a
strong Arab tradition associates Moses and Jethro with
that region.[2] Even in archaeology it is true that: " If
you want new ideas, read old books."

[1] See *The Times*, Feb. 27th and Mar. 5th, 1874.
[2] See *The Gold Mines of Midian*, by Richard Burton, 1878.

A third theory about the Exodus has been recently put forward by a writer who has close personal knowledge of Sinai and its surroundings, acquired by nine years' residence and travelling in the Peninsula as its governor. Colonel Jarvis, in his book, *Yesterday and To-day in Sinai*, agrees with those who reject the southern range of Sinai as the place of the Law-giving, but argues that the desert of the Wanderings and the site of the Revelation are both to be sought in the triangle formed by El-Arish, Rafa, Kossaima, in the northern section. The children of Israel, according to his theory, left Egypt by the road that passed by the coast—the way of the Philistines being the road some ten miles inland which was followed by Allenby's army [1]—the place of the drowning of the Egyptian host and the Sea of Reeds were the Lake of Bardawil; and the Mount of the Law is a limestone massif which rises in solitary majesty and is known still as Hillal, a word of the Arabs that means lawful, and is used especially for the lawful killing of animals. The theory fits some of the probabilities; and it is particularly supported by the geographical features of the northern route, and by the presence in this part of Sinai of quantities of quails and of the secretion of manna in the tamarisk bushes. On the other hand it does not accord with the description of the Mount of the Law in the Bible, or with the description of " that great and terrible wilderness." What may be deduced from these three theories is that the traditional route of Israel and the traditional place of the Mount of Moses have against them the weight of modern research and modern science.

Yet, though the scene which we were visiting may not be the actual scene of Israel's law-giving, it was incongruous to find the fresh tracks of motor-cars when we descended from the plateau to the ravine which leads up to the heart of the mountains. Happly no hoot of a horn came to disturb the solemnity of the place. The Wadi Sheikh is a broad ravine ascending gradually between

[1] See "Egypt in Palestine," p. 142.

rocky masses on either side, that guard it like the avenue
of Sphinxes at the temple of Luxor in Egypt. As we pro-
gressed, the mountains closed in, and the scene took on
an almost dramatic and theatrical character. It was the
fit setting for one of the supreme human epics.

A turn in the Wadi, and we suddenly saw before us the
walled enclosure of the Monastery of St. Catherine and its
garden of cypresses and fruit-trees. Unlike the most
famous Byzantine monasteries in Palestine, Mar Saba near
the Dead Sea, and the Deir Quarantal on the Mount of
Temptation above Jericho, the Monastery of St. Catherine
is not couched on the hills, but nestles in the valley between
two ranges. At a distance it looks almost commonplace,
but as you approach, its embattled walls, dating from
the time of Justinian, mark it as a place of historic
memory.

The Peninsula of Sinai became a place of monastic
settlement for thousands of hermits from the early days of
the Christian Church, partly because of its association with
the Giving of the Law to the Hebrews, and partly because
of its inaccessibility to the persecuting power of the Pagan
Empire. Then, after the Emperor Constantine had been
converted to the Christian faith, his pious mother Helena
visited the hermits' retreats, and was deeply moved by the
sight of a tree said to be the Burning-Bush of Moses,
beneath the Mountain which the monks claimed to be the
Mount of the Revelation. As she had erected a Church
over the place of the Sepulchre in Jerusalem, so she caused
to be erected in Sinai a Chapel over the Bush. The Chapel
indeed contained within its walls the roots of the tree.
Two hundred years later, the Emperor Justinian (527-563)
was moved by the trials of the monks, who were subjected
to raids of the Arabs of the desert, to build around the
Chapel a strong fortress. Doubtless anxiety for the security
of the frontier against the incursions, no less than the calls
of piety, moved him to undertake the work. His fort
stands almost unchanged to this day—it was repaired by

orders of Napoleon Bonaparte in 1799—and the Monastery
of St. Catherine [1] within the fortress walls has been occupied by Christian monks unbrokenly through the centuries. A Mosque has been added to the Chapel of St.
Helena: but the Church has remained the master. A
covered way surrounds the solid walls of the monastery.
It was built of old to give shelter to the monks, when they
emerged from the enclosure for their tilling, against the
arrows of Arab enemies on the mountains above.

Into the enclosure itself we were not admitted, though
we bore letters from dignitaries of the Orthodox Church in
Palestine. The monks declared that they were bound by
a rigid rule only to admit persons recommended by the
Archbishop of Sinai himself, who is independent of any
ecclesiastical authority, lives in Cairo, and scarcely ever
visits his diocese. They hinted also that it was customary
for visitors to come on camels obtained from the branch
of the Monastery at Tor, and that, if we would dismiss our
caravan, and order another from their establishment to
take us to Tor, the rigidity of the rule might be relaxed.
But against this insinuation upon our and their integrity
we were proof; and so we failed to see the holy sites and
the treasures within the walls: the well where Moses aided
Jethro's daughter to draw water, the root of the tree from
which Aaron's rod budded, the famous Mosaics of the
Byzantine chapel, and the famous manuscripts that remain
in one of the world's most ancient libraries. Its precious
code of the Greek Bible was removed years ago to St.
Petersburg; but it still retains the most ancient Syriac
manuscript of the four Gospels discovered in 1893 by two
Englishwomen.

[1] St. Catherine, who, more than Moses, was the idol of medieval
veneration, was a fictitious Christian martyr of Alexandria. Her body
was said to have been miraculously translated to the Mountain of
Moses, and to work miraculous cures there. The principal docks of the
Port of London are called after her, for they were built by the side
of the Chapel to her which the pious Queen Matilda of England
erected in the twelfth century. (See Eckenstein, *History of Sinai*.)

We were permitted to camp in the lee of the massive walls; and the monks let down to us from a penthouse brushwood and coke with which to make our camp-fire. One consolation we had for our exclusion from the guest-rooms. We saw at night the full beauty of the moonlight upon the mountains, giving to them a mystical glamour as wonderful as their austerity in the light of the sun.

On the morrow we ascended the Mountain of Moses by the 3,000 or more steps cut on the face of the rock. We had as guide one of the Jebalia Arabs who for centuries were the serfs and afterwards the servants of the monks, and trace their descent from the Wallachian peasants who were brought to Sinai by Justinian to serve the inmates of the monastery. The stony staircase with its constantly changing views of the mountains, the plateau of Elijah half-way, where a lone cypress-tree rises in the midst of a green meadow, the vision from the summit over the whole range of Sinai and beyond, over the limestone hills of the wilderness through which we had passed, over the Mountains of Arabia In-felix bathed in golden light, and over the waters of the gulf gleaming in the sun; air of crystal purity and aroma of herbs of sharp fragrance as none of us had before known—these things made us feel that, if Jebl Moussa were not the actual, it was the ideal, site of the divine revelation. Fronting it on the west rises the higher peak of St. Catherine (8,500 feet), and to the north-west the massive Serbal, which for long was venerated as the place of the Giving of the Law, and a few years ago gave up inscriptions in a language which may contain the earliest human alphabet.

The monks in a more credulous age contrived to establish the tradition that the mountain above their monastery is the place; and side by side on the summit, and again within their enclosure, a chapel and a mosque bear witness to the veneration of pilgrims, Christian and Moslem, who equally honour the Hebrew law-giver. The Jews were not parties to the tradition, and there is no synagogue. From the mountain of revelation we descended to the Mount of the Willow, Ras Safsaf, so-called because in a dell below the summit stands a willow tree from which, it is said, Moses cut his rod. The highest peak overlooks with a sheer precipice the cup-like plain where tradition, disregarding the words of the Bible that the leader had gone three days' journey from his people's encampment, places the hosts of the children of Israel while Moses ascended the Mount. Tradition also places on this mountain the event of the breaking of the tables of stone when Moses beheld his people worshipping the golden calf.

We returned to the monastery by the zigzags of a road constructed some eighty years ago by one of the members of the Egyptian Royal House of Mohamed Ali, who planned to place a summer palace upon one of the highest mountains in his realm. He was not able to complete the enterprise, and the road remains as his monument. It is interesting that a proposal has recently been made to erect an astronomical observatory on the mountain because of the peculiar purity of the air.

The next day we started our journey from the monastery to Tor by way of the Wadi Isla, the most romantic ravine in the Peninsula. Our Jebali guide had protested that after the rains it was impassable for man or beast, and that if we attempted it, we should have to wade through the water for three hours and would lose our baggage. Under stern cross-examination the three hours were reduced to fifteen minutes. And so, in fact, it happened; though there were places in the great gorge only thirteen feet wide and overhung by enormous cliffs where the rushing water fell in cascades over the rocks and it seemed impossible for a caravan to pass. That hard-worked epithet "Rose-red" applies in simple truth to the walls of the Wadi more than to Petra; and the colours of the cliffs are set off by the palms and tamarisks which border the gurgling stream that rushes through it. We travelled in the region of the granite rock for two days, till, with

amazing suddenness, the wadi debouched through a
narrow opening upon a wide sandy plain without water,
without rocks, without vegetation, without vision. We
had come back to the wilderness, known here as the Kaa,
which rolls flat and featureless to the sea. We made the
last stage on our camels across this picture-book desert,
having the white buildings of Tor to guide us.

We expected to catch a ship of the Khedivial line which
would bring us to Suez. But we were greeted with the
news that, despite the time-tables and the assurances of
Tourist Agents, the steamship had in the memory of man
not been known to sail on the appointed day, and that on
this occasion it was not expected to reach the port for two
or three days more. We thought it might be possible to
sail up the Gulf in a dhow, but the wind was blowing
straight from the north, and it might take four days of
desperate tacking before the boat would make Suez. So
we resigned ourselves to remaining in Tor till we could
contrive some other means of escape.

Tor was a great place of commerce in the Middle Ages.
It was then known as Raithou, and the Archbishop of
Sinai still has his double title. The caravans from China,
India, and the Middle East came overland to its port to
embark their goods for Egypt. The goods were transported over the narrow gulf to Kosseir on the western side,
and thence carried by camel to Damietta or Alexandria,
and transported again by sea to Europe in the Venetian or
Genoese ships. In those days trade followed the monks;
and the road from the seashore to the monastery of Santa
Caterina, and then across the peninsula to the other seashore at Akaba, was one of the highways of merchants.
Benjamin of Tudela, the Jewish traveller, came there in
the twelfth century on his homeward way from India to
Egypt and Europe, and he tells us of a large town of which
the inhabitants spoke Syriac or Aramaic, the language
which the Jewish people spoke in the first millennium of the
Christian era. He and other Jews of the period refer to the

place as " Tor-Sin "—a compendious name which antici-
pates the modern Russian fashion. By the side of the town
he remarked the " Mountain of the Bath of Moses," Jebel
Hammam Sidna Moussa, which is so-called to this day.

The discovery of the passage to India round the Cape
of Good Hope at the end of the fifteenth century took away
the importance of Tor. An attempt of the rulers of Egypt
to dig a Suez Canal, so as to keep the spice trade in their
realm, miscarried. But to-day Tor, for three months in the
year, is again an important place of call, because to it all
the sea-going pilgrims come from Mecca to the north.
It is the site of the largest Quarantine Station in the world,
larger than the Immigrants' Shelters at Ellis Island, and
accommodating at need as many as 40,000 pilgrims at a
time. The station is managed by the International
Quarantine Board under English direction. Empty as it
was when we were there—for during this year the pilgrimage had been almost entirely cut off by the war in the
Hedjaz—we could appreciate the excellence of its organization. Apart from its Quarantine Station, Tor has to
offer to the visitor some hot springs rising in sand hills near
the shore, which, like most things in this neighbourhood,
bear the name and tradition of Moses. It has to offer, also,
a beach strewn with coral and shells, reputed sea-fishing,
and a drinking-house frequented by the mongrel ruffians
of the port. The drinking-house would have been a place
for Conrad to describe. Its clients played some desperate
games of chance with which our presence seemed to interfere. They were of all shades of brown and black; and
several of them in various stages of intoxication from
hashish. But the proprietor, at any rate, fostered sound
commercial principles; for on a big board upon the wall
we read the warning, " *Nullo credito.*"

After a day and a half of these lively surroundings, we
were rescued by a steamship sent for us by the helpful
manager of a Mining Company that is exploiting the oil-
fields along the Red Sea. We coasted along the Gulf of

Suez, having our last view of the gaunt mountains that at this distance appear dead and spectre-like, save when they are lit up by the early sun and the setting sun: and then passing by the sandstone hills nearer the coast in which the mining enterprises of the Egyptian Pharaohs are being re-newed. And so to Suez itself. There, again, we were on the line of the rejected Exodus; for on the east bank of the Suez Canal lies the oasis known as the Ayun Moussa. It is traditionally the place of Elim where, after the crossing of the Red Sea, Moses sweetened the waters. We travelled from Suez to Kantara by the prosaic train, passing stations which still recall the history of the Egypt of Moses, Shalluf, and Serapeum, of which the first is identified by some scholars—who favour the Petra theory of Horeb—with the place of the crossing of the Red Sea, and the second may mark the site of the place of worship to which Pharaoh, hardening his heart, refused to let the children of Israel go out. But from Kantara to Jerusalem, travelling along the northern coast of Sinai by the Sinai Railway, as it is called, we passed by the way of the Philistines through which Moses did not lead the children of Israel, although it was near.

The ancient Egyptian military road led, indeed, along this way, and that was reason enough for the children of Israel avoiding it. The starting-point of the road was a fortress of Thel, which has been identified with a Tell about two miles to the east of the present Kantara.[1] The other terminal point was Rafa, which is now the boundary of Palestine. Sculptured scenes of the road are carved on the walls of the Hippostyle Hall in the Temple of Karnak. There Seti the First, the conqueror of the Hittites, re-corded his victorious march from the Delta to Syria in what is the nearest equivalent of a map from ancient times. The Fortress Thel is seen by the side of a canal full of crocodiles. The canal, which is called " the dividing

[1] See " The Ancient Military Road between Egypt and Palestine," by Dr. Alan Gardner. *Journal of Egyptian Archaeology*, April 1920.

waters," was not the complete predecessor of the Suez
Canal, but passed between the two lakes, Menzaleh and
Ballah. The canal was crossed by bridges, whence the
modern name Kantara, which means simply " Bridge."
To-day, in fact, no bridge exists, either of iron, or stone, or
boats. Yet here through the long ages has been the bridge-
head between Asia and Africa, across which the caravans
of humanity have passed. For on the road from Egypt to
Syria through Kantara the only line of wells and springs
is found in Sinai which makes it possible to march an army
across the desert. To-day the Suez Canal, which with its
narrow stream separates two continents and unites two
worlds, is crossed by a ferry, on the site of the old road
from the Delta of the Nile to the Desert. That road is
superseded, or at least supplemented, by the iron-way
which leads to Jerusalem and Haifa. The railway was laid
by the British Army in 1916 and 1917 when Kantara was
the largest depot on all the war-fronts, the greatest military
town, perhaps, of all time, and its camps accommodated
250,000 soldiers. The hordes have passed: the camps are
deserted; the miles of metalled road are sanded up; but
the railway runs on; and outside the station a board
stands with the legend: " Sinai Railway: for Palestine,
Transjordan, Iraq, and Asia." Daily, the place is
passed by pilgrims of the world who wish to visit Palestine.
You may find there one day a Muslim Hajji returning from
Mecca and Medina to his home in Syria or Iraq, or, if he
comes from India or the Far East, completing his holy
round by a visit to Jerusalem, the third most sacred city
of Islam. Another day you will find a Christian pilgrimage
passing to the Holy Land by way of the Philistines; and
on any and every day you will find Jews coming from or
going to the national home and prattling in Hebrew.

Kantara is the portal of Palestine; and it is the seat of a
kind of Condominium. It is the Government of Palestine
which manages the railway on the eastern bank of the
Canal, although the territory across the Sinai desert as far

as Rafa is within the confines of Egypt. Again, the Police and the Customs House Officers are of Egypt; but the Immigration Officer, whose scrutiny every traveller must pass, is of Palestine; and all the notices on the eastern bank of the Canal appear in the three official languages of Palestine—in English, Arabic, and Hebrew. For at Kantara the prophecy of Isaiah begins to be realized:

" In that day there shall be a highway out of Egypt to Assyria; . . . and Israel shall be the third with Egypt and with Assyria—a blessing in the midst of the land." (Is., xix. 23, 24.)

P

XI

PHOENICIA AND A PAGAN SANCTUARY

We had been for a tour in Northern Syria, to the country once ruled by the Seleucid kings and in the Middle Ages for 150 years a Kingdom of the Crusaders; and we returned to Palestine by the coast road which runs for some 300 miles from Latakia in the North, along that straight shore to Jaffa and was and is one of the highways of trade. Latakia itself was one of the chief Seleucid ports—called after Laodicea, the mother of its founder Antiochus—and is still a considerable harbour with trade in tobacco. Through the Middle Ages it remained an important place; its Jewish congregation was noted by Benjamin of Tudela and its two synagogues by Rabbi Jacob Hakohen the traveller of the thirteenth century.[1] On our journey we traversed the length of the land of the Phoenicians. They were a Semitic people coming from the desert like the Hebrews: and they became the chief mariners and merchants of the ancient world, the predecessors by 3,000 years of the English in their voyages, and the predecessors of the Jews as the carriers of culture and religion from East to West. And the road is strewn with the debris of the passage of their—and other—nations.

Recent excavations of French expeditions at the bay of Ras Shamra, a few miles north of Latakia, have thrown a flood of light on the ethnographical and philological conditions of the Phoenicians in the dawn of history. The story of the finding is romantic. A peasant who was ploughing in 1928 struck his share-point against the edge

[1] *Jewish Travellers*, p. 126.

of a stone slab which, when removed, displayed steps leading down to the door of a beehive-shaped tomb. When the French diggers got to work, they lighted on a large mound to the east of the promontory; and the mound covered a city ten times the size of the fortress of Megiddo, with a diameter exceeding half a mile. Here was one of the chief harbours of the ancient world in the second millennium before the Christian era, a focus of trade and cultures, where the ships gathered from Egypt and North Africa, from the Aegean Islands and Cyprus, and where the caravan routes met from Asia Minor, Syria, and Mesopotamia. The excavation has given up a statuette of the wife of a Pharaoh of Egypt, who ruled between 1900 and 1800 B.C.E., vases from Cyprus, Crete, Mycenae, and Egypt; bronze axes and picks from Cyprus, and a whole museum of pottery. It is now established that the Phoenicians had their part in what is called the Minoan or Cretan civilization, that was spread over the Mediterranean world between 2000 and 1500 B.C.E., and marked the highest stage of art that was known before the Hellenic civilization. Many examples of Minoan art and craft were unearthed at Ras Shamra; but the most striking and unique discoveries were of a library or archive-room of the fourteenth century found in the precincts of a palace or temple.

The library was filled with tablets inscribed in different tongues, but most of them in cuneiform characters. Six languages have been distinguished among them; the Babylonian, which was the diplomatic speech of antiquity, like the French of modern Europe; Sumerian, the language of religion, like the Latin of the Middle Ages; Egyptian and Hittite, both in a hieroglyphic script; Phoenician-Hebrew, written in a cuneiform script; and another unknown tongue similarly written. The reading of the Phoenician script was another romance. Working on the principles of Sherlock Holmes the scholars identified eight letters out of the twenty-six alphabetical designs, and thereafter, from the existing knowledge of the Phoenician language, were able to fill in the rest.[1] The twenty-six simple signs, which do the work of the 300 and more combinations used in the Babylonian syllabic systems, form the earliest known alphabet of signs; and as with the Hebrew script they represent consonants without vowels.[2] They correspond closely with the Hebrew alphabet and they take back the origin of Hebrew writing to the fourteenth century before the Christian era. Remarkable light is thrown also by this Phoenician treasure-trove on the religious ideas and hierarchy of the early Semites. Among the fifty gods and goddesses who have been identified with some probability—but not with certainty—are Elohim, Baal, Dagon, Reshef, Astarte, and Baalath—all of which occur in our Bible; and among the Biblical names of peoples are Hittites, Horites, and Cypriots. The religious writings include an epic poem of a thousand lines containing moral precepts like to those of the Mosaic Law, and expounding the problem of the life and death of Man.[3]

Phoenicia, which means the land of the Palms, includes the whole sea-board of the mandated areas of Syria and Palestine. The southern part of the sea-board was later the land of the Philistines; and so came to be called " Palestine." But the whole was once dominated by the Semitic race which for a thousand years, from 1400 to 400 B.C.E., had an independent and glorious history, colonized and for a time ruled over Cyprus and Sicily, North Africa and the southern coast of Spain, Marseilles, and even English Cornwall, and carried to the north and the west the commerce of goods, of language, writing and

---

[1] See Naish, "Ras es Shamra Tablets," *P.E.F. Quarterly*, 1932, p. 154.

[2] The very word " alphabet " comes through the Phoenician language. It represents the names of the first two letters which were taken by the Greeks to describe the system.

[3] See " The Gods of Phoenicia as revealed by the poem of Ras Shamra," *Antiquity*, Dec. 1931: and Dhorme, " Le Déchiffrement des Tablettes de Ras Shamra," *J.P.O.S.*, xi. p. 1.

culture. They discovered the Western Mediterranean and the Eastern Ocean: and the Phoenician flag, it is said, waved at once in Britain and the Indian Ocean.

The Phoenician merchants of Tyre and Sidon it was who carried the Jewish Diaspora to the Isles of Greece and the northern shores of the Mediterranean. Centuries before the Captivity they were in touch with Hellenistic peoples; and we are told in the Book of the Prophet Joel (c. 800 B.C.E.) that the sons of Judah and Jerusalem were sold by them to Javan that they might move them far from their border (Joel, iii. 4-6). They represent the spirit of commerce and material enterprise which the modern world has come to associate with the Jewish people, but which was not developed among Jews till after the destruction of the national home and their enforced exclusion from the soil. The Phoenicians on the other hand were from the beginning of history merchants and traders; and the Mediterranean was their kingdom.

When the Greeks conquered Asia, the Phoenicians, with the other Oriental peoples, were absorbed in the Hellenistic and Roman Empires and lost their individuality. The religious cultures of many generations have mingled together in their mountains and produced strange mystical sects.

" They are the pools left on the shores by the great waves of opinion which resulted from the struggle of Christianity and Islam against the ancient and fast-rooted systems of Semitic and Persian Paganism." [1]

As Luzzatti, the Jewish Premier of Italy and a champion of freedom of conscience, pointed out, the Arab Caliphs and the Turkish Sultans, with their greater tolerance, preserved the Christian sects from the slaughter which would have wiped them out in the Middle Ages if a Christian

---

[1] See *Heth and Moab*, by Conder, 1883.

Power had continued to rule these Oriental lands.[1]
Among the Moslem sects in these parts are the Druzes,
the Mutwallis, and the Ismailis, who have added to the
fundamental doctrines of Islam mystical ideas of the divine
incarnation that go back to pagan and Gnostic cults.
Among the Christians are Maronites and Melkites, Nesto-
rians and Jacobites, whose creeds are an amalgam of
Hebraic and Hellenistic ideas. And lastly the Jewish community of Aleppo is still devoted to the Cabbala, the
mystical teaching which modified Rabbinic Judaism in the
Dark and Middle Ages.

The most striking of the sects which hold to their secret
creed are the Ismailis. They live in the mountains between the Mediterranean and the River Orontes that
were once the haunt of the Assassins. Those dreaded devotees took their name from the Hashish drug which stupefied
them—and is to this day one of the most insidious curses
of the Orient—and under its influence they were prepared
to carry out any order given by their lord, Rashid el Din,
known as the Old Man of the Mountains. The order was
frequently to kill, and hence the name came to be used for
a murderer. Their first haunts were around the Caspian
Sea; when driven thence by the Mongol tyrant Hulaku,
they came to these mountains between the Syrian desert
and the sea, and maintained their independence against
Saracens and Crusaders, till their fastnesses were taken in
the thirteenth century by the Mameluke Sultan Baibars
who also broke the power of the Latin kingdom. The
Ismailis to-day still live around the mountain fastnesses of
Kadmus and Masyaf, under the lee of the dismantled fortresses. Like the Indians of East Africa, they venerate the
Agha Khan of India whom they regard as a divine incarnation. While they have been brought under the
control of the French Mandatory, and have seen their
mountain retreats invaded by the motor-car, their cult is
still inviolate. So, too, the Druzes, whose cult is secret,

[1] See Luzzatti, *God in Freedom*, Eng. tr., p. 362 *ff*.

are a warlike and exclusive people; and as they showed
in their outbreak against the French in 1925, they combine
ancient fanaticism with modern nationalism.

Traces of the Jewish Diaspora remain in the villages as
well as in the towns where Jewish life has never ceased.
On the coastal road from Latakia we noticed a track leading to a village which is called Beni-Israel; and in the
same region we lighted on a perfect example of a medieval
fortress which bears the name of Sahyoun or Zion. It was
built by the Crusaders who planted in these hills some of
their mightiest works; but its name is perhaps reminiscent
of some early Jewish settlement.

Nearly every town and village along the coast has its
Phoenician name and relics; but three places in particular
are distinguished in Bible history; Tyre, Sidon, and
Arvad. They were each situated on a promontory, with
an island lying close to the land which afforded shelter
to the Biremes and Triremes of these early seamen.
Coming from the north, the first of the three towns on our
route was Arvad, which is reached by boat from Tartus
on the mainland. Tartus is on the site of a new Arvad
which was founded by the Macedonian conquerors of
Phoenicia to hold in check the older city. Its name, indeed,
is a corruption of the Greek Antaradus that means " opposite Arvad." It boasts an imposing Crusader Church from
the Middle Ages; and it was a great fortress of the
Frankish knights.

The island lies some two miles off the coast; you may
still see gigantic ruins of the ancient walls, and the place
instinctively recalls Venice and her fallen maritime power.
The Roman historian Strabo, who wrote in the first century of the Civil Era, recounts that, in his day, the island
was very populous and its houses very high in order to
hold the many inhabitants. The island was the Arvad of
Ezekiel whose mariners served Tyre: the Aradus that
offered a stern resistance to Alexander the Great; the
Ruad or Riad which was occupied by the Allied naval

forces during the Great War of 1914-1918, and used as an outpost of the Intelligence Service. To-day its inhabitants are still sailors and fishermen, but it is also a place of relegation for political undesirables from Syria.

Jews were an important part of the populace in the days of old, as is shown by the mention of Antaradus in the Book of the Maccabees among the places where the authorities were ordered by the Romans to grant privileges to the Jews in their midst (1 Macc., xxxviii. 26).

From Tartus, we continued our way to Amrit where, by the side of the Arab village, are the extensive ruins of the Phoenician city of Marathus. They are more spectacular than the usual maze of wall-foundations which modern excavation reveals. In the middle of the excavated fields conical pillars rise from the mass of tombs; they are known as the Meghazils, and vie with the Pyramids of Egypt in proportion and elegance. The circular basement is flanked by stone lions; above it is a second and third storey of cylindrical shape: and the whole is crowned by a dome. It was on this site that Renan made his famous research into Phoenician culture; here that he conceived his history of the Jewish people, and here that his devoted sister Henrietta sickened with malaria and died.

From Amrit we drove on south-west to Tripoli which was originally a federal centre of the three principal Phoenician towns and established by colonies from each of them. Hence its name: which is the Greek for " the triple city," and is doubtless a translation of a Phoenician word. It was an important place of commerce and learning in the Roman and Byzantine Empires; and till the Crusaders captured it and made it the centre of one of their feudal states, it had a considerable Jewish population. An Arab historian relates that the Saracens planted there a large colony of Jews in the era when the Cross and the Crescent were struggling for the mastery in Syria. The fanatical Fatimid Caliph of Egypt, Ali Hakim, in the tenth century caused the synagogue to be turned to a

Mosque. And the treasury of manuscripts recovered from
the Cairo Geniza contains letters that passed between the
local community and the Jewish leaders of Cairo in the
tenth century with regard to the erection of a new synagogue. At the beginning of the twelfth century, the Academy of the Land of Israel and the Gaonate were moved to
Tripoli when the Crusaders captured Tyre, their last home
within the Land of Israel.

Southwards from Tripoli the road passes over the lovely
Riviera of the Lebanon. The next place of note is Batrun,
the Phoenician Botrys, and rebuilt by Nebuchadnezzar.
After Batrun is Jebail which was the Hebrew Gebal and
the Graeco-Roman Byblos. It was the greatest of all
Phoenician fields of discovery, and has given a wealth of
inscriptions, statues, and jewellery that may be compared
with the treasures of Egyptian Thebes and Luxor. Recent
excavations of a French expedition have revealed that, far
back in the dawn of human history, in the epoch of the
Egyptian kings who built the pyramids some 3000 years
B.C.E., Byblos was a kind of Egyptian colony owing alle-
giance to the Pharaohs and containing temples to Egyptian
gods. In those days there was regular trade between
Phoenicia and Egypt. Syria gave the Pharaohs the wine
and the oil for their ceremonials, and the copper and
timber for their buildings. The name of the place disguised appears in a collection of potsherds, used for magical
anathematizing of the enemies of Egypt, which were found
at Luxor in 1925 and are dated at 2000 B.C.E.[1] And if
Gubal of the Tel-el-Amarna tablets is properly identified
with Gebal, Byblos must have been a principal place of
Egyptian rule in the fifteenth century, when that power
was beginning to reel before the attacks of the Hittites and
other upstart invaders.

Byblos has yielded one of the earliest Phoenician inscriptions on a sarcophagus of the King Ahiram, which
dates from the thirteenth century. The legend on it runs:

[1] *J.P.O.S.*, viii. p. 4.

" This sarcophagus was made by Ithobaal son of Ahiram king of Gebal for his father as his eternal resting place."

A warning follows against the disturbing of the dead man's peace.[1] The inscription establishes that the Phoenicians had a regular alphabet in that remote age; and the excavations at Ras Shamra have confirmed that fact.[2] Byblos was famous in the ancient world for the cult of Adonis and Astarte (the Hebrew Ashtoreth). The whole region, indeed, is honeycombed with relics of those Phoenician deities. The river that runs into the sea near the ruins, now called the Nahr Ibrahim or river of Abraham, was known in ancient times as the Adonis river. It was the central shrine of a worship which was taken originally from Asia to Greece and brought back to Asia with renewed splendour when Hellenistic rulers and Hellenistic culture held the East in fee. Here according to tradition Adonis—whose name corresponds with the Hebrew Adon (Lord)—while hunting, was wounded by a wild boar and perished before Astarte could save him. But the goddess wept over him till he was restored to life.

Lucian, the Syrian satirist of the second century of the Common Era, has described the worship in his treatise on the Syrian Goddess:

" I saw at Byblos [he says] a large temple sacred to the Byblian Aphrodite, and the scene of the secret rites of Adonis. In memory of the calamity every year they beat their breast and wail. And when they have finished their mourning, they sacrifice in the first place to Adonis as to one who has departed this life; [3] and after

---

[1] *P.E.F. Quarterly*, July 1923 and October 1925.

[2] It is interesting that Byblos is the father of our word Bible. The paper that comes from it was called by the Greeks after the place and the book made from the paper was " Byblion."

[3] *Op. cit.*, ch. vi.

this they allege that he is alive again and exhibit his effigy to the skies."

He records that the River Adonis is said to be tinged each year with blood, and loses its proper colour before it falls into the sea. It dyes the sea red over a large space.[1] A rationalist of Byblos explained to him that the Lebanon abounds in red earth, and the violent winds blow down the earth which turns the river red.

Astarte, according to the scholars, was not a Phoenician goddess in origin, but Assyrian. She is identified with Ishtar and also with the Syrian Goddess, the Great Mother. She was, in fact, one of many forms of the worship of the productive powers of nature which was spread over the whole of the ancient world. Her emblem was found in every Canaanite city and shrine which has been excavated. It was her cult which Solomon introduced into Jerusalem for one of his foreign wives,[2] which Jezebel the Tyrian princess brought to Israel, and which Jezebel's granddaughter, Athaliah, tried to impose on the people of Judah. Her images appear in the Canaanite cites of the Shefela, such as Gerar and Ain Shems: in the Philistine towns of Ascalon, Gaza, and Beth-Shan (Baisan), where she is dressed in warlike array and described as the Queen of Heaven (Jer., xliv. 18).

The cult received another transformation and identification when East met West. The Greek goddess of love, Aphrodite, was endowed with her attributes, and adopted her laments for Adonis, who was identified likewise with Tammuz. Save in the Jewish isle of pure monotheism, the unified, or rather syncretized, Syrian-Phoenician-Greek cult was universal in the Graeco-Roman world. Her principal shrine, however, remained by the banks of the Adonis river so long as the pagan Empire stood. The Roman general Crassus, who everywhere sacked temples

---

[1] *Op. cit.*, ch. viii.
[2] I Ki., ii. 5, and 2 Ki., xxiii. 13.

on his Eastern campaign in the first century B.C.E. and despoiled Jerusalem, spent several days counting the golden and silver vessels thereof. The worshippers gathered from far and wide twice in the year. In the autumn when the river flows red, with the god's blood as they believed, they abandoned themselves to wild lamentations: and in the spring, when the goddess of fertility prevailed, they indulged in orgiastic celebrations. Temples lined the banks of the river, but the greatest was at the source, a romantic spot some twenty miles from the coast and nearly 5,000 feet high, where an abundant stream dashes in cascades from a cave in the mountain side. It is a place like to the source of the Jordan at Baneas, hard by the Dan of the Bible, where likewise the Hellenized Syrians located a pagan god Pan, and raised a temple to his glory. Aphaka, the place of the source of the Adonis river, had a world-wide reputation: and its temples with their pagan rites excited the zeal of the Christianized Emperor Constantine who, as we are told by the Church historian of the fifth century, razed their walls and slaughtered their votaries and, as he thought, cut out the roots of the contamination.[1]

We made our way to this place from the coast, but it was not possible to follow the river to its source. The gorge through which it passes is now impenetrable, and we had to climb the mountains above the chasm. For the first part of the ascent we mounted by car up a steep and narrow road to a Lebanese village. There, to our relief, the road ceased: it was not built for motor-cars—and we took to mules. From the village of Faitroun the path lay first through several Christian hamlets set between pine and oak trees and surrounded by vineyards. This is the country of the Maronites, the Syrian Christians who have made the Lebanon more populous than any other part of the Middle East. They have brought to it something of the wealth and material civilization of the New World in which hundreds of thousands of them have made their

---

[1] Eusebius, *Vit. Constant.*, iii. 55.

little pile as immigrants, returning to build their homes
in their beloved mother-land. So one day the hills of
Palestine will be dotted with a population of Jews who
have made their little pile in western countries to enjoy
it in the national home.

Leaving the area of cultivation, we mounted the stony
ridge of the Jebel Hadid, the mount of Iron, of which the
bare limestone is cut into curious shapes. We crossed a
bleak patch at a height of 6,000 feet, and then on the other
side came to glades of pine mixed with spreading walnut-
trees. The cedars indeed, for which Lebanon is famous all
the world over, are now scarce, having been cut down
ruthlessly by kings and generals for centuries; and save in
a few plantations specially preserved, as at the famous
Besherra in the mountains to the north of the river, they
are found only in ones and twos.

The grotto which was the source of the river was visible
for some miles, a gaping hole in the mountain side. Above
us a snowy screen shut out the vision; the " cold mountain," " Sannin," nearly as high as Hermon. When we
approached the grotto we saw the cascades falling from the
mountain; but from the grotto itself, in this season, there
was only a trickle of water. The grotto runs deep into the
mountain side for miles, and the caves around are said
to be the haunt of bears. The stream rushes beneath a
Roman bridge, and ruins of Roman temples are visible
on all sides; but the work of destruction was thoroughly
done by the ardent Christian iconoclasts. The walnut-
trees round the stream were decked with the votive rags
of the women of the Mutwallis who were encamped
around. These women regard the place with veneration,
and they still worship the spirit of Fertility; but the
memory of Adonis and Astarte has passed away.

It is common to find in Palestine and Syria places of
popular worship and pilgrimage which, to-day, are associated with some Bible character or Moslem worthy, but
go back to a pagan cult. There is, for example, the Nebi

Rubein near Jaffa, the reputed tomb of Reuben: the Nebi Usha (recalling Hosea the prophet) in the country below Mount Hermon: and Mar Elias, sacred to Elijah who is revered by the three Faiths, on Mount Carmel. The peasants, from generation to generation, hold to their tradition of a local Saviour though his name may be changed. In the village Arsuf on the coast of Palestine, which takes its name from another Phoenician deity, the fish god " Reshef," the Arabs still congregate at a festival, and worship the local saint in the sea, and barren women bathe and believe that they will be fertile.

On this occasion we came across a strange survival of a Jewish cult at a farm-house by the source of the river, where we spent the night. It was a Saturday, and our hostess told us that she and her family fasted on that day in accordance with the custom of her section of the Maronites. She called it the Sabbath; and the fast may go back to a Judaization of the Roman times when, as we know from the Latin poets, the Sabbath day was adopted as a fast by the pagans—who habitually over-ate. And we were told that the Moslem Mutwallis still observe Christmas, though they regard it as a day holy to Ali, the descendant of the Prophet.

From Aphaka we returned to the coast, and crossing the bridge over the Dog River, walked some way up the gorge on the south side of it. Of all places in the storied East this gorge gives the clearest image of the passage of civilization. The rocky walls which form the bank of the river are like a monumental picture. As a modern writer has put it: " Conquerors passing along this road of the victors have made the lily-sprinkled rocks their visitors' book." [1] Thirty tablets still survive. Egyptian and Assyrian inscriptions are panelled on the hill-side in hieroglyphic and cuneiform script. Here is the seal of Rameses who passed in his triumphant progress against the Hittites to Kadesh, and dedicated tablets to the great gods of Egypt.

[1] See Thompson, *Crusader Coast*, 1929.

Here is the signet of Shalmaneser, Sennacherib, and of
Esar-Haddon who passed in the reverse direction with their
Assyrian hosts to over-run Palestine and enslave Egypt.
Here Marcus Aurelius who built a new road recorded his
work. Here Crusaders and Saracens inscribed their
names and exploits, but not so indelibly. And here, coming to more modern times, the French Expedition of 1860
which, sent to protect the Maronite Christians against the
Druze persecutions, led to the establishment of Lebanese
autonomy, obliterated one of the inscriptions of Rameses,
and proudly proclaimed in its place their own achieve-
ment. The Turks, in their turn, excised the French record
during the war; but the French soon restored it. Here,
more modestly, the Indian division of Allenby's Army recorded its passage; and here, finally, the first French
governor of Mandated Syria, General Gouraud, has described for posterity his work in rebuilding the road and
the bridge.

A few miles south of the Dog River the road comes to
Beirut which was a Phoenician harbour, but became more
famous in the Roman Empire as Berytus. In the first
century before the Christian era it was restored by
Augustus as a military colony and an outpost of Latin
culture in the Greek-speaking and Hellenized Orient; and
in the Empire it boasted a celebrated school of law. It was
again of little importance in the Middle Ages, and during
the epoch of the Crusades; but it had an amazing revival
in the nineteenth century, and from an insignificant fishing village has become one of the chief ports of the Eastern
Mediterranean. The prosperity of the Lebanon region
which encirlces it and the widespread emigration of the
Lebanese brought it trade; and Christian enthusiasm
made it once more a place of learning. Two colleges of
University standing, both missionary in the most enlightened sense of the word, one founded by the Protestants of
the United States and the other by the Jesuits of France,
have moulded and are moulding the minds of the young

men not only of Syria but of all the neighbouring countries, and of the three creeds, Moslem, Christian, and
Jewish. Since the French Mandate was established,
Beirut has advanced its position as the principal city of
the Government of the Lebanon and Syria; and it has
been so thoroughly modernized that it hardly has the
appearance of an Eastern city, but is like a little Marseilles.

The two more famous Phoenician cities, Sidon and Tyre,
which lie between Beirut and Palestine, are not markedly
changed by any modern development. Sidon is the larger.
The main road runs through it to-day, and it has a big
fruit-market; while Tyre is aloof from the road, solitary
by the sea, and has neither maritime nor land commerce.
In the Homeric poems they are already celebrated as ports
and places of trade; and in the prophecy of Israel they
are the marts of nations. They were as the Liverpool and
Southampton of the world of antiquity, the ports from
which men sailed to the West to bring back the precious
goods of other countries. From them the Phoenicians
sailed who founded the great city of Carthage in North
Africa that in the third century B.C. contended with Rome
for the mastery of the Mediterranean. In both places
some few relics of a past glory are still to be seen. Sidon
has yielded to the excavator a vast Necropolis from which
came one of the most perfect works of art of the Hellenistic
epoch. It is a sculptured sarcophagus, called the " Tomb
of Alexander," and represents scenes of war and hunting
with an art which rivals the frieze of the Parthenon of
Athens. It now adorns the Museum of Constantinople;
but a number of sculptured stone sarcophagi are preserved
in Sidon itself, in a local museum. Sidon was a place of
pilgrimage in the credulous Middle Ages. The Jewish
traveller Rabbi Jacob, the messenger of Rabbi Jechiel of
Paris who died at Acre, records that he saw there the
tomb of the prophet Zephaniah.[1] Benjamin of Tudela

---

[1] *Jewish Travellers*, ed. Adler, p. 126.

was there a century later, and found a congregation of twenty Jews. Between Sidon and Tyre lies the village of Sarafand, identified with the Zareptah to which Elijah went when he left the Brook Kerith (1 Ki., xvii. 9).

Little is visible of Phoenician craft in Tyre, the capital of King Hiram the great artificer. The famous city whose "merchants were princes," suffered two overwhelming destructions at the hands of Nebuchadnezzar of Babylon and Alexander of Macedon. And when its material and maritime power was crushed, it had no culture of its own, and became as the surrounding Hellenized towns. A few miles outside the humble port for fishing vessels stands a pyramid reputed to be the tomb of the King himself; and that is all which remains above ground of Phoenician workmanship. Each of the stones which forms the base of the monument is thirteen feet long and nine feet wide and two feet thick.

In our day the doom of the prophet Ezekiel upon Tyre has been fulfilled:

"Thy riches and thy wares, thy merchandise, thy mariners, and thy pilots, thy calkers and the occupiers of thy merchandise, with all thy men-of-war that were with thee, shall fall into the heart of the sea in the day of thy ruin." (xxvii. 27.)

Several times the city has arisen from destruction. In the epoch of the Christian Empires it was one of the strongholds of the Church, and in the days of Crusader Kingdoms it was for a time a place of large commerce with Europe and an exchange of culture. After the Arab conquest of Syria and Palestine it was also one of the principal centres of Jewish population. From the fragments of the Cairo Geniza that, under the skilful handling of Dr. Mann, have thrown light upon the history of the Jews in the epoch of the Fatimid Khalifs of the ninth and tenth centuries, we learn of the importance of the community

Q

and its Rabbis. When Jerusalem fell into the hands of the Seljuk Turks in c.e. 1075 the Academy of Eretz Israel was transferred there for some years.[1] And Jehuda Halevi, who came to the Holy Land on a poet's pilgrimage from Spain in the early part of the thirteenth century, spent some time in the town, and was honoured by the Kahilla. Tyre, called by an ancient poet " the proud mother of palms," was still a beautiful city in the Middle Ages, as is recorded by Benjamin of Tudela. Its population contained some 500 Jews, many of whom owned sea-going vessels and were glass-makers, manufacturing the ware that was prized in all countries. But Phoenicia had ceased to be a national home long before those days, and had become merely a geographical expression.

Phoenician Tyre never recovered from the siege of Alexander the Great and the transfer to Alexandria and Egypt of the commerce of the Orient. That was the dying struggle of her manhood and the destruction of her people. Their Semitic religion and tradition were subjected to Greek ideas; and three centuries later the Semitic nationality was crushed under the might of Rome against which the Jewish people alone was proof. Jewish monotheism and Jewish belief in social justice were principles which neither seductive art nor brutal oppression could shake. The other Semitic people had nothing like it. They retained only their mariners' enterprise and their commercial function: they ceased to be creators or even carriers of culture. And in the Dark and Middle Ages, as George Eliot wrote, it was the dispersed race of Jews who were a new Phoenicia working the cultural mines of Greece and carrying their products to the world.

The passage from Syria to Palestine is over what is called in our maps the Ladder of Tyre, but what the Arabs know fittingly as Ras el Nakura, the Headland of Entry. The name goes back to the Tel-el-Amarna letters of 1500 b.c.e., in which we read of a store-house of the

---

[1] *The Jews under the Fatimids*, Mann, 1920, p. 180.

fortress of Megiddo, Harnakuri. The white cliffs rise sheer to a height of several hundred feet like the English cliffs at Dover, and the modern road scales the Ladder which was for ages a famous barrier. Ancient Phoenicia stretched indeed along the coast of Palestine, in the epoch of the return from the Babylonian Captivity; for the Persian overlord made the Phoenicians masters of the ports and towns which had belonged formerly to the Philistines. They bore rule in Askalon and Gaza as well as in Acre and Jaffa. Hoards of their coins are found in the Tells down the coast. But their civilization has scarcely survived in the southern section. For two years, indeed, after the civil government of Mandated Palestine was established in 1920, the district which included Haifa, Acre, and the coast southwards, was called Phoenicia. The name was not altogether apt, and it was dropped for the more prosaic " Northern District."

The headland of Nakura is literally a portal; for it is the frontier between Syria and Palestine, and at the frontier the road enters a gate by which the motor-car is admitted for examination. And to-day this cliff marks a real division between provinces and populations. On the one side of the line you have the Christian planter and merchant of the Lebanon; on the other side the Moslem and the Jewish peasant or trader of Palestine.

XII

THROUGH THE TOWNS OF SYRIA

Syria is the name given to the whole country that lies between the Mediterranean on the west and the Euphrates on the east; and in this sense it includes Palestine and Trans-jordan. In Hebrew it is known as "Aram," whence comes the "Aramaic" tongue, which is the Syrian language. In Arabic it is called simply "Es Sham," meaning the land on the left, which is contrasted with El Yemen, the land on the right, and covers the whole country above " the island of Arabia " to a person looking northwards. But the name is used more narrowly of the northern part of that area bounded by the Lebanon and the Anti-Lebanon mountains to the south and the west; and particularly of the great plain of Coele-Syria, the " hollow " valley of the Orontes river, which includes the four historic Arab towns of Damascus, Homs, Hama, and Aleppo. In this sense it excludes not only Palestine but also the former Lebanon province—now the Republic of the Greater Lebanon—which embraces the mountains and the coast to the west of the plain. The two neighbouring countries are contrasted as Samaria and Judaea. The Lebanon is known to its inhabitants as " The Mountain," and its Hebrew name, meaning Whiteness, is derived from its snowy peaks. It is predominantly Christian, while Syria, in the narrower sense, is predominantly Moslem. The Lebanon had a separate autonomous Government from the middle of the nineteenth century; and it is to-day a separate mandated State under a French mandate, with a parliamentary constitution and autonomous administration. Syria, which is the subject of this chapter, is likewise a mandated territory of which France is the mandatory. Besides the four big towns, the territory embraces two other places famous in the history of civilization, Antioch in the north, and Palmyra in an oasis of the eastern desert that separates Syria and Mesopotamia. It is a goodly and fertile country, much more productive than the rest of the Promised Land of Israel.

In this historical land the most historical place is Damascus which, like Jerusalem, is contemporary with history. The city wall, twenty feet high and fifteen broad, contains Cyclopean stones builded in a prehistoric age. Its name is recorded in the early Egyptian monuments, and in the earliest chronicles of the Jewish people. Abraham pursued the bands of Cherdoloamer, " Unto Hobah which is on the left hand of Damascus " (Gen., xiv. 15). And it was from Damascus that he chose his faithful servant Eliezer. Through the ages, Damascus has nearly always been the chief city of Syria; it is marked out for this destiny by the wealth of waters which burst out in the plain, and create here what seems to be God's garden. It is not surprising that when Naaman, the Captain of the Host of the King of Syria, was told by the prophet Elisha to bathe in the muddy waters of the Jordan in order to be cured of his leprosy, he was wrath and exclaimed, " Are not Abana and Pharpar better than all the waters of Israel? " (2 Ki., v. 12.)

The Pharpar and Abana of the Bible are the Barada and the Awaj of to-day. These cool streams, rushing from the mountains of Lebanon, have attracted at all times a teeming congregation from the plains and the desert.

> That Paradise the Arab dreams
> Is far less sand and more fresh streams.

One of the Jewish medieval travellers of the twelfth century, Petachia of Ratisbon, records the saying, " If Paradise be on earth, then Damascus is Paradise; and if it be in heaven, then Damascus lies opposite it on the earth." Tradition says that Mohammed, viewing the city from the mountain above, after days of travel through the desert, turned away, saying, "Only one Paradise is allowed to man. I will not take mine in this world."

I have been several times in Damascus; but the most striking impression is that which I received on my first visit in 1908 when I rode from Palestine over the Saddle of Hermon and approached it from the mountains. The sight of its orchard belt stretching some five or six miles on each side, and of the gleaming white towers and domes and minarets of the town, set in the verdure, of the flowery meadows by the stream of the Barada, and of the fountains with their dancing waters here, there, and everywhere, is unforgettable to one coming from the arid Judaea or the parched desert: and makes it clear why the city is associated in the mind of the desert peoples with what is most delectable. It is for them a pearl set in emeralds.

Historically, Damascus is bound up with the story of the Jews, from Bible times to our own days. It was included in the Hebrew kingdom of David and Solomon; but after that short and brilliant epoch of the two Hebrew monarchs, it broke away and achieved independence under its own kings, Ben-Hadad, Resin and their line. These kings were usually allied with Judaea against Israel, their nearer and more powerful neighbour; but later they were combined with Israel against Judaea, an alliance which led the kings of Judaea to intercede with the mighty Assyria. The prophet Elisha is particularly associated with the town, and hard by it there is in the suburb of Jobar an old synagogue erected, the local Jews say, by him.[1] Jobar is identified by the local Jewish community

---

[1] For centuries it has been a place of pilgrimage, partly because it is also the burial-place of a wonder-working sage of the sixteenth century. Synagogues of Elisha are recorded indeed, in most of the towns of Syria which were visited by medieval Jewish travellers, who, like other medieval travellers, were credulous; but this place retains its appeal to our day.

with the Hobah of the story of Abraham. Before the war
when I visited it, the village was inhabited mainly by
Jews. They show in their synagogue the stone on which
Elisha sat when he was anointed by Elijah, and also the
seat on which Elijah sat when he went to the Wilderness
of Damascus to anoint Hazael to be king of Syria, Jehu
to be king of Israel, and Elisha to be his successor as the
prophet of Israel (1 Ki., xix. 15). There is a wonder-
working well in the court of the synagogue, and Moslem
Arabs as well as Jews come there for healing. For Elijah,
known to them as El Khudr, the Green prophet, and the
forerunner of the Messiah, is one of the holiest and greatest
of their saints.

Damascus submitted to Assyria, Babylon, and Persia in
turn, and succumbed to the all-absorbing Hellenism in the
days of the Seleucid Empire. It was supplanted, indeed,
by Antioch as the capital of the Seleucid kings, and became
simply one of the league of ten Greek cities (the Decapolis),
with a new Greek name Demetrias. In the first century
before the Christian era, when the Hellenistic Empire
broke up, and before Rome had asserted her full sway
over the East, she passed to the kingdom of the Nabatean
Arabs who came from the land of Edom and Petra.
Throughout these changes of outward domination the
Jews remained an important part of the population; and
here, as in many other of the Hellenistic towns, they pursued their vigorous proselytism. Josephus records that, at
the time of the struggle with Rome, nearly all the women
of the city were devoted to Judaism. He failed to notice,
however, a new and rival mission which was being
preached in Damascus in his day.[1]

It was on his way to Damascus that Paul—then known
as Saul of Tarsus—zealous for the old faith and determined to put down the Christian heresy which was beginning to make its way, had the vision which converted him.
When he himself started to preach the novel doctrine to

[1] Jos., *B.J.*, II. xx. 2.

the congregation, the Jews rose against him, and he had
to escape in a basket let down from the city wall, from a
house in the street called " Straight." The street—and the
house—are still shown to the believers; and the incident
was vividly recalled when in 1925 Lord Balfour, who was
visiting the city after his journey through Palestine, had
to be smuggled away from his hotel to escape a frenzied
Arab mob demonstrating against one whom they believed
to be the creator of Zionism.

After the Arab conquest Damascus, the city of the
Desert and the Desert peoples, resumed her hegemony of
the East. For some centuries following the period of conquest when Islam leaped over the degenerate Orient, she
was the capital of the Ommayad Caliphs. When they
gave way to the heretical Fatimids and the Abbassid
Khalifs, who had their capitals in Bagdad and Cairo re-
spectively, she lost her pride of place. She was ruled by a
delegate of the Khalif; and in the tenth century, when
the delegate of the second Fatimid Khalif was a Jew,
Menasseh ben Ibrahim, the Jewish community enjoyed
for a period a prosperity that was long held up as a
blessed memory.[1] It is notable that she was never taken
by the Crusaders, or formed part of the Christian Kingdom.

Saladin the Kurd, who, like a Napoleon of the East,
impressed his name and his stamp everywhere, is buried
here. When he ruled at Damascus in the twelfth century,
the city was by its magnificence one of the wonders of the
world. The Great Mosque, which is on the site of an old
Roman Temple and a Christian Basilica, was the supreme
monument. Benjamin of Tudela says of it:

" There is no other like it in the whole earth. They
say that it is a palace of Ben-Hadad (the King of Syria
in the time of Jehu and Elijah). . . . Here is a wall of
crystal glass, of magic workmanship, with apertures

---

[1] See Mann, *op. cit.*, pp. 19-22.

according to the days of the year; and as the sun's rays enter each of them, the hours can be told by a dial."

The crystal wall is gone, and much of the glory was destroyed by fire during Tamerlane's occupation in 1400; but the Mosque is still one of the noblest and the most impressive sanctuaries of the Middle East. The Greek inscription of the Basilica, " Thy kingdom is an everlasting kingdom," may yet be seen on the archway that leads to the Court, to mark the continuity of religion and ages. When Benjamin visited the city, in the twelfth century, he recorded that 3,000 Jews resided there, among them learned and rich men and " the head of the academy of the land of Israel." In those days Jews had their centres of learning and authority in the Moslem capitals outside the Christian orbit; and Damascus had not fallen to the Latin invader.

The Jews have never ceased to be an important part of the population; and their residential quarter, though poor externally, contains palaces which within are lovely with oriental decoration and ornament. The community, indeed, in the first half of the nineteenth century, suffered an ordeal which stirred European Jewry. In 1840 a French Franciscan father was killed; and the story was spread by the monks that the Jews had killed him to obtain his blood. At French instigation 200 members of the community were sentenced to death; but the efforts of Moses Montefiore from England and of Crémieux from France, who came together to the East, were instrumental in saving them; and from their mission sprang the first modern international Jewish body, the " Alliance Israélite Universelle." To-day, when Damascus is under a French mandate, the " Alliance " plays a leading part in Jewish education in Syria: but the community has declined and become stagnant, and is distinguished neither in influence nor in culture.

From Damascus one railway runs south to the Holy

cities of Islam, following the old Darb-el-Haj, the pilgrim way from Syria to Mecca. Another railway runs north-wards to the three towns of Homs, Hama, and Aleppo through the Plain of Syria. It passes first across the high plateau which is bounded on one side by the Lebanon and on the other side by the anti-Lebanon. Dominating that valley is the Acropolis of Baalbek which, as Gibbon said of it two centuries ago, " excites the curiosity and admira-tion of the European traveller." It stands out as magnifi-cently as the Acropolis of Athens; and its ruined temples, which surpass those of Athens in height, nearly equal them in beauty. Greatest of all is the temple of the sun. While Astarte was the supreme deity of Phoenicia, Baal, or the sun, was the great god of Syria. The present name recalls the Aramean god; but in the Hellenistic and the Roman epoch when the temples were built the town was called *Graece*, Heliopolis.

From the first to the third century the Roman Empire, indeed, was associated with the worship of the Sun, and the Emperor was identified with the Invincible Sun. The period of building was from the days of Nero to the days of Constantine (*c.* c.e. 320), who stopped the pagan magnificence. His victory " in the sign of the Cross " over his rival for the Empire marked the triumph of Christianity over the Sun-worship. Some of his successors turned the Temples into Christian chapels; and after the Arab conquest the place was sacked pitilessly by Saracens, Mongols, and Turks. Of the sixty-four columns of the Temple of Jupiter-Sun built by Antoninus Pius in the second century to be one of the wonders of the world, six, each sixty feet high, still stand. Some of the monoliths were brought from Egypt, and it is calculated that their transport must have taken three years.

In the wars of the Crusades Baalbek was a strong fort-ress captured now by the Christians, now by the Saracens. Two catastrophes of nature finally destroyed its strength, and ruined its monuments still more completely than the armies which had sacked it; the earthquake of 1153, which did great damage also in Palestine, and the flood of the River Litany in C.E. 1331. Benjamin of Tudela gazed at its ruins, and identified the place with the Baalath of Lebanon which King Solomon built for the daughter of Pharaoh (1 Ki., ix. 18). He ascribes the huge blocks of granite to the work of Ashmodai, the wonder-working demon of Jewish folklore. And there is something demoniac in these monuments of human toil and imperial magnificence. A block, said to be the largest in the world, reposes in a quarry by the temples, over seventy feet long, fourteen feet high and thirteen feet wide. Its weight has been calculated at not less than 1,500 tons.

The sun was the paramount deity also of the town of Homs, which was the Emesa of the Graeco-Roman Empires, and in the Middle Ages was known as Hems. The temple of the sun-god has not survived in its magnificence as at Baalbek, though columns from it may be seen in the ruined citadel above the town which looms dark with its basalt masonry. It was a priest of this temple who became Emperor of Rome under the name of the deity Elegabalus, the god of the mountain, in the third century, and surpassed the record of self-deification of the whole line of emperors. He sought to make the worship of the sun-god a fundamental part of the religion of the empire, and to subject to it all the gods of Olympus and Rome. But paganism was played out, and neither emperor nor priest could make it prevail.

" Strange must have been the condition of society [says Conder] when the proud Italian race allowed their national divinities to be set aside by this effeminate Syrian, and when senators and populace alike looked with approbation on the procession of the black conical stone from Emesa, when in sweeping Oriental garments Elegabalus paced backwards in front of his idol, accompanied by the dancing girls who were the direct descendants of the devotees of Ashtoreth." [1]

The city of Homs does not go back to a hoary antiquity. But by the side of the lake called after it rises a Tell which is one of the most famous sites of early civilization. It is Kades of Orontes, where the warrior Pharaohs, Thothmes, and Ramases, in the fifteenth and thirteenth centuries, laid low the Hittite armies and established the Egyptian dominion over Syria. It was the most important strategic point in the north, where the route from the Mediterranean to the oasis of Palmrya and Mesopotamia intersected the Via Maris from Egypt to the North. The Hittites were long the dominant people northwards from here; and the ruins of Hittite buildings and Hittite inscriptions are still to be seen strewn about the cities and villages of Northern Syria; and Hittite features, like those on the Egyptian monuments, are common among the fellaheen.

The direct road from Syria to Mesopotamia and the Persian Gulf starts out from Homs, and crosses the desert. Midway you come to the oasis of Palmyra that was for some centuries one of the great meeting-places of peoples and commerce, commanding the high road from north to south and from east to west. Palmyra is the " Tadmor of the wilderness " in the Bible, of which King Solomon, it is said, was the founder (1 Ki., ix. 18); and under that name it is mentioned several times in the struggle between the kings of Israel and the kings of Syria. But it was only after the final destruction of Jerusalem by the Romans that it became a place of great note. Together with Baalbek and Homs, Palmyra was devoted to the worship of the sun; and its temple to the sun-god is as stupendously great as that on the Acropolis of Baalbek. A modern Arab village nestles in one corner of the temple ruins. It gives an idea of the size and grandeur of the town of Queen

[1] See Conder, *Heth and Moab*.

Zenobia—or Bat Zabbai, to give her Arab name—in the third century of the Christian era, to see to-day the mosques, the markets, and the Arab houses gathered in that corner. Beneath it, the ruins stretch for miles, as far as the eye can reach, to the horizon of the sandy hills; ruins of forums, temples and tombs, arches and baths. As Gibbon puts it, "they derive a casual splendour because they rise in the midst of a barren desert broken only by this oasis with its palms." And they derive the charm of romance because they remind us of the bold challenge of a desert queen to the Roman Empire.

The scene is like Petra, but still more desolate. And it is approached, as is Petra, by a gorge lined with tombs. To-day Palmyra is again a military station, and a stage on the motor highway and the air-way between the Mediterranean and the Euphrates. Before the War it was an eight-day journey from Damascus. Now you may reach it in six hours by motor-car, and in two hours by air.

The Jews played a part in its life from the time of the Dispersion. A sepulchral cave in the gorge of tombs contains a series of Hebrew inscriptions, and is known by the natives as "the Jews' cavern." The inscriptions are not interesting in themselves; for they simply record the grant of the burial-places. The most informing tells of a grant given by a freedman to one Simon Bar Abba and his family, "for their eternal honour." [1] Amid the ruins elsewhere a Hebrew inscription with the first verses of the "Shema" was found. They confirm what is to be inferred from the Talmud, that Jews were in Palmyra after the destruction of the Jerusalem Temple; and it has been conjectured from the names of some of the persons mentioned—for example, Wahballat, meaning a gift of Allat, a deity of Palmyra—that in this meeting-place of peoples they were mingled or intermarried with the heathens. That would explain the hostile attitude of the Rabbis towards Palmyra, as in the saying that "the day on which

[1] See *P.E.F. Quarterly*, April 1928, p. 100.

Tadmor is destroyed will be a feast " (Yeb., 16 *b*.). Jews are found in the city after the destruction in C.E. 278 of the kingdom of Zenobia and of the Temple of the Sun, which compares in ruthlessness with the destruction of Jerusalem; and in the early Middle Ages, when their communities were larger in the places outside Christian domination, Palmyra, which had resumed its name of Tadmor, had a large congregation.   Benjamin of Tudela calls it " Tarmode," and mentions that there were about 2,000 Jews in the place:

" They are valiant in war, and fight with the Christians and with the Arabs, and they help their neighbours the Ishmaelites "—[that is, the Moslems].[1]

Rabbi Jacob, the traveller of the next century, records that he saw there the tower of David and wonderful buildings built by the Anakim—the giants—and the tomb of Joel. Lastly, the satirical poet, Alharizi, of the same century, in a fragment of manuscript found among the collection of the Cairo Geniza, writes of the noblest man of Tadmor:

" whom they call Simhah for his generosity; a man of riches, not regarding wealth as profit, and ever in the fear of God."

The poet is praising and satirizing the leaders of the communities which he visited in his travels, apportioning praise or satire according to the measure of their generosity towards him.[2]

From Palmyra a road leads straight to Hama, passing through a number of Beehive villages where the Mutawalli sectaries of Islam have their dwellings.   They show the Persian influence and they wear side-curls like to the Peoth of the Jews.   Hama is on the site of ancient Hamath,

[1] P. 49, ed. Adler.
[2] See *Jewish Travellers*, Adler, pp. 111 and 127.

that is given as the northern boundary of the Land of
Israel (Num., xxxiv. 8). It was included in the Kingdom
of Solomon, who built store-cities in this region. But it
was rather a Hittite than an Israelite stronghold. It was
from Hamath, among other places, that the King of
Assyria, who had crushed the Hittites as well as Israel,
brought men to settle in the cities of Samaria in place of
the Israelites whom he had taken captive (2 Ki., xvii. 24).
Some therefore of the ancestors of the Samaritans came
from the Syrian town. Jews inhabited it on and off through
the ages; and it was the native-place of a celebrated writer
of the fourteenth century who settled in Rome. He wrote,
under the name of Nathan Hamati, works on philosophy
and of medicine, and carried the Greek and Arabic wisdom
to Europe.

The populous city of the present day is half-hidden
beneath the steep banks which form the gorge of the River
Orontes. That river is the thread which binds the civilizations of Syria: Hittite, Assyrian, Hellenistic, Saracen,
and Arab. And the water-wheels, which make their constant music as they pump the water to the fields, are links
between the ages. The river is known to the Arabs as El
Asi, the Rebel, because, as an Arab writer puts it:

"Though most rivers water the lands on their
borders without the aid of water-wheels, the river of
Hama will water them only by the aid of machines."

The river runs its course from South to North passing
through Antioch to the sea near the ruined port of
Seleucia.

Aleppo, which lies between the two places, is built off
its course upon a lofty widespread plateau. Jewish literature knows the town as Aram-Zobah; and both Jewish
and Arab tradition ascribe its Arabic name "Haleb,"
which means milk, to an association with the Patriarch
Abraham who is said to have fed his flocks here and have

given milk to the poor. Aleppo was a Hittite city, and under the name Halman occurs in the records of the campaigns of Shalmaneser, King of Assyria, who took Israel captive. It became more famous in the history of the East after the conquest of Alexander the Great when it was called by the Greek name of Beroea; and again after the Arab conquest. During the Middle Ages it was the chief emporium of trade between the Near, the Middle, and the Further East.

The Jewish tradition of Aleppo goes back to the beginning of the Christian era. The chief synagogue is claimed to be 2,000 years old; and the congregation cherish famous scrolls of the Law that certainly date back to the tenth century.[1] One of the seven gates of the Arab city was called Bab el Yahud, or the Jews' Gate. The famous men among its Rabbis include Rabbi Akhnin for whom Maimonides wrote his Guide to the Perplexed. Saadia, the outstanding teacher of the tenth century, sojourned in the town on his way from Bagdad to Palestine and Egypt, and records that the community contained men of Torah and knowledge.

Like Damascus, but unlike Baalbek, Homs, and Antioch, it was not conquered by the Franks during the 300 years struggle of the Crusades, and so it continued to be a centre of Jewish life uninterruptedly. Benjamin of Tudela found there a Jewish community of some 5,000 persons. Then it was the royal city of Nureddin, the Saracen ruler of the East. Its citadel, which still dominates the town from its steep mound, was built in the next century by the son of Saladin, and is one of the noblest monuments of Arab military architecture. Its bazaars keep unspoilt their eastern character, and have not been vulgarized by trams and galvanized iron as those of Damascus. From the Middle Ages to the nineteenth century, Aleppo remained

---

[1] The synagogue possesses a Geniza, or room of discarded archives which holds out hopes that one day it may yield a treasure of Jewish manuscripts comparable with that found in the Cairo Geniza.

the principal mart of the Levant and of the English Levant Company; and it had its English "factory" from the days of Queen Elizabeth. Shakespeare in his *Othello* tells of Aleppo to which Desdemona's husband has gone. To-day, when the trade of the East goes directly to or from the coast at Beirut or at Haifa, it is losing its place in Eastern commerce, and its Jewish community is dwindling.

Between Aleppo and Antioch you may pass, by a small detour, a famous monastery which is associated with the decline of the Jewish mission to the Gentiles and of Jewish influence in Syria. Kalat Simun (the Castle of Simon) preserves the memory of a monk who was cele-brated in an age of ascetic freakishness by living for some thirty years on the top of a pillar about fifty feet high. Simeon Stylites (of the pillar), was one of the principal religious forces of the early Christian Empire in the fifth century; and it was his influence with the Emperor Theodosius which induced the first Christian persecution of the Jews in Syria—to the greater glory of God.

Antioch is built on a mountain—the famous Mons Casius of the Roman poets—that rises steeply from the Orontes river. It keeps the name of its royal founder, but it has fallen sadly from its high estate in the Seleucid, Roman, and Byzantine empires. It is a small provincial town, more Turkish than Arabic; and the Turkish lan-guage and Turkish coins are current, though it forms part of the territory of Syria. It has less than 10,000 inhabitants. But in the fourth century its population was estimated at half a million, and one may measure the size of the old town by the circuit of walls which scale the flanks of the mountain, and enclose an area four or five times that covered by the present town. The walls are, for the most part, of the Middle Ages, when Antioch was a great city and stronghold during the struggle between Cross and Crescent.

There are smaller sections of the Wall of Justinian. More is likely to be revealed: for an archaeological ex-

R

pedition has begun to dig in this—for archaeologists—virgin soil. Little sign remains within the walls of the ancient splendour from the period when it was the third city of the Roman Empire, next after Rome and Alexandria, and until the foundation of Constantinople, the capital of the East.[1] It was Antiochus Epiphanes, the oppressor of the Jewish people, who aggrandized it above all other towns in Syria so that it was known as "The Golden." Our Shakespeare writes of it as: "The fairest of all Syria." The main street ran along the river, four and a half miles in length, with covered colonnades on both sides and a broad carriage-way in the middle. Herod paved the street with marble; and Titus, when he sacked Jerusalem, saved the bronze Cherubim from the Temple to adorn the gates of the city. The citizens walked in the colonnades protected from sun or rain: and the night was turned into day by the illumination of a myriad lamps. There was, however, no intellectual life at Antioch, such as flourished at Alexandria. The town was famous for its races, its theatres, and pleasances, but not for schools or art. In Antioch, said one historian, there are more comedians than citizens. And another said: "In Antioch the cypresses know how to whisper, but men do not know how to speak." [2] Now it is a rural, sleepy, half-Turkish city. The tall pointed minarets rising from the mountain slopes give it comeliness; and the water-wheels humming by the Orontes, as at Hama, make music. Its bazaars are unspoilt by modernity, and the neighbouring groves are innocent of vice.

From its foundation by the Seleucid monarch in the third century B.C.E., Jews formed a considerable part of the population. They were granted equal citizenship with the Macedonians; and, as we are informed by Josephus,

---

[1] Of the four chief cities of the Roman Empire, Antioch alone has fallen from the position of a great town. And that may help the archaeologists to discover more of her ancient civilization.

[2] Mommsen, *Roman Provinces*, ch. ix.

the grant was recorded on brass tablets which were placed in the market.[1] When after the destruction of Jerusalem the Greek citizens of Antioch besought Titus to drive out the Jews from the city, the Roman conqueror refused, and would not disturb any of their privileges. Later chronicles tell of a synagogue at the west end of the town which was named after Asmunit, the mother of the seven sons who suffered martyrdom at Antioch when Antiochus Epiphanes was persecuting the Jews and Judaism. The story is told in the Third Book of the Maccabees. The synagogue was later turned to a church; and in the credulous Middle Ages the pilgrims were shown in the crypt not only the bones of the seven martyrs, but the rod of Moses, the staff of Joshua, fragments of the Tables of the Law, the knife of Jehu and the key of the Ark of the Covenant. This wonderful selection of relics was said to have been given to Antioch when the Temple was destroyed. Another synagogue celebrated in the chronicles was at Daphne, the most famous pleasure-place of the ancient world, which lay on the Orontes River, a few miles from the capital.

Antioch and the Grove of Daphne were celebrated in a dissolute era for luxury and licentiousness. The town was known indeed as " Antioch upon Daphne," which, as Mommsen says, is as though we should say " Vienna upon Prater." The Jews must have been marked out in the pleasure-loving populace by their exclusiveness from the common cults and by their dour morality. We know from Josephus and the New Testament that they prosecuted vigorously their proselytizing mission in the century that saw both the national disaster and their greatest religious expansion. Nicolas, a proselyte of Antioch, was one of the first deacons of the new sect (Acts, vi. 5). It was in Antioch that the disciples of Jesus congregated after they were driven out of Jerusalem; and it was in Antioch that Paul and Barnabas made the headquarters of the mission to the Gentiles.

[1] C. Ap., ii. 4.

" And it came to pass that a whole year they assembled themselves with the church, and taught much people. And the disciples were called Christians first in Antioch. And in these days came prophets from Jerusalem unto Antioch."   (Acts, xi. 26 and 27.)

The disciples would not have chosen the place for their missionary centre had it not offered good soil for the sowing of the new doctrine. Judaism must have already been mingled there with Greek teachings of mysticism and salvation and of the divine incarnation. Tradition records that Luke who was converted by Paul was a Greek physician of Antioch.

Antioch, indeed, is the place where the Christian branch broke off from the parent stock, and where also Christianity itself split into various sects. Early Christianity, as the doctrine of a sect, is more closely bound up with Syria than with Jerusalem. There was a momentous struggle between Jerusalem and Antioch, between the particularism of Palestine Judaism and the universalism of Hellenistic Judaism; and Antioch prevailed. The question first turned upon the circumcision of the proselytes. " Except ye be circumcised after the manner of Moses ye cannot be saved," said the apostles of Jerusalem (Acts, xv. 1). Paul and Barnabas on the other side maintained at Antioch that salvation came by faith alone, and it was not necessary to require the convert to adopt any national customs or to trouble the Gentiles to keep the Mosaic law. They directed their mission to the Gentiles outside the gates, preaching " the Gospel of uncircumcision " (Gal., ii. 7); and the Christian congregation of Antioch was separated from the congregation of Jews. The victory of the adherents of Paul over the adherents of Peter was assisted by the fall of the Temple and of the national Jewish centre at Jerusalem.

The Church here, indeed, was established as a dominant religious power long before it was strong in Palestine. Some centuries later Antioch was the place where the

Monophysite communities broke away from the Catholic Christianity. The three great sees of the Church in the early centuries of the Common Era were Alexandria, Rome, and Antioch. Each had its Patriarch; and Jerusalem itself was subordinate to Antioch in the ecclesiastical organization, and directly dependent on the Metropolitan of Caesarea, then the Roman capital of the Province. It was not till the fifth century, when the habit of pilgrimage to the Holy Land was moving Christendom, that the Holy City began to take a prominent part in the Councils of the Church. Then a partition of the patriarchal privileges between Antioch and Jerusalem was made, and the Orthodox Patriarch of the Holy City has remained as an institution to our day.

When we visited Antioch, we were shown an underground chamber of a ruined church, outside the limits of the present city, which is reputed to be the place of Paul's ministrations. We could picture in our mind's eye how the slave and the freedman came here, listened to the preaching of the earnest brotherhood, and turned away from the licentious paganism of the Groves of Daphne to the saving doctrine. It was the connection with Paul which gave to Antioch for a millennium a special pre-eminence in the ecclesiastical organization of the Christian Church, so that it was known as " the Eye of Christianity." Council after council was held there. At one of them the decision was taken that the Christian Easter should not be celebrated at the same time as the Jewish Passover, lest the Christians feasting should be confused with the Judaizers. Again it was from Antioch that the Nestorian heresy of the Church had its origin. That heresy spread its teaching to the remoter East, with the aid of Syriac translations of the Greek philosophers, and was, thereby, to preserve the continuity of Hellenistic, Arabic, and medieval civilizations. For, when the Arabs became the dominant element in the East, the Syriac translations were rendered into their language, partly by Moslems and partly by Jews.

The Jewish power in the city was destroyed in the fifth century, when the fanatical and cruel Emperor Zeno almost exterminated the community. He was that Christian Emperor who destroyed the Samaritan power in Palestine. Individual Jews were still found in the city of Antioch when Benjamin of Tudela visited it, though it was under the sway of a Crusading prince. The traveller records that ten Jews—*i.e.*, ten heads of families—dwelt there and were engaged in glass-making. And on our visit in the twentieth century, we found Jewish tailors and traders who maintained the continuity of Jewish residence.

Syria, that was for centuries a hearth of intellectual ideas and religious doctrines, became under the stagnation of Turkish rule a land almost barren of ideas and intellectual stirring. In our day she is quickened with a revival of national life which is parallel with the stirring of Jewish life in Palestine. If the two fertilizing currents of ideas can meet and flow together in a broad stream, they should nourish a Semitic culture that may be as decisive in the history of thought as the culture that came from Syria and Palestine in the first centuries of the Common Era. The fusion of Jewish and Arab thought in the so-called Dark Ages and the early Middle Ages, outside the homes of the two peoples, produced a flowering of art, literature, and philosophy that enlightened Europe.[1] Their fusion in their native lands should surely engender something momentous for humanity.

---

[1] It is a curious sidelight on the Arab expansion in Spain that the town of Seville was called Homs, and the town of Xeres—whence we have our sherry — was called Palestine, because of the number of Arabs from those regions that were settled in them.

BIBLIOGRAPHY

BREASTED, PROF. J. *The Conquest of Civilization.* Harpers. 1926.

SMITH, SIR GEORGE ADAM. *The Historical Geography of the Holy Land.* Hodder and Stoughton.

—— *Jerusalem.*

KRAUSS, DR. S. *Vier Yahrtausende Judischen Palästinas.* Wien 1922.

Jewish Travellers. Ed. E. ADLER. Routledge & Sons. 1930.

The Itinerary of Benjamin of Tudela. Ed. M. ADLER. Oxford, 1907.

MANN, DR. *The Jews under the Fatimids.* Oxford, 1920.

MACALISTER, R. A. S. *A History of Civilization in Palestine.* Cambridge.

CONDER, G. R. *The City of Jerusalem.* Murray. 1907.

—— *The Latin Kingdom.* (P.E.F.)

FLINDERS-PETRIE, SIR W. M. *Syria and Egypt from the Tel-el-Amarna letters.* Methuen. 1898.

ECKENSTEIN, L. *A History of Sinai.* S.P.C.K. 1921.

JARVIS, MAJ. C. *Yesterday and To-day in Sinai.* Blackwood. 1931.

MONTGOMERY, PROF. *The Samaritans.* Philadelphia. 1907.

GARSTANG, PROF. J. *Joshua and Judges.* Constable. 1931.

ALBRIGHT, PROF. *The Archaeology of Palestine and the Bible.* 1931.

CHRONOLOGICAL TABLE

The dates are approximate; and in the case of the more ancient periods, even the centuries are approximate.

	B.C.E.
First period of agricultural civilization of the cave-dwellers	5000
First Semitic invasion of the Amorites	2500
Hyksos Occupation of Palestine and of Egypt	2300 to 1600
Canaanite settlement in Palestine	1800
Egyptian invasions and domination in Palestine and Syria	1500 to 1300
Tel Amarna correspondence	1300 to 1200
Israel's Exodus from Egypt	(?) 1400
Philistine descents on Palestine coast	1300 to 1100
Times of the Judges	1200 to 1000
David Captures Jerusalem	1000
Solomon builds the Temple	950
Division of the Kingdom of Israel and Judah	930
Shishak's invasion of Palestine	928
Omri King of Israel: and building of Samaria	880
Jehu King of Israel	830
The Assyrians capture Samaria: Captivity of Israel	722
Hezekiah King of Judah	727 to 699
Sennacherib besieges Jerusalem	701
Reform of Jewish worship by King Josiah	630
Egyptian invasion of Palestine by Necho	608 to 600
Babylonians under Nebuchadnezzar sack Jerusalem	597 and 586
Jewish Restoration authorized by Cyrus, King of Persia	538
Second Temple built	520

253

B.C.E.

Alexander the Great conquers Syria and the East	333
Palestine under the Hellenistic Kings . .	320 to 142
Rule of the Ptolemies	320 to 198
Antiochus III, Seleucid King, conquers Palestine	198
Persecution of Antiochus Epiphanes . .	175
Maccabean Revolt	165
Simon the Maccabee Prince of Judaea . .	142
John Hyrcanus conquers Galilee and Idumea .	135 to 105
Alexander Jannaeus King of all Palestine .	103 to 76
Pompey, the Roman General, captures Jerusalem	63
Herod the Idumean becomes King . .	40
Herod's Temple built	30 to 20
Herod dies, and Judaea becomes a Roman Province	4

C.E.

Jewish revolts against Rome	30 to 70
Titus crushes the Jewish revolt and sacks Jerusalem	66 to 70
Fall of Masada	72
Jewish rising under Barchochba . . .	132 to 135
Hadrian rebuilds Aelia (Jerusalem) . .	132
Judah, the Patriarch, compiles the Mishnah at Tiberias	200
Helena, the mother of Constantine, lives in Jerusalem	326 to 330
Justinian Emperor	530
Chosroes, the Persian, invades Palestine . .	615
Moslem Arabs invade Syria and Palestine .	632 to 638
Ommayad Caliphs rule at Damascus . .	650 to 750
Abdul Melek builds the Dome of the Rock at Jerusalem	691
Fatimid Caliphs rule from Egypt . . .	900 to 1050

C.E.

Crusaders capture Syria and Palestine . .	1100
Latin kingdom of Jerusalem	1100 to 1187
Saladin retakes Jerusalem	1187
Mongol invasion	1260
Nachmanides settles in Jerusalem . . .	1287
Capture of Acre by Moslems, and end of the Crusaders' kingdom	1291

A.D.

Jews from Spain and Portugal settle in Palestine	1500
The Turks conquer Egypt and Palestine . .	1516 to 1517
Reign of Suleiman the Magnificent . .	1520 to 1566
Tiberias rebuilt by Don Joseph of Naxos . .	1570
Napoleon Bonaparte invades Palestine . .	1797
Ibrahim Pasha, Khedive of Egypt, rules Palestine	1830 to 1840
Turkish power restored in Palestine . .	1840
French Army intervenes in the Lebanon . .	1860
Mikveh Israel Jewish Agricultural School founded near Jaffa	1878
Jewish Agricultural Colonization of Palestine .	1880 to —
The " Balfour Declaration " published . .	1917
British Occupation of Southern Palestine and Jerusalem	1917
British Occupation of Northern Palestine .	1918
The Mandate for Palestine conferred on Great Britain	1920

INDEX OF NAMES AND PLACES

LONDON : CHARLES WHITTINGHAM AND GRIGGS (PRINTERS), LTD.
CHISWICK PRESS, BRUNSWICK PARK ROAD, N.11